Afloat in Time

Dedication

For Eric, Casey and Christine,
Jessie,
Heather and
Brandon

Afloat in Time

by James Sirois

hancock
house

ISBN 0-88839-455-1

Cataloging in Publication Data
Sirois, Jim, 1930-
   Afloat in time

   ISBN 0-88839-455-1

   1. Sirois, James, 1930- 2. Gildersleeve family. 3. Ocean falls
(B.C.)--History. 4. Loggers--British Columbia--Biography. I. Title.
FC3826.1.S57A3 1999   971.1'1   C99-910596-5
F1088.S57 1999

We acknowledge the financial support of the Government of Canada through the
Book Publishing Industry Development Program for our publishing activities.

Editor: Nancy Miller
Production: Nancy Miller and Ingrid Luters
Front cover photos: Top photo by Almon and Lloyd Owens, circa 1940. Bottom
photo is Doc Gildersleve's camp, Burke Channel, circa 1924.
All photos courtesy of the author unless otherwise noted.

Two earlier publications of the author are the *Kimsquit Chronicles*, 1996, ISBN-
0-9683362-0-5 and *Gildersleeve-Owens Pioneer Loggers in Coastal British
Columbia*, 1997, ISBN-0-9683362-1-3.

Published simultaneously in Canada and the United States by

HANCOCK HOUSE PUBLISHERS LTD.
19313 Zero Avenue, Surrey, B.C. V4P 1M7
(604) 538-1114 Fax (604) 538-2262

HANCOCK HOUSE PUBLISHERS
1431 Harrison Avenue, Blaine, WA 98230-5005
(604) 538-1114 Fax (604) 538-2262
Web Site: www.hancockhouse.com *email:* sales@hancockhouse.com

Contents

Acknowledgments

I wish to thank the following who read the manuscript and made useful suggestions: Chuck Charlesworth, Jim Grieg, Bill Lawrence, Joe Ouellette, Merrily Enquist, Audrey (Sirois) Schlinger, Cherie (Sirois) Bauer, Marilyn (Gadsden) Wilson and Pearl (Gildersleeve) Evans.

Thanks, also, to those who contributed to historical information: Clyde Gildersleeve, Virginia (Owens) Wilson and Mary (Leavy) Gazolla.

The map and glossary were edited by Clyde Gildersleeve and Viv Williams.

A special thanks to the following who contributed anecdotal information: Phyllis (Gadsden) Gildersleeve for her story "Where Are We?"; Virginia (Owens) Wilson for her story "Dirty Socks"; the late Carl Chrismas for his story about a dog named Pat at Gildersleeve's Tallheo Point Camp, first reported in a story called "The Dyno Dog" written by Carl and published in the magazine *The West Coast Logger*, April/May issue, 1993. I have paraphrased that story and use it by permission of Mrs. Chrismas, Carl's widow.

Lastly, I am indebted to Merrily Enquist and Cec Calverley for their help in editing the final manuscript.

Introduction

Six miles below the headwaters of Dean Channel, on the British Columbia coast, the Dean River flows graciously into salt water. This spot, known for centuries as Kimsquit, is a place of outstanding river, sea and mountain beauty. My residence, a log cabin, is situated on land contiguous with the Dean River, world famous for its run of summer steelhead.

Living amid this wilderness splendor, lately I have engaged myself in the recollection of my boyhood activities growing up in this coastal area during the thirties, forties and fifties. It pleases me to reflect on the times that I shared with interesting people that I loved, admired or respected. I had the good fortune as a boy, to be raised under the influence of my grandparents, Amy and Doc Gildersleeve, and their extended family that included long-time employees and friends.

The Gildersleeves were gypo logging contractors who for thirty-nine consecutive years, beginning in 1917, ranged from Smith's Inlet in the south to Gardner Canal in the north working to put logs in the water for Pacific Mills Limited later to become Crown Zellerbach Canada Ltd. Gildersleeve Logging was conducted from large floating log rafts that were towed from place to place logging a year or two at each location.

In 1930, the year I was born, the Gildersleeve Camp was operating in the South Bentinck Arm off Burke Channel. The state of gypo logging art in the twenties, thirties and forties on the steep British Columbia coastal hillsides heavily involved the high lead logging system. The system was designed to lift at least one end of a log or logs off the ground, avoiding stumps and other fallen debris on the way to be stacked in a pile, called a cold deck pile, at the base of a spar tree. The high lead system employed steam donkeys, skylines, wooden spar trees, large cold deck piles and finally A-frames mounted on large floating rafts to skid the logs from the cold deck piles into the salt chuck.

When I asked grandfather why at age twenty-six he had moved to British Columbia from Oregon, his reply was, "Because all of the big timber in Oregon and Washington has been cut."

As a boy, most of the people who impressed me were educated, as Grandmother would say, "in the school of hard knocks." They all shared the same "opportunity," which was to go to work and make something of themselves. They taught me that life as we live it is not fair—but then, so what. These mentors showed me that the sooner I accepted this "fact," the sooner I would do tolerably well with the gifts I had—good health, a willingness to work and the horse sense to get on with it. Because my parents had divorced and times were hard, my sisters and I went to stay with our grandparents. My own early education was somewhat haphazard. I took the first two elementary grades at the school in Ocean Falls, B.C., where my two sisters and I lived in my grandmother's house, on Tenth Street, number 1058.

The summer of 1938, following the second grade, Grandmother gave up the house in Ocean Falls and we moved out to Grandfather's logging camp. There, with my sisters Audrey and Cherie, I took Canadian government correspondence courses. For me it was grades three and four. We learned to read, write and do arithmetic. That was about it. We went to classes on what could be called the kitchen table, mornings only. After classes, I did minor chores and then accompanied my sisters on rowboat search and discovery expeditions.

It is my hope that these anecdotes will encourage my children and grandchildren to remember me as someone who vigorously pursued finding my niche in a contradictory but challenging world. The following quotation is one of my favorites:

Do what thy manhood bids thee to do,

From none but self expect applause;

He noblest lives and noblest dies who

Makes and keeps his self made laws.

—Sir Richard Francis Burton, 1821–1890, Explorer and Writer

I do believe in luck and that a stroke of good fortune can be a deciding factor toward success in pursuing any of life's goals. However, I also fervently subscribe to the words of Thomas Jefferson who said, "I have noticed that the harder I work the more luck I have." It has been said by Kenneth Thompson, who purchased control of the Hudson's Bay Company (HBC) in 1979 for $640 million cash, that "If you wish to prosper you must be ambitious. You must be prepared to sacrifice leisure and pleasure." The ambitious understand and accept this truth wholeheartedly. For them pleasure is in the "doing" and so long as they note progress being made every day is a holiday.

Another quotation, from an unknown author, that always makes me chuckle goes something like the following:

There are people that make things happen,

There are people that watch things happen,

and there are people who wonder what happened.

The question is, I think, which category do we choose to be in? I feel that many of life's annoying contradictions are man-made if not self-made. If this is true, then arming ourselves with a sense of humor may assist in lubricating us through many tough situations. Believing in oneself is of vast importance and when your sense of humor fails you, as it will from time to time, a stand for what you believe in has to be taken. Otherwise, you will never mature and grow to be an individual who is someone to be reckoned with and admired.

Searching inward for our individual sense of responsibility, strength of character and self respect is our best shield against the enormous amount of distasteful peer pressure so prevalent in today's society. Getting through life while maintaining a sense of dignity, a sense of self respect and, most important, a sense of humor is a serious challenge. It's tough, but in some strange and mysterious way, it is worth the best shot one can give it.

JAMES SIROIS
1999

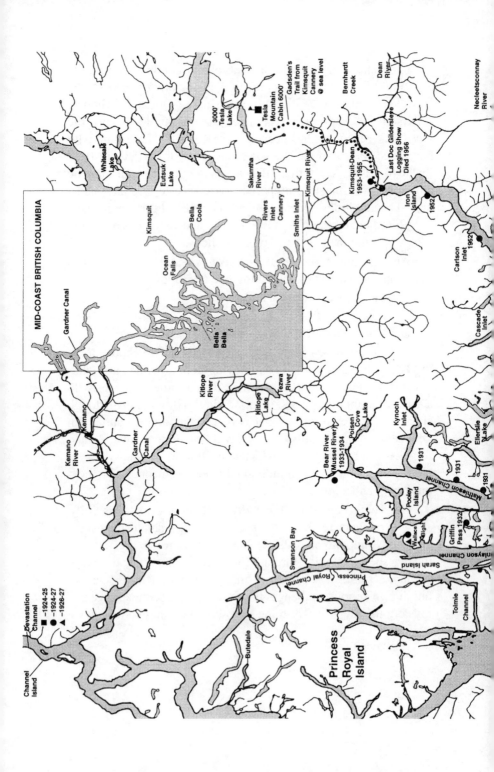

MID-COAST BRITISH COLUMBIA

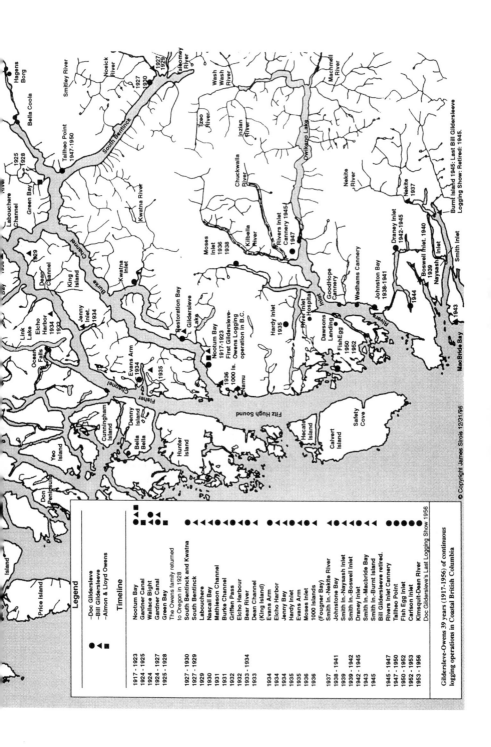

Legend

●	–Doc Gildersleve
▲	–Bill Gildersleve
■	–Almon & Lloyd Owens

Timeline

1917 - 1923	Nootum Bay	●■
1924 - 1925	Gardner Canal	●■
1924	Wallace Bight	■
1924 - 1927	Gardner Canal	●▲
1925 - 1928	Green Bay	●■
	The Owens family returned to Oregon in 1928	
1927 - 1930	South Bentinck and Kwatna	●
1927 - 1929	South Bentinck	▲
1929	Labouchere	●
1930	Nascall Bay	▲
1931	Mathieson Channel	●▲
1931	Burke Channel	●▲
1932	Griffen Pass	▲
1932	Elcho Harbour	●▲
1933 - 1934	Bear River	●▲
1933	Dean Channel (King Island)	●▲
1934	Evans Arm	●
1934	Elcho Harbor	▲
1934	Jenny Bay	▲
1935	Hardy Inlet	●▲
1935	Evans Arm	●
1936	Moses Inlet	▲
1936	1000 Islands (Fougner Bay)	▲
1937	Smith In.-Nekite River	●▲
1938 - 1941	Johnstone Bay	▲
1939	Smith In.-Nayeash Inlet	●▲
1939 - 1942	Smith In.-Boswell Inlet	●▲
1942 - 1945	Draney Inlet	▲
1943	Smith In.-Macbride Bay	▲
1945	Smith In.-Burnt Island	▲
	Bill Gildersleeve retired.	
1945 - 1947	Rivers Inlet Cannery	●
1947 - 1950	Tallheo Point	●
1950 - 1952	Fish Egg Inlet	●
1952 - 1953	Carlson Inlet	●
1953 - 1956	Kimsquit-Dean River	●
	Doc Gildersleve's Last Logging Show 1956	

Gildersleve-Owens 39 years (1917-1956) of continuous logging operations in Coastal British Columbia

Glossary

.30/30: A popular (in its day) rifle of caliber .30/30. A cartridge having thirty grains of powder with a .300-caliber bullet.

A-frame: A tall 150-foot arch of timbers mounted on a floating log raft and used as a high fairlead (pulley mount) to haul logs from nearby sidehills to the salt chuck using wire cable.

Bag boom: Loose floating logs encircled by a string of boomsticks.

Bawdy house: House of ill repute.

Bite of the line: Standing dangerously close to a slack line where, when the line becomes taut, one is in danger of being struck by it. Now used as an expression relating to any dangerous or uncomfortable position.

Bolts: In the lumber industry, a bolt is a very short log, perhaps only a few feet long. For example, shingle bolts used in the manufacture of shingles.

Boom of logs: Logs tightly stowed, side by side, within a rectangular framework of chained together boomsticks, using swifters or riders pulled across on top at right angles and chained to either side to maintain the rectangular shape; for example, a five-section boom.

Boom chain: A heavy linked chain (about eighty pounds when new), seven feet long, with a large ring at one end and a toggle at the other. The toggle end hangs down through a four-inch hole drilled in the ends of the boomstick and is picked up with a pike pole and threaded up through the four-inch hole in the next boomstick where the toggle is spread across the hole to secure the chain.

Booming grounds: Protected waters where loose logs are temporarily stored in bag booms while they are being sorted into species or made into rafts for towing to sawmills, etc., for further processing.

Boomstick: A long log, sixty feet or better, with a four-inch hole drilled vertically through each end with a boom chain hanging in one end. When these boomsticks are chained end to end, they are used to enclose floating logs for safekeeping. (See boom chain.)

Brush out: To clear an overgrown pathway of bushes and branches.

Bucker: Man who saws felled trees into specific lengths prior to their removal from the forest.

14

Bug: Hand-held electrical switch that initiates on contact through palm pressure and is used by the whistlepunk to relay signals to the donkey puncher (engineer).

Bull block: In high-lead logging it is the pulley block at the top of the spar tree through which the one-inch main line cable runs and attaches to the butt rigging. (See butt rigging.)

Bull bucker: Man in charge of fallers.

Bull cook: Assistant to the camp cook, splits wood, makes beds, lights fires, tends the water system and fixes whatever.

Bull of the woods: Camp superintendent.

Bushed: Tired.

Butt rigging: The short length of chain and shackles that connect the one-inch main line cable to the one-half- to three-quarter-inch haulback cable and also from which hang the one-inch chokers.

Camp tender: Functions as a boat that transports both personnel and supplies as well as assists in towing logs to and from the booming grounds.

Cat road: A skid road cut through the bush by a Cat dragging logs.

Cat skinner: Caterpillar tractor operator.

Catawampus: Expression meaning out of line, bent, twisted, not square with the world.

Chaser: Unhooks the chokers from the logs at the spar tree.

Chivaree: A mock serenade to newly wed couples performed with tin pans, cooking pots, horns, etc.

Choker holes: Holes existing or made under a log where a chokerman pushes the choker knob through to the other side.

Choker: A one-inch steel cable approximately thirty feet long with a steel knob swagged onto one end and with a "bell" apparatus that can slide the length of the cable. The knob end is pushed under the log, pulled up around the log and locked into the sliding "bell"; thus, the log is choked.

Chokerman: The logger who attaches choker cables to the logs.

Claim: A patch of surveyed timber to be logged off.

Cold deck pile: A large pile of logs yarded out of the woods and stacked up at the base of a spar tree as a temporary storage prior to removal by truck or railroad to another location.

Coleman: Gasoline lantern or camp stove.

Commissary: A camp store with basic supplies of boots, socks, rain gear, Stanfields, pocket knives and watches, liniment, laxatives, tobacco, gum and candy, writing paper and stamps, etc.

Company town: A town with a single employer that also provides all goods and services including housing accommodations.

Cordwood: A cord of wood is a stack eight feet long by four feet high by four feet wide, or 128 cubic feet.

Cork boots or corks: Caulk shoes; boots with steel points (caulks) embedded in the heels and soles of the boot to prevent slipping on round, slippery logs.

Corking: Placing one's gillnet in a position to obstruct another fisherman's net.

Cruiser (Timber): Estimates the quantity and quality of standing timber in an area.

Davis raft: Invented by Bert Davis, the Davis raft was built up by parbuckling (rolling) logs onto a previously woven mat of logs and cables and securing each succeeding layer with heavy steel cables until the original mat was several feet below the surface. The completed raft, like an iceberg, was more beneath the surface than above.

Dead head: A water heavy log that floats near vertically in the water, sometimes only a few inches above the surface and often several inches below the surface, as a serious water hazard.

Deadman contacts: Normally open electrical spring-loaded contacts that close with hand pressure but spring open when pressure is released.

Donkey engine: A sled-mounted engine at the foot of the spar tree used to yard logs to a landing with wire cable on drums; could be steam, gas or diesel fueled.

Donkey puncher: Man who operates the donkey engine.

Dory: A boat with a narrow, flat bottom, flaring sides and high ends.

Double bitted: An ax with two blades.

Drag saw: A steam or gasoline motorized crosscut saw used at landings to cut logs into rounds of wood.

Draw knife: A knifelike blade with a handle at each end at right angles to the blade. Usually used on wood by pulling or drawing tool toward operator and thus removing thin shavings.

Drubbing: Spanking or sound thrashing.

Empyema: A collection of pus in a body cavity, especially in the pleural cavity.

Eye splice: An (eye) loop made in the end of a cable or rope by looping the end back and splicing it in to secure the loop.

Faller: A logger who cuts down trees for a living.

Float camp: Large moveable rafts of logs, usually supporting houses, machinery and sheds for logging purposes.

Flunky: Person who assists in preparing food in the cook house and waits tables.

Friars balsam: An aromatic ointment used for medicinal purposes that soothes and restores breathing passages.

Friction tape: Electrician's tape.

Gilchrist jack: A heavy duty hand-operated mechanical jack used by hand loggers to lift and skid logs to the water.

Gin pole: A leaning spar fitted with a fairlead pulley and line for lifting and loading and/or dumping logs or whatever.

Gofer: Go for this, go for that.

Grease trails: Trails long ago established by coastal Natives to transport their trade goods including oolachon grease from the salt water to the interior tribes.

Grub: The white larva (about one inch long by three-sixteenths diameter) of certain insects, especially beetles. Also, refers to meals (food) that loggers eat.

Gumwood: The wood of a gum tree, especially eucalyptus of Australia, often used as an outer sheathing at the water line on wooden boats to protect the hulls against rough usage.

Gunny sack: A strong burlap sack made from hemp used early on for sacking coal and bulky produce; latterly used derogatorily to mean "all washed up."

Guy wires:Gypo logger: An independent logger who does not own timber rights and so contracts for those that do.

Hand logger: Coastal logger who works alone or with a partner. Usually they work steep slopes to the salt chuck where gravity is used to aid in skidding logs downward. Early hand loggers were restricted from using power tools.

Hang up: Any obstruction that prevents a "turn" of logs having a speedy trip to the landing.

Haulback block: Is hung on the spar tree usually close beneath the bull block. The half-inch haulback cable runs through the haulback block and out to the tail blocks and thence back to the butt rigging.

High lead logging: System using a spar tree and donkey to drag logs, at least one end off the ground to avoid obstructions such as stumps, into a landing.

High rigger (high climber): A person who climbs the tree with belt and spurs. Hanging from his belt was an ax and a saw. After limbing and topping the spar tree the high rigger was then responsible for rigging the guy wires, blocks and cable systems for high lead logging.

Hooker: Man in charge of the yarding crew and responsible for setting up the block and cable systems to be used on the yarding roads pulling logs from stumps to the landing.

Iron Chink: Machine used in coastal canneries that automatically guts, cleans and slices fish. It was first used about 1903 and displaced several human workers, often Chinese men.

Jack snipe: A small, short-billed bird.

Klahowya: Chinook greeting; "How are you?"

Konk knots: Growths on a tree caused by a parasitic tree fungus; in other words, rot.

Konky or conky: Poor quality tree usually containing rot.

Kwakuitl: Native people occupying central B.C. coast islands, specifically Vancouver Island.

Landing: Place at the base of a spar tree near the donkey where logs are loaded onto trucks.

Lignum vitae: A hard and extremely heavy wood; often used to make wood bearings.

Log dump: Where logs are unloaded at the booming grounds.

Manila rope: A Philippine hemp rope made from the fiber of the abaca plant used extensively prior to the introduction of plastic ropes.

Mastoid: A reference to the temporal bone behind the ear.

Matrimonial cake:

Cookie mixture:	Filling mixture:
1-1/4 c. sifted flour	2 c. pitted, chopped dates
3/4 c. butter	1 tsp. soda
1 c. brown sugar	1 c. water, 1 tbsp. lemon juice
1-1/4 c. rolled oats	1 tbsp. lemon juice
	1c. brown sugar

Combine cookie mixture ingredients and spread 1/2 of it into shallow 10" x 12" pan and press down. Combine filling ingredients and cook over a low heat until thick. Cool slightly and spread over first mixture. Sprinkle balance of cookie mixture over the date filling. Bake at 325 for 45 minutes. Cut into bars.

Mesachie: Chinook jargon for bad or evil.

Misery whip: A two-man crosscut saw, sometimes fifteen feet long, replaced by modern chain saws.

Molly Hogan: A logging term meaning a circle of wire rope used temporarily as a link between two eye splices. Also, a wire strand removed from a steel cable and used through a hole in a pin in place of a cotter key.

Mug-up: Take time for coffee and cake.

Net loft: Storage place inside a fish cannery where gillnets were hung during the winter.

Oolachon: Small candlefish. Many Natives still render the fish for their rich oil, often called grease, which they use in cooking.

Packer: Before modern refrigeration fish packers picked up the daily catch from gillnet fishermen and transported same to the nearby canneries.

Pass line: Light 1/4" by 5/16" cable (usually the straw line) used to take a high rigger up and down a spar tree and to hoist all the blocks and cables up the tree when rigging up.

Peavey: A tool having a straight heavy wooden handle with a steel point and free swinging hook, used primarily for rolling logs.

Pecker pole: A small tree hardly worth logging.

Peeler log: Usually a large diameter log free of large knots, cracks, splits and rot, that can be used for peeling off sheets for the manufacture of plywood.

Pike pole: A wood or aluminum pole often thirteen or more feet long with a pike on one end and used by a boom man to maneuver logs in the water.

Point-to-point navigation: Dead reckoning navigation by water following points of land to destination.

Pole cat: An ill-smelling, long-haired member of the weasel family, resembling a marten and sometimes referred to as a skunk.

Poleax: An ax, usually with a hammer opposite the cutting edge, used in stunning and slaughtering animals.

Poleaxed: Hit on the head as if by a poleax (a battle ax with a long handle).

Potlatch: An event in Native society where wealth is given away for the purpose of achieving status in their culture.

Powder monkey: A fellow who handled dynamite, usually stumping power (20 percent to 40 percent) and blew up obstructing stumps and rocks.

Pulling slack: Unspooling strawline from the donkey drum and pulling it through the bush by hand (manpower) to thread the tail blocks and back to the donkey to pick up the haulback cable. Spooling in the strawline threads the haulback out through the tail blocks and back to the butt rigging once again.

Push: Foreman of a logging camp.

Putt boats: A 1930–40s boom boat with an Easthope or Vivian gas engine and a wet exhaust that in operation made a kind of putt-putt sound.

Rafted up: Log rafts secured together for storage or towing purposes. Also several boats tied side by side; sometimes tied to a wharf, sometimes anchored in a bay.

Raising a spar: Often a suitable growing tree was not available in a logging area where one was needed and so a spar would be brought in and raised for that purpose.

Rigging slinger: The man who pulls the rigging through the bush to the fallen and bucked logs. Second in command on the rigging crew.

Rigging: A network of pulleys, cables and chokers that dragged, hoisted and loaded logs.

Road: The path from the active logging area to the spar tree along which logs were dragged or skidded. As each strip of timber was logged the road was changed (rerigged at a new location) by the hooker.

Rowing Indian fashion: Standing in a skiff facing forward and rowing with sweeps.

Salal: A dense evergreen shrub of the West Coast bearing edible fruit. The berries make wonderful pies and jams.

Salmonberry: Edible, sweet berry having an orange to red color about the size and shape of a blackberry, but not as firm or tasty.

Salt chuck: Salt water as applied to the ocean and coastal inlets.

Sasquatch: A large, hairy manlike creature reported to inhabit areas of the Pacific Northwest. Sometimes called bigfoot.

Scaler: A person using a scaling stick who classifies, measures and calculates the volume of wood that can be cut from a raw log.

Schoolmarm: A tree with two main trunks instead of one.

Scissor-Bill: A stupid logger.

Scotchman: A buoy marking the end of fishing gear (halibut line) or traps. It should also have the owner's identification visible.

Self starter: An individual who seldom has to be told what needs to be done and needs little or no supervision.

Shift: A straight, loose-fitting dress worn with or without a belt.

Show (logging): Any logging operation such as a high-lead show or a side-hill show, or skidder show, etc.

Sidehill show: Coastal logging term for a steep slope to be logged.

Siwash logger: A beachcomber.

Siwash: Originally Chinook jargon for a Native Northwest Indian. Sometimes meaning to divert a line around an obstacle for a change of direction where a pulley is not readily available. Latterly, it's applied to any lazy person.

Skookum: Chinook meaning "powerful."

Skyline system: A heavy steel cable (1-1/2" to 2-1/2" diameter) strung between two spar trees up to 2,000 feet apart with a traveling carriage. From the carriage hung chokers (steel cables) that transported logs into the air and over rough ground to the trackside or landing.

Snag: Standing dead tree.

Snoose: A Swedish invention of finely ground moist tobacco. It is commonly used by loggers under their lower lip in place of cigarettes.

Spar tree: The tall standing or raised tree used in high-lead logging stabilized with guy wires and where running cables pass through blocks (pulleys) hung high up on the spar.

Springboard: A board about five feet long used by fallers that was inserted in notches chopped in the tree trunk. Among other functions, the springboard raised the faller above the swelled butt, making less work chopping or sawing.

St. Vitus' Dance: An acute nervous disease of children (chorea) characterized by uncontrollable muscular twitching of the face and limbs.

Standing boom: Semipermanent string of boomsticks with stifflegs to shore often functioning as a safe deepwater tie-up area for log booms, barges or boats.

Stanfields: Warm winter underwear, usually wool.

Steam pot: Steam donkey.

Steel Straps: A short length of steel cable (10' to 15') with an eye splice in either end.

Steelhead: A sea-going rainbow trout.

Stetson: A felt hat with a broad brim and high crown.

Stiffleg: A boomstick used in conjunction with a standing boom to hold a float or standing boom away from shore; sometimes called a jillpoke.

Stowing logs: Securing log rafts or bags to a standing boom for safe keeping. Also, the act of using individual logs to build five-section flat rafts.

Strawline: The smallest diameter steel cable spooled on a donkey engine.

Stumping powder: Low grade dynamite; 20 to 40 percent dynamite.

Sunshine logger: Applied to anyone not wanting to work on the wet B.C. coast in the winter. Also applied to anyone who won't work in the rain.

Sweeps: An extra long pair of oars.

Swing: Moving logs from place to place prior to reaching salt water. For example, from the back of a claim to a cold deck next to a spar tree (swung once). From the cold deck skidded into the salt chuck (swung twice).

Tail block: A pulley the farthest point out (back end of the setting) through which the haulback cable runs. These blocks also control the angle and position of the yarding lines with respect to the donkey.

Teredo worm: An aquatic, wood-boring worm that attacks floating logs as well as wood-hulled ships.

Thimbled: Struck anywhere on the cranium with a human finger wearing a steel sewing thimble.

Tide flats: Shallow shoreline exposed to air as the salt water recedes with an ebbing tide.

Towing bitt: A strong post (often in pairs) on the back deck of a tow boat used for anchoring the tow line when towing.

Trackside: A logging setting with a spar tree at a road or track.

Turn of logs: A unit of logs "yarded" or hauled by cable in one trip to the landing.

Turnout: A wide spot in the road where trucks can pass.

Whistlepunk: Signal man that relays operating commands by signal wire or radio from the hook tender to the donkey engineer who normally cannot see the operation.

Whooping cough: An infectious disease of the respiratory mucous membrane, especially of children.

Widowmaker: Any leaning tree, standing snag, dangerous or rotten tree tops or limbs, etc., that might prove a threat to fallers.

Windjammer: Vessel propelled by sails.

Wood log: A log that is to be cut up for fuel to fire the steam donkey or the camp wood stoves.

Yarding: The act of skidding logs to a central location such as a trackside or landing.

Yew wood: An evergreen coniferous wood being fine grained and elastic.

Gildersleeve History in B.C.

In 1916–17 George Harrison (Doc) Gildersleeve, my maternal grandfather, came to British Columbia from Oregon with his brothers-in-law, Almon and Lloyd Owens. They were loggers. In 1916 the three men established a logging operation at Nootum Bay in lower Burke Channel. Doc, Almon and Lloyd lived in tents when they first set up camp at Nootum in 1916 and began to clear space near the beach for cabins that were to come later.

Steam power was still very much in vogue in 1917. The first year or two they had contracts for cutting cord wood to fuel cannery steam plants in the nearby coastal area. One method of getting the wood to the beach was by way of the Nootum River. The trees they felled produced logs too long and heavy to move in the narrow river waterway and so they were "bucked" (sawed by hand) into short-length bolts that floated easily down the river to the tide flats where they were then split into cord wood.

Handlogger is the term that described what people like my grandfather were in those early days in British Columbia. M. Allerdale Grainger, a man who assisted in writing the first Forestry Act in British Columbia, in his 1908 novel entitled, *Woodsmen of the West*, had this to say about handloggers:

> The first morning light would see them already at their place of work, perhaps a mile's rowboat journey from their home. There they would slave all day, carrying their sharp, awkward tools up through the hillside underbrush; chopping and sawing, felling big timber; cutting up logs, barking them; using heavy jackscrews to coax logs downhill to the sea. At evening, tide serving, they would tow such logs as they had floated round to where their boom was hung, and put the logs inside, in safety. Then they would go home and dry their clothes, and cook supper, and sleep like dead men.

According to Allerdale, handloggers scorned elaborate logging apparatus and were content to work close to the beaches, wanting only that timber they could haul out "easily." Their work rarely reached as far as 1,000 feet inland from salt water.

Doc and brother Bill with Almon and Lloyd Owens broke out of the handlogger mold in the early 1920s when they had an A-frame and cold deck outfit operating in the Restoration Bay area of Burke Channel. The loggers first created a cold deck pile around a designated spar tree. Often when the fallen timber was far enough back from the salt chuck, more than one spar tree was used. The cold deck pile was then moved (swung) from spar tree to spar tree using a donkey engine. The final swing was into the salt chuck using a 150-foot-high lead A-frame and steam donkey situated on a large floating raft made of logs.

Later on, Doc progressed all the way to truck logging. His first truck outfit was at Rivers Inlet Cannery at the head of Rivers Inlet. Due to the swampy nature of the ground alongside the Wannock River and Owikeno Lake, about eight miles of plank road were required. Later, in 1947–50, he employed trucks in logging the slopes of Tallheo Point in the South Bentinck.

In 1917, Doc Gildersleeve was twenty-six years old, being born May 3, 1891, at Sunnydale, King County, Washington. Many years later, when I was nine, he told me that he had come to B.C. to log because in Oregon and Washington most of the available big timber was gone, all cut by 1917. I did not understand then, but fifty-eight years later in 1999, one sees the logging industries in Oregon, Washington and now British Columbia as remnants of much better days.

Doc Gildersleeve and my Grandmother Amy Isadore (Owens) Gildersleeve were married June 1, 1909, in Lane County, Oregon. He was eighteen, she was twenty. In 1918 they moved their family north into British Columbia from Oregon, bringing with them the three children they had at the time. The oldest child, my mother, Elsie Gertrude, was eight; Richard George was three; and Hattie Ella Mae Gildersleeve was one.

Doc built a cabin on the beach at Nootum Bay for Amy and their kids and established their home for the next five years.

24

Three more children were born to Doc and Amy in their Nootum cabin. The first was Frank, 1919; Pearl, 1921; and Keaton, 1922.

In those early days of encampment at Nootum Bay (1917–24), Doc had little means for getting around the country to places like Bella Bella, Bella Coola or Ocean Falls, where there was a hospital. All three were roughly fifty to sixty miles distant and transportation was possible only by water. At first, if they needed to get to Ocean Falls on an emergency basis or even to pick up groceries and mail, they rowed a flat-bottomed skiff about eighteen feet in length. They rowed standing up facing forward, "Indian fashion." Working with the wind and tide might take three days each way. Later the primary means of transportation was the *Mary S.*, his twenty-five-foot, heavy built wooden work boat powered by a three-cylinder gas engine with a wet exhaust. When underway the exhaust made a "putt-putt" sound. Craft of this type became known to all family members as Putt Boats. Because the *Mary S.* lacked speed (six to seven mph) and passenger accommodations, Amy chose to deliver Uncles Frank, Keaton and Aunt Pearl in the cabin at Nootum rather than in the hospital at Ocean Falls. The idea of expecting the weather to cooperate in undertaking an eight-hour trip in the *Mary S.* to Ocean Falls near the time of her delivery evidently did not appeal to Grandmother, tough as she was. As a boy, I was told that Granddad delivered Grandmother's last three kids himself. I have no reason to disbelieve this and perhaps, during that time, he helped deliver other children in that remote area. It was also said that his midwifery prowess was the reason that he acquired the nickname "Doc." Whatever the reason, it stuck with him from then on, all the rest of his days.

Doc and Amy

Doc was of average height for his generation, being five-foot-ten with a wiry compact physique. He had a long, intelligent, friendly face with high cheek bones featuring a prominent, narrow, Roman nose and a mouth ready to smile. It was said that his father, my great-grandfather, John Franklin Gildersleeve was half

Cherokee Indian. His mother was Harriet Dunham. George Harrison Gildersleeve was fifth of eight children.

Granddad liked to tell us kids that he ran away from home when he was eleven years old and never went back until he was seventeen. He was sent out by his mother to pick gooseberries for dinner and never returned. He claimed that during those early intervening and enlightening years he managed to eat regularly by hiring himself out as a "gofer" to one bawdy house proprietor or another.

Doc was the dominant figure, the patriarch in his family and extended family of grandchildren, longtime employees and close friends. Due in part, I believe, to the fact that he was very hard of hearing, his manner could be distant and stern to his children and grandchildren. And yet to others who knew him well, he was open and friendly. I never knew of anyone who would have judged him other than generous, fair and above all honest.

Grandma Amy Gildersleeve was short, five-foot-one, born November 29, 1889, in Cottage Grove, Oregon. In later years, when I was still a boy, she had what Granddad called an "ample figure, warm in the winter and shady in the summer." Her face was small, round and delicately featured with a pixielike quality, especially when she smiled or laughed, which she did a lot.

Grandmother was one of seven children and the only girl. Word had it that her mother was somewhat of a tyrant and raised her daughter as the workhorse of the family. I can easily believe this to be true as Grandmother could do just about anything in the way of cooking or sewing and do it exceedingly well. Her culinary skills were legendary. She put up preserves of meat, fish, vegetables and fruit. She sewed and made everything, including quilts, drapes, her clothes, our clothes and more. She commonly had several pairs of knitting needles going, turning out socks and sweaters, and for relaxation she crocheted and embroidered. For hobbies, she gardened and in much later years, she collected sea shells with a vengeance, traveling over much of the B.C. coast in search of her prey. Grandmother Gildersleeve was a generous person. She was a giver, always ready to help and do much more than her share. She was a positive thinker and, I believe, optimistic by nature. She tried to see good in everyone, though with some people I felt that she had to squint awfully hard.

Amy was a self starter and always enthusiastic, yet she never seemed to want much for herself. I never heard her utter an oath or complain to anyone, let alone to my sisters and me. God knows, I personally caused her fits. On top of her other myriad responsibilities and after raising her own family of five kids under trying circumstances, she often had to shoulder the task of looking after my two sisters and me. She fed us, clothed us, comforted us when we needed it and boxed our ears when we needed that.

When she teased us, we were "rapscallions" or "scalawags." When we teased her, we were "young jackanapes." If we upset her or scared her it was "tarnation" or "thunderation." If we confused her, it was "great Caesar's ghost."

Amy usually wore a light cotton shift to well below her knees. For comfort on her feet she wore broad, brown moccasin shoes with thick crepelike soles that planted her solidly on terra firma. As far as we kids knew, Gram was the boss.

Everyone called her Gram. We kids loved her, relied on her and had full confidence in her. I never understood why she wept so easily when family members were leaving home or coming back home. The circumstances made little difference; she wept anyway.

Gram was born with a minor congenital defect to both of her little fingers. It prevented her from straightening them out as a piano player would need to do. I inherited Gram's crooked little finger gene, so I too have crooked pinkies. She instructed me that massaging the tendons of my small fingers would help in straightening them out as I grew older. So, in tucking me in at bedtime, she would tell me in a whisper to rub my small fingers, equally, until I fell asleep. Every night I would begin with the right little finger and fell asleep soon after. Today years later, my right little finger bears testimony to her good advice, while my left remains very crooked.

Gildersleeve • Owens • Wheeler Family Tree

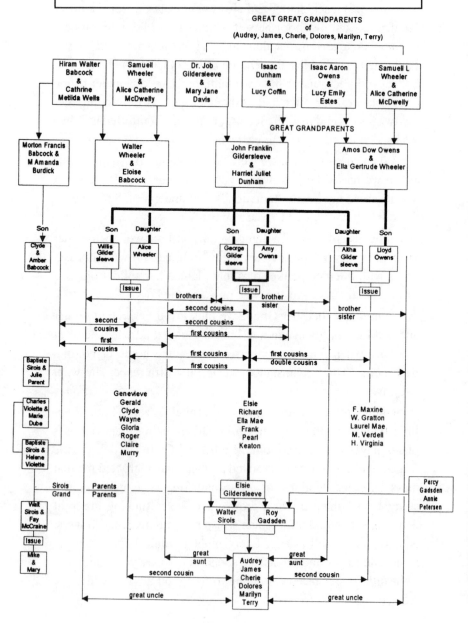

GREAT GREAT GRANDPARENTS
of
(Audrey, James, Cherie, Dolores, Marilyn, Terry)

Hiram Walter Babcock & Cathrine Metilda Wells

Samuell Wheeler & Alice Catherine McDwelly

Dr. Job Gildersleeve & Mary Jane Davis

Isaac Dunham & Lucy Coffin

Isaac Aaron Owens & Lucy Emily Estes

Samuell L Wheeler & Alice Catherine McDwelly

GREAT GRANDPARENTS

Morton Francis Babcock & M Amanda Burdick

Walter Wheeler & Eloise Babcock

John Franklin Gildersleeve & Harriet Juliet Dunham

Amos Dow Owens & Ella Gertrude Wheeler

Son — Clyde & Amber Babcock

Son — Willis Gildersleeve

Daughter — Alice Wheeler

Son — George Gildersleeve

Daughter — Amy Owens

Daughter — Altha Gildersleeve

Son — Lloyd Owens

Issue

brothers
second cousins
brother sister
brother sister
second cousins
second cousins
first cousins
first cousins
first cousins
first cousins double cousins
first cousins

Baptiste Sirois & Julie Parent

Charles Violette & Marie Dube

Baptiste Sirois & Helene Violette

Genevieve Gerald Clyde Wayne Gloria Roger Claire Murry

Elsie Richard Ella Mae Frank Pearl Keaton

F. Maxine W. Gratton Laurel Mae M. Verdell H. Virginia

Sirois Grand

Parents Parents

Elsie Gildersleeve

Walter Sirois

Roy Gadsden

Percy Gadsden Annie Petersen

Walt Sirois & Fay McCraine

Issue

Mike & Mary

great aunt
great aunt
Audrey James Cherie Dolores Marilyn Terry
second cousin
second cousin
great uncle
great uncle

28

The Pioneers

Pioneering was not a new idea to the Gildersleeve family in America. Richard Gildersleeve, a Puritan, was born in 1601 in County Suffolk, England. Sometime prior to 1635, Richard Gildersleeve sailed for America with his wife and young son, Richard II, and joined other Puritan settlers at Watertown, Massachusetts, thus becoming the pioneer founder of the family in America more than 350 years ago.

An excerpt from the book *Gildersleeve Pioneers*, by W. H. Gildersleeve, dated 1941, published by The Tuttle Publishing Company, Inc., Rutland, Vermont (p. 20) has this to say expressing the sort of welcome the Puritans experienced as their little ship, after eight weeks at sea, approached the shores of New England:

> No friendly lighthouses, no passing ships nor pilot boats spoke a welcome. No charts and soundings warned them of hidden rocks on which they might sink and perish. Primeval wilderness and native desolation brooded over sea and land. A vast dense forest was before them, sparsely inhabited by savages and a few isolated bands of Europeans.

Doc Gildersleeve, born in 1891, became a part of the tenth generation in America—descendant of Richard Gildersleeve, the Puritan.

One can easily believe that the experience of going ashore at the wild and remote beach of Nootum Bay, B.C., in 1918 as a family of five was every bit as concerning to Doc and Amy Gildersleeve as Puritan Richard Gildersleeve's experience was for him and his family 285 years earlier, going ashore at Watertown, Massachusetts, with uncertainty surrounding them.

The greatest similarity of situation in my view is that, for better or worse, both families were assuming responsibility for their actions and their welfare. They were making the effort to gain control of their destinies. Can any family be expected to do more for themselves? They were fully prepared to sacrifice for their future well being and for what they believed in. Above all, they believed in their own abilities to cope with challenges, whatever they might be.

What sort of men and women were they that left their friends and relatives, took their children and their meager possessions, traveled hundreds and hundreds of miles to a foreign shore to settle in a remote place in the wilderness? They exposed themselves and their children to untold hardship and danger. Almost anything that needed doing for creature comfort, or just plain survival, was going to be damned difficult to do.

Just think of it, now, this was no weekend picnic, where, when the food ran out, or the sun went down, or the mosquitoes got too thick, they could pack up the kids and go home. No, they were home. They had arrived in a place on a rocky, sandy beach almost surrounded by heavy forest, with a shallow stretch of water extending out into what was called Nootum Bay.

Nootum Bay is situated in lower Burke Channel, four miles south of Restoration Bay. Captain Vancouver, in his exploration of the Pacific Northwest Coast in May, 1793, repaired his leaky ships at Restoration Bay, as if this had a pinprick of significance to Doc and Amy Gildersleeve as they waded ashore with their belongings and kids that first day in 1918.

Doc, Almon and Lloyd had built shacks for their wives and families during the previous year when they were living in tents and getting their cord wood operation started. The shacks would shed rain and block the wind, but not necessarily cold drafts or mosquitoes.

There was no place to shop for food, clothing or anything. If one had not thought to bring it, then, tough beans. Make it or go without. A shopping trip might be planned back to Ocean Falls sixty miles away in the rowing skiff, where Doc and Amy had first arrived by steamer from Oregon. That, however, would require absence from daily labor and potential wages.

I can imagine that thoughts and questions similar to the following were going through their minds. Well, we must have food. Are there any fish in the bay? Did anyone bring fish hooks? You say we can hunt deer, goats and bear? Where do we hunt them? You mean we have to climb up there? I wonder how long meat will keep before it goes rotten? Did anybody pack that book on curing wild game? I wonder if these wild dandelion

30

greens are edible? They look okay, but, to be sure, Dad, you'd better try some.

There was no interest in turning back now. They had a dream and, prepared or not, were eager to face their future.

This brings to mind a very famous poem by Goethe (1749–1832), the German poet. The truth contained in it should be an inspiration to all those who aspire to pioneer—whatever the purpose. I quote as follows:

Until one is committed, there is hesitancy,
The chance to draw back
Always ineffectiveness.
Concerning all acts of initiative,
there is one elementary truth,
The ignorance of which kills
Countless ideas and endless plans:
That the moment one definitely
Commits oneself,
The providence moves too.
All sorts of things occur to help one
That would never otherwise have occurred.
A whole stream of events issues from the decision,
Raising in one's favor all manner
Of unforeseen incidents and meetings
And material assistance,
Which no man could have dreamed
Would come his way.
Whatever you can do or dream you can, begin it.
Boldness has genius, power, and magic in it.
—Goethe

Aquatic Chickens

These pioneers were not green as grass; they had, in fact, hunted, skinned and cured wild game in Oregon. Yet, it did take some time for them to adapt satisfactorily to their new environment.

Someone had brought along several chickens with the idea that they would be able to raise chickens and have a constant supply of fresh meat. The idea actually was good. In off-loading their belongings and supplies that first day, darkness overcame them and not everything was transported and placed high up on the beach. The chickens were not high priority and also not thought perishable, and so remained down on the beach where they were placed after being rowed ashore. During the night the tide came in and all the chickens drowned. So much for chicken stew. Tides were a factor that they were not used to but they quickly adapted to the phenomenon.

I am quite sure that Doc and Amy landed in the wilderness expecting to be able to handle their challenges. They were prepared to roll up their sleeves and go to work. Yet, is anyone ever prepared to put up with the unexpected that pioneers such as they ran into? I believe that it is a unique mindset that carries and sustains people of their caliber. The truth is, as with so many other pioneers, they did not know that surviving and flourishing as they did in the wilderness on practically nothing was next to impossible. They just went ahead and did it anyhow.

A typical example of the unexpected occurred as the Owens and Gildersleeve children were playing on the beach one sunny morning. Frank Gildersleeve, now three years old, was playing with a short, sharp stick. Young Frank fell, holding the stick before his face and jamming its end into his eye socket. The result was one of gouging the eyeball out of its socket to flop loosely onto his cheek. The other children, shocked out of their wits at seeing Frank's macabre expression, ran screaming to get help. Apparently, without much fanfare, Grandmother sloshed Frank's face and dangling eyeball with fresh, clean water and then proceeded, using two spoons, to coax the eyeball back into its socket. Amazingly, he suffered no lasting ill effects from this ghastly incident and recovered completely.

Tragically, later in 1924, Amy's third child, Ella Mae, drowned while playing alone on slippery logs.

In many ways, Doc and Amy were just ordinary people who managed to accomplish extraordinary tasks. Above all, they were doing what they wanted to do and anything they managed to build was theirs.

Gildersleeve-Sirois History in B.C.

Elsie and Walt

Elsie Gildersleeve was eight in 1918 when she arrived on the beach at Nootum Bay, B.C. The family resided there for about five years while her father Doc Gildersleeve learned to log on the sidehills of British Columbia.

The beach environment was potentially hostile to young children, that is, at least until they became acclimatized to the dangers surrounding them. For example, children being careless of an incoming tide might suddenly be trapped by surrounding deep water, and separated from the safety of high ground. The specter of one of the children drowning was ever present.

Sharp tools, another danger, were everywhere and careless handling could cause a sudden loss of fingers or toes, or worse. Also, predator animals such as bears, wolves and cougars that prowled the forest and underbrush encircling Nootum Bay were a constant worry for parents.

Periodically, Amy Gildersleeve would leave the beach to assist Doc with tasks that required an extra pair of hands. During these times Elsie, being the oldest, had charge of her siblings, being anointed with the necessary amount of authority.

On a certain occasion, when Elsie was about twelve years old, she had been put in charge while her mom and dad left in their gas boat for the day. Later when her parents were overdue on returning, Elsie, worried, had gone alone out to a place on the beach called the "Point," in hopes of seeing them approaching up Burke Channel.

The Point, for some reason, was a place that had danger associated with it and all siblings, including Elsie, were strictly forbidden to go there, especially when their parents were gone, no

33

matter that it was a vantage point to view boating activity in Burke Channel. Later Amy and Doc returned safely and were informed of Elsie's transgression by one of her siblings. The result to Elsie was an unfortunate lecture that left her with a disappointing memory of the incident. To her it seemed gross injustice to be reprimanded for actions caused by her sense of responsibility for her siblings and worry for her parents.

Once when I was thirteen, in a moment of lapsed judgment, I sassed Elsie. After she slapped me across the face, she informed me that "she was my mother and where I was concerned she was to be obeyed even though she might be wrong." She demanded respect from her kids. No doubt as her mother before her expected it. She also insisted on her children calling her "Mother" and would not tolerate maw or mom. Now that I have absorbed parenting lumps of my own, it is clearer to me that, among other simple truths, when young one must learn to take orders gracefully before being successful later on at giving them.

By any yardstick, Elsie's upbringing was authoritarian. Her character was shaped by no-nonsense parents and honed by adult responsibilities before she was twelve. In her early teens Elsie already had shown a flair for artistic achievement when she began to sketch and paint in oils. Over the years, although she was entirely self taught, she developed into a creditable artist and completed many canvases to the satisfaction of relatives and friends.

In personality, Elsie favored her father, Doc Gildersleeve. She said to me on one occasion that she wished that she had been born a man. "Men are allowed to do so much more," she said. She never hesitated long to speak her mind, especially if she felt that her integrity was being questioned.

Elsie was no complainer. She also was not one to confide in her children; to her we were too young to understand her problems and from us she never looked for sympathy. During times of family upheaval, I would watch her cry quietly alone and could do nothing to help her. Considering her austere upbringing, however, I feel that she was a good mother to her children. She worried about our formal education or lack of it. Academic achievement was not the central focus of life in the logging camp and after two years of correspondence courses, Elsie made personal sacrifices to see that my sisters and I attended a regular school. For example, her pursuit of our elementary school educations took her to Dawson's Landing in Rivers Inlet and later Ocean Falls to live apart with us from our stepfather, Roy Gadsden, many months at a time, while he supported us financially from grandfather's logging camp. By this time Elsie was looking after five of us—sisters Audrey and Cherie Sirois, Marilyn Gadsden, brother Terrence Gadsden and myself.

By 1927 Elsie Gildersleeve was seventeen years old and attending school at Battleground, Washington. It was during this period that she met Walter Sirois (Anthony Arthur Sirois) whom she married November, 1928, when she was eighteen and he was twenty-two.

Walter Sirois was born February 1, 1907, in Van Buren, Maine, on the St. John River and the International Boundary between Canada and the U.S.A. His forebears were descendants of Acadians, the early colonizers of present-day Nova Scotia and New Brunswick. They were exiled in 1755 after their land passed from French to British rule. Though many Acadian families at that time found refuge in Louisiana and coastal New Brunswick, a small handful later became the first colonizers of the Madawaska region, along the St. John River. (See *National Geographic*, Sept. 1980, Madawaska.)

My paternal grandfather J. Baptiste Sirois, born September 24, 1877, was killed accidentally (buried and suffocated in an earthen cave-in) when my father was a young lad of ten. His mother, my paternal grandmother, Helen (Violette) Sirois, born March 25, 1881 (and died July 5, 1940), then married his father's cousin, also a Sirois, who had a young daughter (Stella). My father could not get along with his stepfather nor with his newly acquired stepsister, so at fifteen years of age he split.

For the next year or two Walter Sirois worked when and where he could. One winter it was a lumber camp, the following winter a sawmill and in summer it was on a gravel train. At the age of seventeen, with his mother's approval, he had applied for and received induction into the army and was stationed at

Vancouver, Washington. It was while in the army that he became interested in wrestling and it later on became his professional activity.

At the time he and Elsie Gildersleeve were married, he was out of the army and working for the Zellerbach Company at Camas, Washington. In March, 1929, he quit the paper mill at Camas, Washington and with Elsie, who was pregnant with Audrey Sirois, he took the coastal steamer to Ocean Falls, B.C. Grandfather (Doc) Gildersleeve picked them up in the *Crusader I* (camp tending boat) and he took them to his logging camp, which was now at a site in South Bentinck Arm. They arrived in the wet snow and rain, typical for early March in that part of the world.

By now Doc and Bill Gildersleeve had parted company, but Doc's younger brother Jack, who had an R.N. (Registered Nurse) certificate, was at the camp as first-aid man. It was a responsible position, especially in those days, when they were a long way from a medical doctor or hospital should anyone be hurt. (No radios or telephones meant little or no communication with the outside world.)

Amy Gildersleeve was not in camp either, as she was still at their place in Battleground, Washington, where her kids, Richard, Frank, Pearl and Keaton, were going to school. So, there was a dearth of both women and kids in camp at that time.

Audrey Darlene Sirois, fifteen months my senior, was born August 7, 1929, in the hospital at Ocean Falls, B.C. That September Doc's camp shut down for the winter. The men left except for a skeleton crew that was to look after the camp and equipment during the freeze-up. Doc and Elsie took Audrey, who was barely two months old, and left for Battleground, Washington for the winter.

Froze In

Four men were left in camp as caretakers; they were George, Scott, Bobbie Haines, Jack Gildersleeve and my father, Walt Sirois. According to Walt, by November that year, the South Bentinck Arm "froze solid from the head clear to Tallheo Point. No boats could come in or go out. We were snug as bugs in a rug.

Pretty quiet it was, no means of communication, not even a damn radio. We were froze in until March before the ice broke up and started to go out. If one of us had got sick or wounded, it would have been too bad." (I can recall hearing stories about that winter, although I was not to be born until the following December.)

Granddad and his men lashed large log poles on each side of the *Crusader I* at the water line. The poles extended a few feet in front of the bow to serve as ice breakers, preventing the wood hull from being chewed up as the boat smashed its way back into camp that March in 1930.

During the long winter Walt had a trapline that occupied much of his time. He was also the hunter and meat getter. "Deer were plentiful and ducks and geese were all over the tide flats." As Walt put it, "I would sneak over to the sloughs with Doc's shotgun, a double-barrel Fox, in the early morning and come home with a goose or a couple of ducks."

The following fall of 1930, Elsie, who was pregnant with me, did not leave camp to go to Battleground. Instead she took Audrey and went into Ocean Falls about October to wait for my birth. Late in December, Doc and Walt ran into Ocean Falls in the Crusader I. I was born Walter James Sirois, December 31, 1930, some time just after noon. Soon after my birth, Elsie and Walt headed south with two babies, Audrey and myself, to Battleground, Washington. Walt returned to the camp in the spring, March 1931, without Elsie. She remained in Battleground with Audrey and me.

In May of 1931, Walt was hit in the eye with a tree limb that severely damaged his eyeball. He spent two or three months in and out of the general hospital in Vancouver, B.C. That injured eyeball, according to Walt, ended his logging career.

Once he decided to leave the logging business for good, about 1932, he took up wrestling again and later developed into a world-class wrestling champion. He wrestled all over the globe in many major foreign and domestic cities until World War II, when he enlisted in the army. He was attached to an engineering battalion, was in the D-Day invasion of France, and remained overseas until war's end.

The fall of 1931 Amy took a house in Ocean Falls and the Gildersleeve kids moved into town for school. Thus began the pattern for the next several years—summers at camp, back to Ocean Falls to attend school in the fall.

Returning to British Columbia

Elsie Sirois was now twenty-one years old with two children and pregnant with her third. Audrey Sirois was two years old and I was ten months. Elsie and Walt remained in Battleground, Washington, where Walt took up rabbit farming. Sister Cherie Lee Sirois was born March 30, 1932, in Vancouver, Washington. At about two years old I recall a scene where my father was stretching a rabbit hide over some kind of drying rack; not a very pleasant memory, but one of the very few from that far back. Great-grandfather Gildersleeve lived just down the road. His vegetable garden was a blessing to us as our father Walt was out of work for long periods.

The depression of the 1930s hit many families very hard. Because of that, and other reasons unknown to me, ours was one family that did not endure. In September of 1932 our mother left our father at Battleground, Washington, and returned with us three kids to British Columbia and our Grandmother's house on Tenth Street in Ocean Falls; a stable environment, all things considered, for those days and times. Cherie was six months old, I was almost two, and Audrey was almost three.

I can imagine that my mother's decision to leave our father was difficult. Knowing her in later years, however, taught me to realize that when her mind was made up, right or wrong, that was that. I believe now that her decision to leave our father was right and best for all of us. For many years I felt the sting of not being close to my natural father. However, I don't regret being raised, for the most part, in my grandparents' family and to have come under their instructive influence.

Uncles Richard, Frank and Keaton and Aunt Pearl had already returned to the logging camp in 1931, having been absent seven years, since the drowning of their sister, Ella Mae, in 1924.

So it was in 1932 that Audrey, Cherie and I were back in British Columbia. It was a homecoming of sorts. Unknown to us at the time, it was a returning that was going to stretch into the years ahead, influencing the development of our individual characters in an important, if not significant way.

Not long after our return to B.C., Elsie, along with Aunt Pearl and Uncle Keaton, came down with a virus that attacked their ears and throat. All three were hospitalized at St. Paul's Hospital in Vancouver, B.C. Mother and Aunt Pearl required mastoid operations. Aunt Pearl recovered rapidly, but our mother remained hospitalized for two months and had a very difficult recovery.

We were told early on not to refer to our uncles and aunt in that fashion. It was to be Frank, Pearl, Keaton and Richard. Thus, we were treated as brothers and sisters in one large family. It was as though I grew up with three brothers, Richard, Frank and Keaton, rather than none; and three sisters, Audrey, Cherie and Pearl, rather than two. By the time sister Marilyn Gadsden and brother Terry Gadsden came along, I considered myself grown up at twelve.

My last recollection of Walt Sirois for the next fifty years, was in early 1936. I was five. He came to Ocean Falls to see our mother. He knew she was planning to marry again and he might have been wondering about his three children. I remember well my mother introducing me to Walt saying, "James, this is your father." I was shy and felt very awkward. I recall two other minor details. He wore black wingtip brogues that I tried to polish for him. And he sprinkled salt on his apples. Walt and Elsie did not resolve anything between themselves and he left within the week. Later on during World War II, he wrote to me steadily while he served overseas with Patton's American Third Army.

In 1935 the Gildersleeve floating logging camp was towed to Evans Arm, off Fisher Channel, and later the same year further south to the West Arm of Moses Inlet, now Hardy Inlet; and in 1936 to the North Arm of Moses Inlet.

By 1938 Granddad was ready to move again. Three large fish packers ran up from Wadhams Cannery in Rivers Inlet, to tow the camp to Johnston Bay, a place we called the Hole-in-the-Wall. It was slightly west of Wadhams Cannery, where Johnston Creek empties into it.

In the fall of 1941, Gildersleeve Logging Company was moved into Draney Inlet and remained there for the duration of the war.

Uncles Frank and Keaton joined the RCAF in 1942 and were gone till the war's end. Uncle Richard remained at home with Granddad to work in logging, considered an essential war industry.

At war's end, the camp was towed out of Draney Inlet and about fifty miles east to the head of Rivers Inlet. Three years later, in 1947, the camp was moved north to Tallheo Point at the confluence of the North and South Bentinck Arms, off Burke Channel, and remained there until 1951, when the camp was moved to a site (now charted as Gildersleeve Bay) inside Fish Egg Inlet at the head of Convoy Pass. By 1954, Gildersleeve Logging was in Dean Channel tied to the shore in Carlson Inlet. Andy Torkelson and my old friend Pete Gazzola were still with Grandfather after almost thirty years.

The last logging show for Gildersleeve Logging was at Kimsquit Bay near the head of the Dean, 1954–56. In 1956 the camp and equipment were sold to Neal Duncan, a logging contractor from Vancouver Island.

Amy Gildersleeve predeceased Doc on January 13, 1955, of a heart attack, at the age of sixty-five years and is buried at Ocean Falls, B.C. Doc Gildersleeve died of a heart attack a year later at age sixty-four on April 7, 1956. He is buried in Vancouver, B.C. In recognition of the Gildersleeve family as working pioneers in the development of this B.C. coastal area, modern charts note Gildersleeve Bay lying inside Fish Egg Inlet, also noting Gildersleeve Lake situated 500 feet above salt water, out of which Doc Creek plunges steeply to Burke Channel. Amy Creek not far away meanders into the Nootum River, reaching salt water at the head of Nootum Bay.

Early Years

Bald Eagle

Soon after our return to British Columbia in 1933 at Bear River (now called Mussel River), on a warm sunny day, our mother took snapshots of my sisters and me on the mud flats and left us there to play. We were probably less than twenty yards from the camp floats that, since the tide was out, were settled high and dry in the mud and sand. Suddenly there was a great flapping of wings as a giant brown bird swooped out of the sky with talons outstretched as if to pluck one of us up to carry aloft. Indeed, apparently that was the bird's intent. Aunt Pearl, who was watching over us at the time, gasped and yelled for us to run as the great bird returned and swooped at us time and again. We ran, all three, and made the safety of the float logs. We were small enough to hide under the float against the barnacles and marine growth attached to the logs. The immense bird pulled up in flight and plunked itself on the edge of a woodpile directly over our hiding place, immediately cocking its head to peer down at our dark and smelly refuge. My sister Cherie was the smallest and most certainly was the one the eagle was after.

Uncle Keaton, who was twelve, ran to get his .22 rifle. The great bird of prey was so intent on his potential quarry that he paid no heed to the fuss he was causing. Keaton shot him minutes later. A family picture records Aunt Pearl and Uncle Keaton holding the dead eagle with outstretched wings. It was a bald eagle, with wing tips measuring seven feet across. Later in the day, Grandfather avowed that this bird could have carried sister Cherie away.

The above episode certainly was not a typical occurrence by any means. However, there were also numerous grizzly bears and black bears roaming the swamp and mud flats near the camp, hence the name Bear River. From then on, we kids were fairly restricted in our freedom to roam until we got much older.

Ocean Falls

I came to realize, years later, that the summer of 1933 was, for me, the beginning of a most wonderful childhood. That fall, when Grandmother returned to her house in Ocean Falls with Aunt Pearl and Uncle Keaton so that they could attend school, we three kids went along too.

Ocean Falls was what one would call an isolated coastal town, with no roads in or out, situated approximately 350 miles north of Vancouver, B.C. at the head of Cousins Inlet on the central B.C. coast. It was a "company town." In 1933 the town's residential housing and pulp mill were owned and operated by Pacific Mills Company Limited. After World War II the Pacific Mills Company Limited name was changed to Crown Zellerbach Canada Limited

Prior to World War II, the mill employees numbered around 1,000 and total town inhabitants were more than double that figure. The employee turnover was low and the town economy seemed very stable. Everyone knew everyone and everyone else's business. Doors could be left unlocked; crime as regards misdemeanor activity was virtually nonexistent.

Most persons living in Ocean Falls at this time were employees of "the company," with only a few exceptions. They were banking people, or government employees, such as the provincial police officers, or forestry and fisheries people, to name most of them. To my knowledge, at that time there were no self-employed people living in any of the company houses, except for our family, supported by my grandfather who was a logging contractor for Pacific Mills. There was not even a town bum or vagrant of any kind. I heard it said many times back then that Ocean Falls was a great place to raise a family, and perhaps it was, depending upon what one considers specific to the task. The world has changed dramatically since those days. At that time, with a large part of the western world in the middle of a bad depression,

Ocean Falls was probably a good place to be. Isolation may have been one of its key assets.

The town officers and adults, in general, I feel were good to the town kids. Certain days of the year were, as I remember it, exceptional for everyone. There was May Day where a pretty young girl was selected as queen with two maids of honor and where other young ladies suitably attired danced around the May pole as a prerequisite to later activities. The first of July, Dominion Day it was called then, hosted parades, sports and prizes. Halloween brought trick or treating (no razor blades), and at Christmas a town tree provided gifts for all kids.

Marbles

I am not sure how it happened, but at one of the Dominion Day celebrations I became the marble champion for my age group— six to eight, I think it was. Overnight I shot to fame on my block. I have not been as well recognized among my peers since. One could say that I flamed out at an early age. A year or two later it seems that I had captured all the marbles in existence. We champions played only for "keeps," with anyone who dared oppose us. Whatever marbles we won in any given game we kept, it was that simple. Eventually all my opponents either ran out of marbles or lost a taste for the game. What to do with thousands of marbles? I had many gallon cans full. For amusement in my attic bedroom one rainy afternoon, I solved the problem by dumping the lot into the cubbyholes behind the attic walls. Picture hundreds and hundreds of marbles rolling around between the joists on the ceiling of the rooms below. However, they never became a problem, at least as long as we lived there. If some later tenant tried to repair or move a ceiling light fixture, he may have been pelted with hundreds of half-inch colored marbles pouring out the fixture hole. I'll bet the mice had a rough time getting around too, tippy-toeing on all those glass balls.

In 1985 when I again visited Ocean Falls, for the first time since 1955, thirty years had passed. All of the houses on the hills had long been removed by the government, enabling the land to grow trees once again. I climbed up through the rock gullies, small creeks and thick brush, to where Tenth Street and our house number 1058 had stood. I found alder trees, six to eight inches through, growing on the spot. Since house 1058, along with all the rest, had been burned, I started looking for marbles in the dirt beneath the moss, but disappointingly, I found nothing. Possibly I was not in exactly the right place. Someday, a future archeological team may come across all those marbles and who knows what they will think; perhaps, that it was the site of an ancient marble factory, and not far away they may also discover the remains of an early history pulp and paper mill.

Whooping Cough

During the winter of 1936 I came down with the whooping cough. In those days it was a pretty serious ailment. The phlegm rose up out of one's lungs when coughing started and proceeded to plug one's windpipe. The consistency of the phlegm was comparable to the white glue we used as kids to paste pictures in scrap books. Often there was not a whole lot families could do about it and kids choked to death.

My grandmother had fashioned a bed sheet to form a tent over my bed. Alongside my bed sat a big tea kettle on a single-burner electric hot plate with newspaper rolled to form a tube from the kettle spout to exhaust under the tent. Friar's Balsam fumes poured from the paper tube day or night when needed. One older member of the family would take turns tending me, sometimes all night. They would spoon a mixture of honey and lemon juice down my throat as soon as coughing started. The acidic mixture was about the only treatment to break down or cut the phlegm. This family ordeal went on for months. Finally, I started to get better and then they realized that they might survive as well. I was weak for many more months afterward, but once fully recovered, I have never had a serious chest or bronchial ailment of any kind.

Electrocution

With physical health restored, my normally active imagination, which had been dormant for several months, began to boil out of control. It became obvious that, although my physical health was much improved, my good mental health was not confirmed. First evidence of this fact came when I was able to talk my older sister Audrey into poking a metal toy into the empty socket of a hanging light fixture. The resulting rainbow of blue, yellow, green and white sparks, thoroughly penetrated with Audrey's impressive screams, brought my Aunt Pearl running. Audrey was spread eagled, face up, on the unused bed and mattress upon which she had been standing to reach the hanging light socket. Her face and lips were quite blue, due to a lack of oxygen. Mouth-to-mouth resuscitation unfortunately had not been invented yet; however, Aunt Pearl made do by grabbing Audrey by the shoulders and shaking her violently, alternating with generous whacks to both cheeks until she started to breathe and opened her eyes.

Lye

My next maneuver was with my younger sister Cherie. Grandmother boiled the hard-to-clean laundry in a copper tub atop the kitchen wood stove and often used Gillette lye (sodium hydroxide) in the wash water. The lye she used came in the form of thin flakes with an interesting translucent blue-white cast to them. I was fascinated by the aesthetics of the flakes but my sense was that in some way they were dangerous. I told Cherie that it was sugar and offered her a spoonful, which she took into her mouth. This time, my grandmother came running and immediately saw the situation. With Cherie crooked in one arm she began pouring cooking oil into Cherie's mouth and throat, successfully floating the lye crystals out of her mouth in a foaming mass. How fortunate we all were for my grandmother's quick reactions. How lucky Cherie was not to be badly hurt. As it happened, Cherie had some burn scars inside her mouth, but none of the lye crystals, it seems, got as far as her vocal chords; I thank my lucky stars.

Feen-a-Mint

One would think that after the above episode, I would begin to smarten up. Right? Wrong! No more than a few weeks later I dis-

45

covered a box of Feen-a-Mint laxative in the bathroom medicine chest. For all the world they looked to me and probably anyone else, like Chiclets sold in those days over the counter as chewing gum. Feen-a-Mint laxative was candy coated like Chiclets and chewed like gum, as well. One Feen-a-Mint "candy" was a standard laxative dose for a child, as I recall. But I fed most of the entire box to my sister Cherie, who had not yet realized that for some reason I was out to do her no good. Cherie had to camp on the toilet for days, poor soul, upsetting everyone in the process and also alerting family to my continuing miscreant acts.

For some reason, I cannot recall being punished for that particular misdemeanor, although I am certain that I was. The following incident may clarify the exact meaning of the quotation, "What goes around, comes around."

Canary

A few months after the Feen-a-Mint caper, Grandmother left our house unattended to go to the local general store for supplies. Previously she had made it abundantly clear to us three kids, and especially to Cherie and myself, that we were not to enter the house, for any reason, or under any circumstance, in her absence. One might say that due to certain recent happenings of one kind or another, Grandmother had made this a law.

You can imagine how stunned I was then, when about a half hour later, Cherie, who was Grandmother's favorite, approached me with the innocent comment that "the canary was out of its cage and flying around in the house." When I asked Cherie how this was possible since we were not supposed to be inside the house and the canary certainly could not get out by itself, she replied that she "really did not know," but wanted me to help her catch the bird and get it back into its cage. "No way," I told her. "The rule is that we don't go in there, and that is that." So we went in. Among my other peculiarities it seems that I am a sucker for a sob story. Cherie did not know what would happen to her if I did not help, etc., besides, I did owe her.

Unbelievably, I did manage, after quite a spell of chasing that canary all over the house, to catch it, while Cherie helped by blocking doorways and such so that I could corner the bird. The *coup de grâce* came when I had to stand on the kitchen table in order to reach the open door of the cage to insert the bird. (This does add a slightly interesting note as to how the bird escaped in the first place). I was closing the cage door when, to my chagrin, in walked Grandmother, her arms full of groceries. My karma has always been to face the music and take what I have coming with dignity, but not necessarily without a last word. The clouds forming on Grandmother's face looked pretty stormy and as I opened my mouth to try to explain, she bellowed, "What in thunderation is going on here?" My mouth was still hanging slack jawed from fear when Cherie offered instead her explanation: "Jim let the bird out of the cage." I should pause here to say that Grandmother's canaries were next to godliness with her. The picture of me standing there on the table, having obviously manhandled her bird, I suspect was about all that she could take from me; especially, after the electrocution scenario with Audrey, the caustic soda and Feen-a-Mint scenarios with Cherie, and others, and now this. The canary during its freedom flight had discovered bits of liver and blood on the kitchen sideboard and, in pecking at it, had managed to stain its breast feathers so that to Gram the bird appeared wounded. She grabbed me with a ferocity that bordered on frenzy and getting me down on the floor, beat the heck out of my back side and any other part of me that got in the way. That drubbing I did not forget. Cherie, too, felt Gram's wrath, with a switch from the "familiar" alder tree out back. Gram favored the limber ones that "sang" in the air. I had no regrets over the incident, since I had had it coming for some time. Did I not read somewhere that Al Capone was eventually convicted for income tax evasion and not the many murders he reportedly committed?

Most important, even though my grandparents were strict with us three kids, we always could tell from their actions that we were loved, and we loved them. As I grew older, I felt the responsibility of their love and trust, and felt that I owed them much more than I would ever be able to repay.

47

Bread and Milk

The years from 1930–36 were difficult for everyone that we knew. As far as possessions went, they did not seem all that important, since no one had any. There were times when we did not have a lot of variety in what we ate, but I can never remember going hungry.

Gram baked bread constantly, it seemed. Many of our meals consisted of homemade bread broken into spoon-sized chunks, covered with milk and sprinkled with sugar. Then there was boiled rice laden with raisins, covered again with sugar and milk. Spanish rice was another favorite dish for us kids. Also, I have never eaten bread or rice pudding as tasty as the way Gram used to fix it.

For breakfast we often had oatmeal or Red River cereal and if there was any left over, Gram would lightly fry it for lunch. Sprinkled with brown sugar it was great. (If you have not tried this, don't laugh). Even in 1934 manufacturers of breakfast food put inducements in and on cereal packages. I remember being very proud of my Tom Mix ring and Red Ryder badges that I had to send in cereal box tops to receive.

Prior to first grade, I had one or two pairs of bib overalls and a couple of shirts. Later on, Grandmother made trousers for me from scrap material she had scrounged. If ever I was unhappy with anything that my grandmother did, it probably was the trousers with no pockets that she made for me. There was no fly either. How in the world can a young boy manage without pockets? I had no place to put stuff. As for no fly, I was always reminded that girls' trousers had none. I felt my pants were sissy pants since I had to drop them to pee, something the other boys did not have to do. I loved Gram though and never wanted to hurt her feelings, so I kept my thoughts about my pants to myself.

We did have shoes but wore them mostly for special occasions and never in the summer. If by today's standards we would have been regarded as poor, then everyone we knew was poor. You could have fooled me, though. I had the time of my life.

Woodshed

In Grandmother's house in Ocean Falls, the woodshed was an area of major functional importance. The rear entry of the house was through the woodshed. Immediately through a door to the left was the kitchen, where the sink and drain board to the right allowed one to dump armloads of groceries.

Odors that permeated that shed's damp atmosphere were so pungent that recalling them today transports me instantly to that room more than fifty-five years ago. At the far end of the shed, opposite the outside back door, was the coal bin that easily held a half dozen sacks of lumpy coal. Along one wall, fir firewood was stacked for the kitchen stove. Leaning against the wood pile were gunny sacks containing spuds, carrots, onions, turnips or what have you.

The smell of the coal bin was the dominant odor with the fir wood a close competitor. However, the scent of moldering bulk vegetables sought recognition, as did a low grade aroma of tom-cat urine that somehow was always present and must have filtered into the shed from under that end of the house.

But this was not all—in the fall, wild game, such as deer or goat, was hung in the woodshed. Wild fowl such as ducks and geese sometimes were hung along the wall "to ripen," as Grandma would say, prior to plucking the feathers and cleaning the critters for the stew pot. I remember having to help pluck a few birds, but mainly Grandma and my sisters did that tedious work. Grandmother often kept some of the feathers and down to be used for pillows.

My main job then was to fill the coal scuttle with coal for the potbelly stove in the living room. The lumps in the coal bin were often as big as dinner plates and that meant I had to break them into fist-size pieces that would fit through the top front door of the stove. The whacker I employed to break up the larger lumps was the blunt side of a single-bladed ax, as it also served for splitting the wood blocks. The technique I employed was to raise the ax over my head, blunt side forward. I lined up with the coal lump and at the bottom of my swing seconds before impact I would turn my head to the side, with face and eyes scrunched up.

Coal splinters flew in all directions, but it seemed that most of them speared my face and neck. Quite often more than one whack was necessary to subdue the more reluctant pieces of coal.

Perhaps my memory of this place is keen because it was the "proverbial woodshed" where I often wound up to receive my comeuppance after many a failed flight into fanciful doings. Often I was required to go to the back yard and select a fresh limber branch from a nearby alder tree; then a brisk switching to the legs would follow. The stinging sensation to the legs was ferocious, probably physical agony at its absolute worst, as I am sure I thought then, recalling my usual loud bellowing. In fact, remembering the pain from a previous drubbing would trigger bawling from me at the outset of the next thrashing prior to being struck. Curiously, though, I don't remember any welts on my legs that lasted more than a few minutes. I guess the lickings were not as horrific as they seemed at the time.

Attic Bedroom

The potbelly coal stove was situated in the living room below a heat register placed in the ceiling directly above. Upstairs, the register was a great place to stand on cool mornings and evenings while dressing or undressing. It was also a great place to be when any of the adults had guests of an evening. Conversation was easy to monitor. If cigarette smoke accompanied the sound of voices, then we knew that someone special was down there. No one in our family smoked, except my grandfather, and he was usually at camp sixty to ninety miles away. The people downstairs could tell when we were spying on them and would admonish us in a loud voice saying, "You kids get into bed."

The potbelly stove with its great nickel-plated ornament and nickel-plated doors sat behind a huge black bear rug. I never knew for sure, but I imagine that Granddad had shot it, in the days prior to my time. They shot several bears for food in their early years in B.C.

The bear rug fur was thick and a lustrous shiny black, with the usual green scalloped felt attached underneath. The head was completed so that the bear's mouth and jaws were in an open snarl, showing all of the teeth. I have no idea what ever happened to that rug, but it was a beauty.

Upstairs in the attic near the heat register and next to my bed hung an old wolf hide. It was stiff as a board and had a terrible odor if you put your nose to it. It hung there for years and it also mysteriously disappeared.

Running Away

Along about 1937, one morning there was great excitement in the house. My Uncle Keaton, who was fifteen and eight years my senior, was missing. He failed to appear when he should have been igniting the morning fire in the kitchen stove.

Grandma was beside herself and had all manner of terrible thoughts about what might have happened to him. Then it turned out that the neighbor boy, Tommy Morris, was also missing from his house. A few hours of sleuthing and questioning of their pals determined that Keaton and Tommy had left town the previous evening on the Union Steamship boat that called weekly into Ocean Falls. They had stowed away, it turned out later, in one of the lifeboats.

At Powell River, an RCMP official came aboard and "accompanied" them to Vancouver where Tommy's aunt met the boat and took them into her custody. Tommy and Keaton spent the next two weeks attending the Pacific National Exhibition in Vancouver, which was their intent and destination all along.

Just more than two weeks after their departure, they were back at home in Ocean Falls and were received by their peers as conquering heroes. Grandma took Keaton's running away as a personal affront and was pretty sour on the episode. Granddad on the other hand, upon hearing that Keaton had run away, laughed and thought that it showed spunk on Keaton's part. After all, he had run away from home himself when he was eleven and never returned for years. When I asked Keaton what he planned to do after the exhibition, if they had not been caught, he replied that he "had not thought that far ahead." At the outset of WW II Tommy Morris joined the RCAF and later was lost in a raid over Germany.

Saturday Movie

For some reason that I still do not understand, on Saturdays Gram often gave me fifteen cents to go to the local movie (maybe to get me out of her hair). I say that I don't understand because back then fifteen cents was a lot of money.

Often Uncle Keaton would take my fifteen cents and buy himself a ticket, telling me to sneak in by walking close to him in the crowd past the ticket taker, as if I was his shadow. For some inexplicable reason on those occasions no one ever asked me for my ticket. In later years, I figured that Keaton and the usher had a scam going. Keaton likely still had the fifteen cents Grandma gave him and maybe he split it with the usher. Hey, there has to be some explanation.

One Saturday I arrived home to Grandma's house after the movie with a large wad of chewing gum bulging my cheek. We never had chewing gum, which was a luxury and cost another five cents. Grandma demanded to know where I got the gum and so much of it. I explained to her, unabashedly, that I found it under the theater seat that I occupied (As if I was also asking, doesn't everyone?). It still had, as I recall, plenty of flavor. How could anything that tasted that good be bad for me, I reasoned in my mind. When first I snapped it off the seat, it was rock hard and some varnish came with it, but a little aggressive mastication soon put the bounce back into it.

Grandmother's face went white, and with one hand over her mouth and the other firmly clamped on my ear, she marched me on my tippy toes to the kitchen sink and the bar of Fels-Naphtha soap. In very short order I had my mouth thoroughly scoured out with a toothbrush and plenty of soap. The horse had left the barn as far as sterilizing my mouth was concerned. It took me some time to understand that the soap treatment was meant to educate and influence my judgment on where not to look, in the future, for things to chew on. After all, it was only months previous to this that in another episode, I came bawling home with green slime drooling from my mouth. Everyone thought that I had gotten into rat poison. With some detective work on Grandma's part, it turned out to be the yellow heart of a skunk cabbage plant that my buddies and I believed was corn on the cob.

Grandmother and Aunt Pearl (who was still a high school student) certainly had their hands full with the likes of me and my strange behavior. Perhaps my parents' separation and divorce had something to do with my unruly attitude. However, I doubt it.

Our mother, not being married and having three kids, was not typical in Ocean Falls in the 1930s. Consequently, all three of us took a fair amount of razzing from the neighborhood kids. I took it upon myself, consciously or not, to stand up to the abuse and so unwittingly became a neighborhood tough. I beat up on everyone I could who I thought sassed me or our family.

Late one afternoon, a neighbor boy a little older than I smacked me across the face with a cedar shingle, stunning me and knocking me to the ground. I was getting the worst of it when all of a sudden sister Audrey appeared out of nowhere and like a wildcat jumped on my opponent's back, yelling for me to run for the house. Being fairly intelligent, I saw the logic in her thinking and took to my heels. The neighbor boy was no match for Audrey in her frenzy and he ran for it too.

Unfair Advantage

Girls were very difficult to fight. Grandmother had instructed me never to hit my sisters, or any girls, in the chest. It was a bad thing. The girls could develop tumors she said. I was not able to follow Gram's thinking, but was willing to accept her judgment in the matter. Perhaps my peers, the neighbor boys, had been told the same thing, I don't know. However, it gave the girls around our age a decided advantage, in my opinion, since they were as gangly as the boys, and when grappling, smelled just as bad.

One afternoon I found myself under attack from a neighbor girl, name of Agnes Jones, and soon realized that I was in real trouble. The mental handcuffs regarding no chest hitting left me very little target, it seemed, for me to strike at. Before I could figure out my strategy, she had hit me with her fists, arms, elbows, knees, pulled my hair, got me down, spit on me and rubbed my face in the dirt. Embarrassing yes, but since there were no observers, I decided to absorb my punishment gracefully. Earlier I had "beat up" on her younger brother for calling me names, so I guess it was tit for tat.

Neighborhood Tough

Not long after my muscular comeuppance at the hands of this wily female I remember a police officer appearing at Gram's front door. Through the door window I could see the head, shoulders and beaver hat of a provincial police constable. Opening the door and before the constable could say "Jack Robinson," Gram asked "What's he done now?" as she gave me her beady eye.

Apparently, as the constable explained quietly, also fixing his gaze on me, some of the neighborhood mothers were complaining about my aggressive behavior. There was even a report that I had been pushing the girls around. That comment relative to the Agnes Jones fiasco offended my sense of dignity. This official visit from the local police force certainly impressed me and Grandmother, also. As soon as the constable departed, Gram thimbled my head, grabbed me by the ear and marched me tippy toe to the woodshed, an area of the house with which I was already very familiar.

On occasion any reasonable small piece of stove wood was suitable to Grandmother and after giving me several good whacks on the legs with it, she turned me loose saying, "All right, now, young man, perhaps that will teach you to behave yourself." Eventually, I believe the whackings did have a positive effect. Perhaps it was just that I finally started to grow up to match my glands because gradually I started to act like a fairly normal seven year old.

Girl in the Bushes

The second grade in Ocean Falls, as I recall, seemed rather sublime. Not very much happened. I did not commit any near atrocities, that I remember, and probably our family life was just plain dull for a spell. However, during this doldrums period, I had heard via the grapevine that getting a girl into the bushes and getting her pants down was a big event. Soon after, I enticed a neighborhood girl who lived close by, into the bushes. Naturally, since she was about six or seven she did not know why I wanted her in the bushes any more than I did. I had to bribe her. The promise of five cents (that I did not have) did the trick. Once in the bushes, upon request, she removed her panties. As I stood examining her appearance, at close range, I was confused as to what this was all about since I had two sisters and I could see nothing to write home about on this one either.

Another detail that I had heard about was that the boy must get on top of the girl and get his peter into her. I had no problem in getting her to lie down, as I recall, but when I tried getting my limp noodle between her legs, the only emotion I remember was my disgust at the bum information the rumors had given me. All of a sudden, to make matters worse, my penis jumped up like a pole cat stiff as a sucker stick. I was now really confounded because for all practical purposes it was pointing up and I needed it to go down. After a little more futile activity, I decided that I was the butt of someone's joke. The angles were all wrong. Besides, the girl was getting upset too, letting me know with loud shouts of, "I wanna go home." We both went home. That afternoon my young girlfriend approached me as I sat with my mother on the front porch steps and asked me for her nickel. "What nickel," my mother wanted to know. Somehow my tongue had turned to stone. I learned, early on, what it feels like to be caught "red handed." Again, I cannot recall what punishment was meted out to me for this crime. It was many years, however, before I again found myself "in the bushes." I often wonder though, what ever happened to that nice little girl. I hope she soon forgot that terrible experience with me.

Easter Eggs

Easter for us kids seemed almost as important an event in our lives as Christmas. A visit from the Easter bunny was a much-heralded event. Like most families in those days, there was not much loose cash to be spent on such frivolous items as chocolate bunnies and chocolate eggs. Nevertheless, come Easter Sunday morning, all kinds and sizes of candied eggs would be hidden everywhere; under pillows, behind books and inside vases. At the appropriate time my sisters and I would be turned loose on an egg hunt that would leave us breathless.

In advance of one memorable Easter, Grandmother had purchased a number of porcelain egg cups. She set them on the window sill of her bedroom behind the drapes and out of sight of snoopers, or so she thought. In each of the egg cups she had placed a hollow chocolate Easter egg. A few days after coming upon this hidden cache of chocolate eggs and suffering a brief moment of weakness, I nibbled a small piece from the bottom of one of them. Not to worry, I replaced the egg so that the nibble was not visible. On succeeding days when my good judgment was at a low ebb, I would return to the egg cache and proceed to nibble more chocolate. Eventually all of the eggs were nibbled so that only half of each chocolate egg remained intact. Careful placement of each half egg in its respective egg cup caused all to appear well and normal.

On Easter morning, after our usual energetic hunt for candied eggs, Grandma, with an unusual flourish, produced her surprise of real chocolate eggs in egg holders to an enthusiastic group of aunts, uncles and us three kids. As I remember, one chocolate egg for each family member.

With a yelp, Gram discovered the heinous skullduggery of the nibbled eggs and looked straight at me for an answer. No doubt the guilt on my face was throbbing like a neon sign. "Why you young Jack Snipe," she cried, as I burst for the hallway door, but Grandma was faster, and grabbing my ear, tippy toed me once again out through the kitchen to the woodshed for another character-building session. A few judicious whacks to my bare calves with a medium-sized chunk of firewood tended to help restore Gram's sense of dignity. She let go of me while I continued to perform my version of St. Vitus's Dance, a jerky variation of running on the spot in an attempt to avoid as many blows to the legs as possible. Gram left me crying in the woodshed and returned to speak with the others, whereupon I could hear a lot of laughter. That's another thing about adults that puzzled me. There I was, out in the woodshed, banned as it were, with throbbing calves, and they were laughing. It seemed to me then, and I guess it is still true today, you never can tell what people will think is funny.

Audrey's Pneumonia

Not long after I had recovered from the whooping cough, my older sister Audrey came down with a cold that developed into a case of pneumonia (empyema). The same sort of illness today may not be considered very serious since it probably can be treated satisfactorily with a modern antibiotic medicine. Back in those days, however, 1939, medicines such as the ubiquitous penicillin drug just were not available. The nasty result was that Audrey had to be hospitalized in the Ocean Falls Hospital.

Her condition grew steadily worse and after a month of confusion, the doctors had to operate. From under her arm they inserted a tube into her lung cavity in order to drain away the infectious fluid they found there. Sulfanilamide was a relatively new drug then and the doctors in some desperation gave her huge doses of it. Although this medical procedure may have saved Audrey's life, she did not have a rapid recovery. As I recall, she convalesced in the hospital for a month or two after the operation. The large doses of sulfanilamide drug, they conjectured, may have been the cause of the strange "blackouts" that Audrey began to suffer as she gradually got well. Fortunately after many months of these blackout spells, they gradually stopped for good.

It was only when Audrey was well on her way to recovery that Cherie and I were allowed in to see her. Prior to that we had to stand outside the building and wave at her through the window. During her convalescing period she was allowed a few special favors and one that I enjoyed immensely, right along with her, were copious quantities of Welch's grape juice. The only time that I could get my hands on any was during a visit with Audrey.

A little later, when Audrey was eleven, she had another close call, but of a different kind. She nearly drowned. Audrey had been attempting to follow Aunt Pearl and some of her friends along a string of logs (boomsticks). She failed to make a successful jump across a wide gap in the logs and fell into the water without the older girls noticing anything wrong. After going under a time or two, Pete Gazzola, who had been watching Audrey from a distance, hurried to the spot. Looking down into the water, he saw her swirling hair floating beneath the surface. Reaching down he grabbed a fistful of hair and yanked Audrey out onto the logs. She came to, lying on a bed in the house with everyone fussing over her. I firmly believe that when your time is up, there is nothing to be done about it. Up until now Audrey had survived my light socket attack, her pneumonia attack, and now this near drowning. Her time just was not up in these incidents. When it is your time to go, you are going, make no mistake about it.

Grades One and Two

My first grade teacher, a Miss Davis, was middle aged, tall, with a broad flat face, short and thick curly brown hair parted to the side, slightly hooded eyelids, a prominent humped nose, large flat yellowing front teeth, generous lips and slightly receding jaw. She wore no makeup that I remember. If she had, it might have helped to conceal an unhealthy pallor.

My second try at the first grade (the first was cut short by the bout with whooping cough) was successful in that I managed to get passed into the second grade. Miss Davis may have wanted to flunk me the second time for being a nuisance, which undoubtedly I was at times.

A talking in class incident, one day, got me fifteen minutes after school sitting rigidly at my desk with my hands behind my back. After being let go, another young lad and I were pretending to lock the teacher in the building by putting a stick in the front door padlock hasp. She must have heard the two of us skulking around the door because just at the instant I dropped a small twig in the hasp, she tried to open the door. Finding it blocked, she panicked and started screaming and rattling the door for all she was worth. She may have thought that our next move was to set the building on fire.

The screaming terrified me and my initial reaction was to run for it. We both did. Only a short distance away I reversed course and ran back to the door in an attempt to remove the stick. In her frenzy, Miss Davis was still rattling the door so hard and fast that I could not get the stick out right away. The first instant the door stood motionless, I quickly removed the twig from the hasp and attempted my escape. My partner in crime was long gone. Unfortunately for me, Miss Davis was too fast and leaped out to grab me by the collar before I could get off the porch. I was sentenced on the spot, after a stern lecture, to another fifteen minutes staring straight ahead at the blackboard. That was not all. I had to carry home a sealed note to my Grandmother relating details of my dastardly deed that I am sure Miss Davis figured would result in a sound spanking at home. Little did Miss Davis realize that this episode was literally child's play when compared to what Grandma was used to from me. All I recall getting from her this time was a quick thump with her steel thimble plus a light boxing of the ears and an order to get coal in from the woodshed for the potbelly stove in the living room.

My second grade teacher, Miss Green, was a pistol. She was tall, middle aged and bony. She had a flaky, thin, white face. It appeared to be dried out and starched, except for the spidery red and blue capillary lines around and over her nose. She often wore a too-tight Kelly green suit, a color I have always detested. The worst thing about Miss Green that I sensed right off was that she disliked kids; I thought, me in particular. I never was a brilliant student and could not understand why some teachers, like Miss Green, would openly take advantage of us less fortunate kids. I will not forget the day she revealed her latent sadism. She embarrassed me by holding up my spelling paper and announcing to the class, that "here was a boy that still could not tell the difference between 'there' and 'their'." No doubt she was right about my confusion, but still for second grade that was pretty heady stuff. I figured the others might have been faking it.

Fortunately for our grade two class that year, spring finally arrived and we were freed from the clutches of Miss Spider Nose. I had a treat in store for me that no others in my class would share—my sisters and I were going out to the logging camp for the summer.

I did not know it then, but I was not to return to school in Ocean Falls until I entered the fifth grade. The next two years of schooling for myself and my sisters would be through government-sponsored correspondence courses.

Thimbled

Even though my poor treatment of Audrey and Cherie indicated that I had some sort of grudge against them, I did not. On the contrary, I thought that we got along quite well.

On occasion, when Cherie and I caused some minor infraction that irritated Grandmother, we got to sit on stools facing into a corner of the room, Cherie in one corner and me in another. We had to be absolutely still and quiet, and were not supposed to turn around to look at each other. In a short while I would hunch over and peek under my arm at Cherie across the room and she often would be peeking under her arm at me. That would set us off again, giggling and snorting uncontrollably. Gram would approach, thimbled finger poised, menacingly, and that shut us up fast. I was always impressed with the intensity of pain that a thump from her thimbled finger produced.

Grandmother was an expert when it came to thimbling young heads. She had developed several options that I recognized, but she no doubt had others too. Her regular option was simply a flick with her thimbled finger directly to the back of my head as I was going by at a trot. This never hurt much as she was aiming at a moving target; besides, that part of my head seemed devoid of nerves. Another option was a flick to the side of my head just above the ear where the meat is thin and the nerves gather in bunches. That one got my attention. A thump straight down on the crown of my head was a grabber too and usually had me massaging the spot briskly. The fiercest blow of all with the thimbled finger, I felt, was a straight jab to the forehead. For all practical purposes it felt about the same as if being struck with a .45-caliber bullet, only without as much penetration.

Cherie and Audrey never got thimbled as much as I did—Audrey, hardly ever, since she was older and seemingly so well behaved.

Wedding Bells

By the fall of 1938 my mother decided that she would marry again. The man to be my stepfather was Roy Percival Gadsden. I hardly knew Roy Gadsden as a person prior to their marriage. As a boy of eight I had already bonded with my Grandfather and felt that I did not require another voice of authority to have to contend with. It turned out, however, that Roy Gadsden was a fine fellow, as grownups went, and any differences of opinion that we had later on were likely more my fault than his.

The wedding took place on November 15, 1938. It was a house wedding with the Reverend Peter Kelly, of the United Church of Canada, presiding over the ceremonies. Everything seemed to be going smoothly until near the end when most of the women started to cry. I was witnessing what I thought to be a peculiarity of women, crying for no apparent reason. However, I had no time to dwell on this phenomenon because the wedding chivaree was about to begin outside from the front porch.

The groom had put my Uncle Keaton in charge of the chivaree detail. He would be tossing a few dollars in coin, a king's ransom in those days, to a waiting crowd of neighborhood kids. The groom perhaps did not realize it, but putting Keaton in charge of handling the coins was like putting the "fox in charge of the hen house." Keaton had prearranged to have some of his cronies stand in a certain spot on the lawn and I was to stand in another place. The plan was simple. He would toss the coins directly to us so that we would have no trouble scooping them up; then we were supposed to split fifty-fifty with him later. The few remaining coins were scattered to the rest of the crowd to keep things looking on the up and up. As I recall, the plan went well. All in all, it seemed a win-win situation.

Mother bore my third sister, Marilyn Ann Gadsden, March 3, 1940, when I was ten. Two years after that she bore her second son, Terrance Keaton Roy Gadsden, February 13, 1942.

Growing Up in Camp

Living a major part of our early lives at the floating camp of the Doc Gildersleeve family was for myself and two sisters probably the most memorable time of our lives. It has been said that what you do not know does you no harm. For me, this old saying holds a lot of truth. I believe that kids can adapt readily to their environment. They accept it for what it is, their reality. Kids are not concerned about what they do not have, if they have no awareness of it. Their imaginations can help create a satisfying world around themselves. For us three, it was like being invited to live on a friendly planet—a place where kids go about in relative innocence, looking, listening and learning to assume minor chores tuned to a child's growing awareness. My sense is that strength of character, where high moral judgment is valued, is a slow cook process. It cannot be hurried and mixed signals will surely spoil the soup (i.e., too many differences of opinion from unqualified sources, such as youthful peer pressure and TV).

Buildings and Floats

In camp our world was the length and breadth of several large log floats (rafts) that supported houses, machinery and other equipment and altogether was perhaps 500 feet long and 200 feet wide. The extended world was a quarter of a mile of immediate shoreline either side of the floating dwellings.

The camp was secured to the shore by means of a "standing boom" (a string of logs chained together at their ends). They, in turn, were tied to the shore, with wire rope and "stiff-legged" away from the shore. This system prevented the whole floating affair from hanging up on the beach as the tide ebbs and floods twice every twenty-four hours. The outer world existed only on special boat trips away from the camp to such places as a fish cannery where there might be a post office, machine shop or grocery store.

The number of buildings in camp varied from time to time, but generally numbered about ten to fifteen. Among these were four or five personal family dwellings. Then there were several bunkhouses for the hired men; a cook house and dining room for between twenty and forty men at a sitting; a wash house; a blacksmith shop; an office and commissary; various large sheds for storage. Most of the time there were two putt boats (work boats) for pushing logs and log rafts around. A larger camp tender, about forty feet long, was used primarily for towing logs and for transporting people and supplies between the camp and the so-called outside world.

Each family dwelling had its own individual float. In this way the homes could be moved around among the other floats or towed away all together to a distant location. The log floats were constructed from several large spruce logs, and were held together with a cross log on top at each end. The cross logs were laced tightly to each individual float log with wire rope held by staples.

Some of the main camp floats were much larger than the private-dwelling floats and supported more than one building; however, all floats were constructed and held together in the same manner.

The most serious maintenance problem with the log float was the control of the teredo worm (ship-boring worm). If not for the existence of the teredo worm, a well-constructed log float would last a lifetime and then some. Even with the worm, our log floats had lasted fifty or sixty years. The only preventive maintenance procedure that I ever heard of for teredo worm control on log floats is an underwater dynamite blast using a light charge. Hydraulic shock, supposedly, kills the teredos, but I have no idea how one would determine effectiveness of this process.

Teredos also enjoy boring into wooden boat hulls. In that case, about every six months the camp boats, all of which had wooden hulls, were beached near the camp on a makeshift grid. At the age of eleven, I began making myself useful doing minor caulking on the wooden hulls, as well as applying teredo-killing copper paint. (Copper paint is now banned due to the lead content—turns out it isn't just harmful to worms.)

Links with the Outside World

Of course, there was no telephone and TV had not been invented. Of an evening, we listened to the radio that was powered by a twelve-volt wet cell battery. The major radio programs we listened to were *Jack Benny, Fibber McGee and Molly, I Love a Mystery, Amos and Andy, Henry Aldridge, The Great Gildersleeve* (no relation to my Grandfather Gildersleeve), *The Green Hornet, The Shadow, Jack Armstrong* and a religious soap opera in the mornings called *Light of the World*.

The only other contact with the outside world was through visitors to our camp on their boats. They included salesmen, some selling logging equipment, while another by the name of Ted Goldbloom sold tailor-made suits, watches and fine jewelry to the loggers. Then there were the commercial fishermen, gospel boats, government officials such as fisheries, forest and police, and a few tourists cruising the coastal waters in their pleasure craft.

Camp Location

The principal factor in deciding where a float camp such as ours was to be located was the simple commodity of drinking water. Any place close to the logging show was okay as long as there were a flowing stream and shelter from the wind and waves.

The very first task upon moving to a new location was to run out the water lines. The creek was dammed high enough up the hillside to provide sufficient water pressure for the wash house, cook house and private dwellings.

All houses had hot and cold running water. The cook house stoves were wood-burning stoves as were the wash house and bunkhouse stoves. However, most of the private homes had converted to oil-burning stoves by 1937. Nevertheless, the hot water systems were the same for wood or oil burners. A heating coil in the stove firebox leading to the hot-water tank back of the stove provided a hot water reservoir for use in the kitchen, or for bathing and clothes washing.

Doc Gildersleeve, Ocean Falls, B.C., circa 1957.

Amy (Gram) Gildersleeve with Marilyn Gadsden, circa 1943. *Photo: Courtesy M. Gadsden*

Doc and Amy's first home in B.C. at Nootum Bay, 1918. Left to right: Rosco Owens, cousin Verdelle Owens, Uncle Lloyd Owens, Aunt Altha Owens, Doc Gildersleeve, Aunt Ella Mae Gildersleeve, Amy Gildersleeve, Uncle Almon Owens, Elsie Gildersleeve, cousin Maxine Owens, cousin Laurel Owens, Uncle Richard Gildersleeve.

Gildersleeve Logging, Restoration Bay, Burke Channel, B.C., circa 1924.

Gildersleeve Logging, Burke Channel, B.C., circa 1924.

Above: Uncle Jack Gildersleeve and a grizzly at Nootum Bay, B.C.

Right: Uncle Lloyd Owens and Doc Gildersleeve, circa 1918.

Aunt Pearl, Gram and Uncle Keaton Gildersleeve. Keaton shot this bald eagle that was after Cherie Sirois on the beach at Bear (Mussel) River, B.C., circa 1933.

Above: Elsie Sirois and Spunk at Moses Inlet, B.C., 1936.

Left: Aunt Pearl, Uncles Frank, Richard and Keaton Gildersleeve at Moses Inlet, circa 1936.

Below: Audrey and Cherie Sirois at Moses Inlet, circa 1936.

This picture of a whale feeding was taken from a float house. This was a daily occurence. Fish Egg Inlet, B.C., circa 1950.

First grade—Jim Sirois is in the back row standing next to the teacher Miss Davis.

Keaton Gildersleeve and Jim Sirois with dogs Curly and Spunk in Moses Inlet, 1936.

Elsie Adams, Aunt Pearl and Uncle Frank in Frank's home-built speedboat at Ocean Falls.

Jim, Cherie and Audrey Sirois in Ocean Falls, B.C., circa 1937.

Roy and Elsie Gadsden at Dawson's Landing, B.C.

Marilyn, Terry and Elsie Gadsden and Doc Gildersleeve.

Graduation class of 1949. Left to right, back row: George Davies, Jim Sirois, Roger Killin, Leo Portelance, Ron Robinson, Barry (can't recall surname), Allen Gilchrist, Sid Fosdick. Front row: Maureen Brown, Doreen Wheaton, Donna McLeod, Doreen Miller, Katherine McKay, Berel Vanatter, Rosa Spence.

Jim, Cherie and Audrey at Ocean Falls, circa 1947.

Jim during his first year at University of B.C., 1949.

Uncle Almon Owens, Doc Gildersleeve, Uncle Lloyd Owens and Uncle Jack Gildersleeve at Nootum Bay, B.C. circa 1920. They are wearing the goat skins in which they had to sleep overnight to keep warm.

The famed picture of Dirty Socks—the man who shot five bears at one time.

This photo shows logs alongside the steam donkey stiffleg waiting for the flood tide to transport them away. South Bentinck, B.C., circa 1929.

Stowing logs in Burke Channel, circa 1924.

Doc Gildersleeve's early powerboat in Burke Channel, B.C., circa 1924.

Doc Gildersleeve Camp at Mathieson Channel, circa 1932.

Uncles Almon and Lloyd Owens' railroad logging operation in Green Bay, B.C., circa 1925.

Photo: Courtesy Gordon Douglas

The Union Steamship vessel *Cardena* unloads equipment, groceries and mail at the Tallheo Camp, 1950.

Gildersleeve Logging cold deck pile.

Right: An old steam donkey was used for cold decking in the woods, and for yarding logs to the salt water from a cold deck pile.

Ocean Falls, circa 1970.

Gildersleeve Truck Logging at Tallheo Point, B.C., circa 1950.

Gildersleeve Camp float housing at Tallheo Point in South Bentinck Arm, B.C. Uncle Dick and Aunt Phil's house is in foreground, circa 1949.

Above: Camp tender *Crusader* on ways for its semi-annual copper paint job.

Left: Frank Gildersleeve, Andy Torkelson, Johnny Monks (aka Old Curmudgeon) and Roy Gadsden, circa 1935.

Doc Gildersleeve's camp tender *Crusader 1* at Griffin Pass, circa 1930. It was powered by a 55-hp. Vivian diesel engine.

Gildersleeve Camp at Tallheo Point, circa 1949.

The rigging crew at Johnston Bay in 1939. Left to right: Andy Torkelson, Keaton Gildersleeve, unknown, Roy Peters, Peter Gazzola, Harold Jefferies.

Left: Jim Sirois bucking logs for scale, 1949.

Below: Crown Zellerbach Logging employees. Left to right: Scottie Pete, Jack Vanderzee, Jim Sirois, Horace Gullett. Ocean Falls, circa 1954.

It was normal on a cold fall or winter morning for us kids to elbow our way into position around our oil-burning kitchen stove, the only source of warmth. We soaked up heat while our breakfast pot of rolled oats cooked, erupting small spurts of steam.

All family laundry was hand washed in tubs using the old scrub board. The bed linens for the bunkhouses were shipped out once a week via Union Steamships to a laundry in Vancouver—one set of sheets going, one set coming and one set in use.

The wash house's main function was to provide space for the loggers to clean up after work each day and do their personal laundry. Hot showers were vital.

None of the private homes had showers, as I recall, only bathtubs in later years. During the day when there were few men in camp, the ladies would take advantage of the wash house showers, where there was plenty of hot water available.

Charles Atlas

My grandmother's house had a bathtub in the bedroom, behind thick drapes. One day I had bathed and was dressing when Grandfather unexpectedly entered the bedroom and proceeded to disrobe. Off came his "corks" thudding to the floor. I was timid about being caught in there, not having had a chance to leave before he began to undress. I waited a few minutes and peeked out through the curtains, expecting him to be dressed. Instead he was still stark naked, admiring himself in front of the large mirror atop the bureau. I ducked back, embarrassed, figuring to give him another minute or two. When I peeked again, he was now puffing up his chest and making like Charles Atlas. Since Grandfather was hard of hearing, he did not hear me scuffling about behind the drapes. At last, I figured, I had waited long enough and with bad timing I bolted from behind the curtains just as he had bent over with his buttocks toward me. Since I was ten years old and not very tall, the view was quite startling for both of us. He saw my bugeyed expression in the mirror.

Realizing that I probably was spying on him while he was performing in front of the mirror, he grabbed a rubber boot and caught me perfectly in the rear as I sped for the curtain draped doorway. The force of the boot assisted me through the opening to a knee knocker landing on all fours, close to Grandmother, and the kitchen sink. "Great Caesar's ghost!" she blurted out startled, "What in tarnation are you up to?" as my grandfather's roar of laughter followed me from behind the curtain.

Planters

A few of the family floats were planked over and fenced in to provide safety for small children and pets. Grandmother's float was not only planked, but also covered with planter boxes full of dirt. The soil had been gathered from small dirt pockets on the rocky hillsides and put into five-gallon pails. From there it was transported via rowboat to her many planter boxes where she cultivated countless flowering plants, both wild and domestic.

Boardwalk

A plank boardwalk about four feet wide delineated a path from float to float and led all around the camp. The loggers' caulk shoes chewed up the surface of the planks so that hundreds, if not thousands, of sharp splinters presented themselves to our bare feet. Nevertheless, we kids ran around barefoot on those splintery planks all day long and rarely, if ever, did we feel pain or get slivers in our toes.

The boardwalks went past the doors of all of the buildings including the bunkhouses and being inquisitive like any kid, I had a pretty good idea of what was going on and where. One of the rules that I was supposed to heed was to stay out of the bunkhouses; not because anyone thought that I was in any danger, but more likely thinking I might be exposed to rough language. It's also possible that they wanted to protect the men from me. I could be a real nuisance, asking a lot of questions, etc. Once in a while I did go in the bunkhouses on legitimate errands, but basically, it was off limits.

Private Space

Each man's bed was his home away from home. You did not sit on a man's bed without asking permission. This was his own small kingdom for his length of stay in camp, which in those days could be many months. He sometimes erected a few shelves for personal items and pictures and put traveling bags under the bed.

The bunkhouses were heated with wood-burning oil drum stoves that could throw off a tremendous heat. On wet days men would drape their sopping garments on wire hanging racks from the rafters above the stoves. By the following morning all would be dry, or hopefully so.

The bunkhouse doors were rarely closed. They were the prime means of ventilation in allowing the hot humid air from drying clothes to escape. With several pairs of sweaty long johns, socks and pants drying out, the breathable atmosphere became rather limited.

I laugh when I hear today's loggers, with their private rooms and TV, grumble of having several days remaining before their twenty-seven days in the wilderness have earned them ten days leave in the city. The same guys wonder why things they need to buy cost so much. But as others have noted, with tongue in cheek, "this is progress."

Bullcook

The bullcook was one of the few employed men who stayed in camp to work. His job was to apply himself to a goodly range of duties that kept the camp running smoothly. His main line of responsibility was service to the cook and the other hired men. He split and supplied wood for the cook house stove and all other camp stoves. It was necessary to have several days worth of split and drying wood on hand in case unexpected events arose. In addition to the above, the bullcook swept the bunkhouses, made the beds every day and changed bed sheets once a week. He also fixed plumbing, kept the water supply flowing, cleaned the outhouses, did carpentry work where it was needed and much more. A good bullcook was a real asset to a logging camp.

Cook House

The cook house was always one of the largest buildings and the brightest inside. The long tables covered with white oil cloth and white tableware contributed to a bright, clean appearance. The floor was mopped and scrubbed regularly. Caulk shoes were never allowed in the cook house, which helped keep the floor clean. At place settings, plates were put face down with saucer and cup on top of each plate, flatware along side. Condiments on the table might be changed for breakfast, lunch and dinner.

Protocol was that every man in camp had his own place at a specific table. A new man arriving in camp had to be careful to find a place that was not currently being used by anyone, otherwise tempers would flare.

When the triangle bell rang calling the men to eat, the food was already on the tables, put there by flunkies (aids to the cook). As the bowls or platters of food were consumed, the flunkies, standing by, would snatch up the empty dishes and return quickly with full ones. Quite often the hungry men would try to hurry the flunkies with either encouragement or threats, sometimes in raw language. A logging camp never was a place of opportunity for the faint of heart and many flunkies could dish out as good as they got.

Blacksmith

The blacksmith's shop, to me, was the most exciting and wonderful place. It smelled of coal smoke, hot oil, fire and brimstone. There was always plenty of clanging and banging going on. Things of intrigue and interest were continually being produced.

Huge vises were available for clamping. All sorts of hammers were available for bashing and hacksaws for whacking off chunks of metal. Best of all, it was virtually impossible for me to damage anything there. The blacksmith all but ignored me, and so long as I was not standing in his way, he left me alone to amuse myself.

The best part, when I was ten or eleven, was being allowed to turn the forge blower crank for long periods. This enabled me to witness white-hot metal emerge from the forge, get hammered a time or two, then be quenched in a bath of oil or water with a great crackling burst of hissing, snapping and bubbling, attended by volumes of smoke and steam. I thought, for sure, that it was a swell place to be and that to be a blacksmith must be the very pinnacle of achievement.

Later on, when I was twelve, the blacksmith was able to use me at the anvil to the point where I was actually beginning to learn something and make myself useful. Hooks of all kinds, straps, shackles, bolts, nuts and spikes for pike poles were produced constantly. The blacksmith regularly made tools for himself that were necessary for him to complete certain jobs.

After selecting a rusty chunk of iron from any one of several metal junk piles, he would toss the piece into the glowing forge and leave me working the blower while he turned his attention to another project. In turning the blower crank handle, air was forced through a pipe to accellerate combustion of the smouldering embers. I had learned that high air velocity or too much air overheated the fire and burned metal. Thus, I provided a slow, steady flow of air that in time created a cherry red glow to the metal that the "smithy" wanted. Soon he would be back. Grabbing the cherry red metal with appropriate tongs, he swung the sizzling hot chunk to the anvil. Tapping a spot on the glowing metal with his long stick was my cue to hit that exact spot with a certain force. As my hammer struck, he would tap again with his stick, sometimes in the same spot, sometimes another. As the metal cooled, back into the forge it went for more heat. This activity might go on for quite a while and I was constantly amazed at what was created from an unassuming chunk of iron. Though only twelve, I did not tire swinging the nine-pound hammer as, most often, only a few blows were required prior to more heat being needed and so I rested a lot between heats. As the blacksmith cautioned me on several occasions, it was accuracy that was needed with the hammer blows, not a lot of force.

Commissary

The commissary was a small store in camp for the benefit of the men. Socks, shirts, pants, caulk shoes, jackets, tobacco, flashlights, soap and shaving supplies, liniment, Eno's Fruit Salts, pocket knives and watches were among the many items that could be purchased, as well as candy bars and pop.

The man in charge of the commissary was the timekeeper. In addition to dispensing the above supplies to the loggers, the timekeeper was in charge of payroll and purchasing. Supplies acquired from the commisary were duly noted by the timekeeper and the cost deducted from the loggers' bi-monthly pay checks. I can remember two or three timekeepers, but the most colorful was a man by the name of Charlie Rippington. Charlie, it seemed to me, was very pious in his outlook and could even be embarrassed for others around him who were not. Even to us youngsters he appeared to be very gullible.

My Uncle Keaton and I had little trouble snitching candy bars and gum from right under Charlie's nose. A little planned diversion was all it took and old Charlie never seemed to catch on, or so we believed. Just in case, we had several secret caches around camp. We took extraordinary measures in disguising where we hid our filched candy bars, as if we expected Charlie to descend upon us and demand a confession of our misdeeds. Sister Cherie's means of obtaining candy was I think typical of young female audacity. No cunning plots, no cloak and dagger swagger; she merely stood around smiling when the men came to the commissary to buy things. In this way, she usually would have a candy bar or package of gum "forced" upon her.

Charlie

Charlie at this time was about forty and, although compactly built, was already a little stooped in posture. His hair was light brown, straight and side parted, but closely cropped all around, like a Marine. His face tended to be craggy, with thick magnifying eye glasses and a prominent thin nose hooking at the end. He had a small lipless mouth that exposed the upper gum limit of his false teeth whether he was grinning or not.

However, aside from a few interesting personality quirks, Charlie was a pretty fine fellow. Almost always he had a positive and enthusiastic attitude. Most importantly, Charlie was an honest man who needed little supervision and was a man my grandfather could rely on. In retrospect, I wonder if he was more aware of our candy bar filching than we knew.

Charlie's most interesting quirk, or so I thought at the time, was his attitude regarding swearing—not anyone else's, it seemed, just his own. Charlie was a practicing Christian and he worked at it as a lot of others do not. I don't remember hearing him comment against anyone who used foul language, and I never heard him swear, except once he came close. If Charlie wanted to give vent to his enthusiasm or rising emotion, he would sort of shift around on his feet like a boxer and repeat the words "man-o-man, man-o-man." If he really got excited he just said it louder and faster.

One day I happened to be present in the commissary when Charlie bashed his finger, a good lick, with a claw hammer he was using to hang up a small display. He fell from his stool in pain, all cramped up, bending over to cradle his throbbing finger. His face was contorted, with lips twitching. I could see the possibility of an ugly oath taking shape behind his ill-fitting false teeth. Looking at me with pained eyes, I barely heard him utter the word "curses." I was exceedingly impressed with this, because "curses" was the one word that to me expressed all the worst swearing I had heard up to that point. Soon though, Charlie regained his composure and hopped around holding his finger repeating "man-o-man, man-o-man," as if he was hoping to forget his close brush with temptation.

Camp Tender

From 1928 to 1942 the camp tender for Gildersleeve Logging was the *Crusader I*, a thirty-eight-foot wooden-hulled vessel. It had a fifty-five-horsepower Vivian diesel engine, a wood and coal cook stove for cooking, a fold-down galley table for eating and four bunks for comfortable sleeping.

The camp tender's function was to ferry people and supplies to and from camp, plus performing towing duties around camp and elsewhere when required. The *Crusader I* had a full-time skipper in pursuit of the above tasks. He was Roy P. Gadsden, the eldest son of Percy Gadsden, an old friend of Doc's from the Nootum Bay 1920s. Roy, at the age of seventeen, came to work for Granddad to run the *Crusader I* and stayed for twenty-three years. He was the perfect employee—a self starter, conscientious, hard working, honest and got along well with everyone.

Log Stowing

The booming grounds, where the logs were "stowed" once they "hit" the salt chuck, often was right beside the camp or in a bay a short distance away. In any case, the best spot was away from the wind and waves and close to the logging show.

Most of the time the camp itself was close to the logging operation. This, of course, was the best setup, since then the men had only a short distance to travel to and from work. The sorting and stowing of logs close by the camp automatically became a major part of the camp world that we kids explored as we rowed to the beaches and back to camp. The evenly stowed logs of a five-section raft (boom) presented an interesting challenge to our nimble young legs as we practiced our skill at racing back and forth across the uneven log surfaces while they bounced rapidly up and down under our weight. On other occasions we dared each other to walk barefoot along a slimy boomstick pretending that sharks or other hungry monsters would rise up and devour us if we fell in. As small children we had to wear life jackets. I must have been nine or ten and ecstatic when I finally was allowed to go without one. I felt free, like a turtle jettisoning its shell.

Learning to Swim

Once my Uncle Richard, swinging me like a sack of potatoes at arm's length, on the count of one, two, three, flung me out into the salt chuck with no life jacket. I was seven years old at the time. I went screaming all the way, landing about twenty feet out in the deep water. I sank like a box of rocks and can remember clawing my way to the surface for air, where I rapidly discovered the dog paddle. Uncle Richard swam up beside me, in case I needed rescuing, but found me dog paddling back to the floats, bawling loudly, as I was scared to death.

Falling off the floats into the chuck was a great danger. The float logs were often too high out of the water for kids with limited strength to gain a handhold and crawl out. Life jackets were a good idea for that reason. A good set of lungs, however, usually brought help in a hurry.

In those days thunder and lightning flashes terrified me. Uncle Richard would take me outside in an electric storm, presumably to show me that I would not be harmed. I wasn't easy to convince and jumped sky high as I felt sure that every lightning bolt shot right through my gizzard.

Fire

Before 1950 there were no electric lights in camp. Coleman lanterns were used in all of the houses. One of my jobs was filling lamps and lighting them as it got too dark to read or play cards. One fall evening an unusually strong breeze blew window curtains against the hot mantles of a Coleman lantern and, before anyone noticed, the whole wall in Uncle Frank's bedroom was aflame. The call of "fire" brought the entire camp of twenty-five or so running to help. A bucket brigade was formed and there not being enough fire buckets for a situation like this, cooking pots were commandeered from the cook house. The bucket line started at the water's edge and extended about thirty feet to the building on fire. Salt water was scooped from the chuck and passed hand over hand to be tossed onto the flames by the strongest men. The scene was pandemonium and besides the bucket brigade, other individuals were running to the water's edge, scooping water and then dashing back to the fire to douse the flames. In the melee people running with buckets collided with each other and still others in confusion threw their buckets onto the fire along with the water. My grandfather was seen dashing with a bucket of water and just before reaching the fire, he stepped into a hole between the float logs, twisting his leg severely.

All things considered, Grandfather was lucky they were able to get control of the blaze and extinguish it before any serious damage was done. Otherwise, it would have spread to the other buildings and that, no doubt, would have meant the loss of the entire camp and all that Grandfather and Grandmother had worked years to build.

Playing Cards

Back then there was not a lot to do in the evening but read, play cards or tell stories. Poker, cribbage and rummy were the three card games of choice. Almost every night men would gather in the poker shack either to play or to watch. I would hang around and watch because often either Uncle Dick or Granddad would be playing. The first few years I made myself useful as a "gofer," running errands to get more cigarettes, candy bars or soft drinks. Gradually, through watching, I saw how winning hands were developed and how they were played by a few skillful players, my grandfather being one of them.

As in other areas of activity, I learned that timing in poker playing, in order to win, is very significant. It's an understatement to say that holding good cards is important, but probably not as important in winning consistently as how one plays the cards one is dealt. In general, if you have a good hand you should endeavor to keep as many players in the game as long as possible, contributing to building the pot in the betting after each round of cards is dealt. In this way, the pot will soon grow large enough that even the players with the poorest hands are reluctant to drop out as they may feel from the cards showing that they could eventually win by catching the right card on the last round. The game of poker I have found is like the game of life; if you put nothing into the pot, the chances are you will not get much out.

Once the pot is sizable, it may be time to make your move if no one else does, to enlarge the pot even further by betting more heavily. Some will drop out, but a few will follow, hoping that you are bluffing or hoping that they will improve their hands dramatically on the last card, if indeed there are any more cards to come. Even if you hold good cards, you may want to "check" your cards to them and let them bet, thus allowing yourself the pleasure of calling them while studying their moves for future reference. Confuse them the next round by raising the bet. The pot will grow even larger as a few will call you, especially since they may think that you are trying to "buy" the pot. This could go on even further, but it does indicate, I think, that timing plus skill in betting is exceedingly important to a successful poker player.

This is not to say that other skills are not equally as significant in poker, as the song says, "you have to know when to hold them and when to fold them." Even the very best poker players can lose. Luck plays an important role, but knowledge and skill over the long haul is what makes a winner.

Once when I was about sixteen, I found myself way over my head in a poker game that had started out with a twenty-five-cent limit on bets. Not long after the game got underway a few forceful players decided that higher stakes were required and no one complained so we played on. I soon realized that this game was no social event between friends and the pressure had me very nervous. About this time in a hand of draw poker, I was dealt a jack-high straight flush in the first five cards. The mathematical odds against this happening are great, especially with five players in the game. Try as I might to control my emotions, I could not. My hands shook. Suddenly I felt a steadying hand on my shoulder and a voice asking me what I thought I should do "with that mess of cards." Looking over my shoulder, I recognized one of the older cook house flunkies, himself an inveterate poker player. He had seen my nervousness and sensed that speaking to me would calm me down. After the other players drew cards and I drew none, they all smelled a rat and folded. I won a small pot that could have been much larger if only I could have contained my emotions and disguised the fact that my cards were essentially unbeatable.

Importantly, one should adopt the habit of never letting your opponents see your cards at the end of a hand unless they pay to see (call your bet). Showing opponents your cards when they do not "call" you tells them too much about what sort of a player you are. I feel that it is a bad practice, even among friends. Keep them guessing; show them nothing unless they pay to see. There are some players who will insist on seeing your cards when they have decided not to call your bet and will get very angry when you refuse them. Stand your ground—the rules of the game are with you.

I was in another game in a bunkhouse where a player jumped up to grab a look at cards that beat him, even though he had decided not to call and had folded his hand. He hoped he could prove to himself that the winner was bluffing. The incident ended with one man hoisting the other over his head and throwing him onto the oil-drum wood stove. The stove and stovepipe were sent flying. Amid sparks, ashes and smoke, ten feet of hot stovepipe spewed black soot over the poker table and all of us players. Needless to say, and not to make a pun out of it, that ruckus put the damper on any more card playing that night. Unfortunately, I cannot remember which of the players it was that got the hot seat, the good guy or the bad guy. In poker, as in everything else, life can be unfair as well as exciting.

During my university years money was always hard to come by, but often I won enough at small weekend poker games with fellow students to buy an extra hamburger or two. One memorable weekend I found myself a significant winner in a poker game where finally articles of clothing were accepted for betting. One of the students at my boarding house was a particular snob. He had lost all of his remaining allowance of cash to me. As the game wound to a close, he happened to get what he thought was a pretty fair hand and eventually just he and I were left to challenge each other over the pot. From experience, I knew this fellow to be an emotional hot head and judged that he could be fooled into thinking I was bluffing, when I really held excellent cards. I feigned nervousness and made a substantial bet, whereupon he called my bet with a brand new pair of Scotch brogues, his dress shoes. His face turned sick when he saw my cards that overcame his. He was beside himself and insisted on having his shoes back, pointing out that they were not even my size. I sold the shoes to a classmate for ten dollars, about one-third their value at the time. I have often wondered if that fellow ever reflected on that game, considering what lesson it may have taught him. My response, always, to anyone who hasn't done his homework and suffers from it, is tough beans.

Moses Inlet

The summer of 1939, Gildersleeve Logging was in Moses Inlet, an arm of Rivers Inlet. The tides on the northcentral coast of B.C. are fairly large; about eight to ten feet run out on average from high tide is not unusual. At high tide the water depth beneath the floats nearest shore might be only a few feet deep; thus, at low tide that portion of the float camp would be high and dry on the beach. During a minus tide event, which would occur only a few times a year, possibly all of the camp floats could be aground, surrounded by barnacled rocks, seaweed, mud and sand. Seldom seeing so much beach stretching before us, we kids wasted little time in getting off the floats and onto the tide flats where we could begin exploring. We began by turning over rocks to marvel at the many small creatures, including tiny crabs scurrying for another cover. The sea life abounded. Most fish, except for bull-heads trapped in sea water pools, were gone, but jelly fish, starfish, sea cucumbers, sea anemones, sea urchins, crabs and many other spiky-shelled creatures were everywhere, not to mention mussels and clams.

Moses Inlet was also a great place for wild berries. My grandmother was an inveterate searcher for wild berries, especially red and blue huckleberries, mountain blueberries and salal berries. She and my sisters would often be seen disappearing from view along the shoreline in one of the many rowboats. This suited me fine, as picking berries was about as interesting to me as jumping off a cliff. Gram had tried to enlist my services, but she soon learned that I was just "in the way."

At this particular time my Uncle Keaton, who was fifteen, and I, seven, were engaged in building a smokehouse on shore behind the camp. Actually, to our minds it was more of a hideout.

Whenever there was distasteful work to be done, we could disappear to the smokehouse and pretend to be working.

One warm afternoon when even our smokehouse project seemed tedious, we decided to explore the rocky bluffs back of the camp. We took along our .22 rifle in case we met up with wild animals. Keaton's idea was that as soon as we were out of sight of the camp we would be able to relax and have a smoke. Since we were clever fellows, we decided to fill the .22-cartridge boxes with tobacco in case we were searched, carrying the cartridges loose in our pockets. Who would ever think of looking for tobacco in .22-cartridge boxes, we felt, even though empty of cartridges they were almost weightless. As clever as we thought we were, we did not realize that no one cared anyway.

Away we went and climbed high up on the shrubby bluffs where we found a shady ledge covered with moss and salal berry bushes. Making ourselves comfortable we got out our "makings" and started rolling cigarettes. We then laid back, lit up and puffed, taking care not to inhale.

Soon our conversation turned to important stuff, such as girls, and how some girls had to get married and what that was all about. Keaton, being older than me, naturally was my mentor. He asked me if I knew how babies were made. I said "sure," which was a lie. He knew that I was fibbing and so proceeded to explain everything with hand gestures, and undulating body gyrations, all intended to make it clear for me. I was confused. Why would grownups put up with all of that "rigmarole" just to get kids.

After much more puffing and pretend inhaling on my part, Keaton decided that we had better get back. Without thinking, I tossed my slimy cigarette butt into the nearby brush without first crushing it out. We both instantly leaped to the spot where I thought the butt disappeared and began a frenzied search for it. In our imaginations that butt was a smoldering bomb. Time and time again we were told that forest fires were the worst calamity that could befall us, and carelessness with cigarettes was how fires were started.

After a fruitless search, we reluctantly decided to give up and leave. We lingered a while longer, rubbing blueberry juice in our eyelashes and eyebrows to dye any singed hairs. This was another of Keaton's clever ideas to prevent detection that we were lighting matches and smoking in the bush. It never occurred to me or possibly him either, that my two blueberry stained eye sockets might arouse suspicion. I probably looked like I was "made up" for a role as *Phantom of the Opera*.

Lying nervously in my bed that night, I expected at any minute to hear the call of "fire." I slept very little the next few nights, thinking that a lump of moss now smoldering slowly was ready to burst into flames. Eventually it rained, and I quietly thanked God and only then did my fears subside.

"Bulldogs"

During the summer months in Moses Inlet the large horseflies were a real nuisance. The months of July and August were particularly bad.

These horseflies are so large that we kids called them "bulldogs." Others referred to them as bombers or B-29s, because of their size; they could be heard coming from a long way off. Their bite was very painful. It's been said by some, that a bulldog bites a steak from you, then flies to a tree to rest and eat.

While this may be exaggeration, the bulldogs themselves are not difficult to swat. After the morning sun warms things up, they will land upon you sometimes in clusters where a hand smash can often take care of several. Loose clothing is the best way to foil these critters. The worst scenario is tight clothing, i.e., tight trousers. The bulldog can land unnoticed, and his stinger can penetrate even heavy cloth to nail you good.

My friend Pete Gazzola showed me how to deal with a bulldog I captured trying to bite me. First, he pinched off a small piece of the fly's rear end, opening up a hole into which he inserted a flat toothpick. When released, the fly revved up his wings and roared off trailing the toothpick behind, much like an airplane dragging an advertisement.

Once I was shown how I could deal with bulldogs, I began to experiment on my own. First I replaced the toothpick with a piece of white cigarette paper. This worked exceptionally well. It was a less aerodynamic burden to the fly and it could be seen going away from much further off.

Next I made small paper gliders and glued bulldogs to the leading edge of the wings like several motors on a bomber. This worked only moderately well. I think, perhaps, the glue made the flies drunk and so they likely were not putting out their rated power.

Another experiment with bulldog motive power was on the toy boats that I made. Normally, I attached a string to the bow of my toy boats and pulled them along in the water beside the floats. I used common pins to secure several bulldogs in line to the bow of one of my boats. When they were all buzzing in unison, attempting to fly, they actually moved the toy boat smoothly through the water. However, there were two main problems. One was to insure that all flies pulled in the same direction. (They often would spin around on the pin that held them to the boat.) The other major problem was to get them all buzzing together. Half of them would be revving up while the other half were shutting down and vice versa. Very exasperating. This, I finally decided, was not a task worthy of my attention and so, eventually, turned to other activities.

Tragedy

On another very hot day that summer of 1939 I can remember the long, intermittent wail of the steam donkey whistle crying out to us in camp its message that someone was badly hurt; all work stopped. Soon the entire work force returned to camp from the woods with one of their number on a stretcher. I watched them put the body in the poker shack back of the commissary. The victim was covered with an old gray blanket. As boys will do, I climbed on a block of wood to look through the window to stare and wonder at the long shape under the blanket. Is that what a body looks like, I wondered? Who is it? Did I know him?

Soon I was told that Jimmie Gadsden, a young brother of my stepfather Roy Gadsden, was killed blowing whistles (sending in signals via electric wire to a horn on the steam donkey) that day.

96

I did not know him well for he had been in camp only a short time. He was seventeen.

Less than a year later a young logger I got to know, whose name I now cannot remember, was whittling a toy sailboat for me from a piece of red cedar. Each evening I watched with admiration while whittling progressed and the boat began to take shape. I could easily see how beautiful it was going to be when finished. I could tell, too, that he enjoyed my enthusiasm over his progress as much as he enjoyed the whittling. One evening he made the remark to me, "Tomorrow we may be able to start on the masts."

Those long mournful wails from the steam donkey whistle reached us once again and we all waited with fear and foreboding. In the men came, silent, eyes averted, for again one of their number was cut down. They all understood the significance of the moment. "There but for God's grace go I." My friend, the whittler, was gone.

Crossbows and Fish Packers

Uncle Keaton had a small woodworking shop behind one of the bunkhouses and among his tools was a woodworking lathe. He got pretty good at turning wooden bowls, lamp bases, etc. Also, he turned long mahogany darts for the crossbows that two of the loggers in camp had made in their spare time using simple tools. The bow itself was fabricated from a piece of yew wood cut from the hills. The darts were about twelve inches long, including the eagle feathers at the trailing end. Each dart had a three-inch finishing nail inserted into the front end in a carefully drilled hole. The one and one-half inches of nail that protruded was ground to a needle point. The crossbows were beautiful examples of hand craftsmanship and wonderfully accurate. At close range they were deadly.

Keaton and I invented a game where we stalked each other with these crossbows except we used relatively nondangerous darts (sans nail), although they did produce large welts, especially if hit in a fleshy spot. One evening, during a spectacular and exciting exchange of darts, I shot out one of the bunkhouse windows that happened to be next to Pete Gazzola's bunk. The immediate result, not to mention shouts of indignation, was that Pete presented me with a replacement piece of glass plus glazing putty and then proceeded to supervise my first experience at installing a window pane.

That fall Grandfather had three fish packers come up from Wadhams Cannery in Rivers Inlet to tow the camp to a new location. As all the shore lines were let go and the camp slowly began to move away from the beach, Uncle Frank, myself and the two crossbow men were on hand. A large, very old sun-bleached snag still rooted on the shore became a receding target for the bowmen. As we were picking up speed, two mahogany darts sped to the snag and lodged themselves securely side by side into the wood. A comment was made then, wondering if the darts would ever be found. That was fifty-eight years ago and I also, now, wonder if the darts are still there.

The logging camp was headed for new territory. The loggers looked forward to a new timber claim, trees to fall and swing into the salt chuck, boom into rafts and send via tugboat to Ocean Falls. For my two sisters and I, the new location would provide fresh territory for investigation, new tide flats to roam and possibly new and different sea creatures to discover.

The new campsite was Johnston Bay two miles west of Wadhams Cannery, a place we called Hole-in-the-Wall, into which flowed Johnston Creek. This oblong little bay was about one mile long and one-half mile across.

Hole-in-the-Wall

We arrived late in the afternoon and the first chore was for the bullcook to run out the water lines. Without water, there is no hot food or hot showers for the men. Grandfather used to say that a man can stand almost any miserable cold and wet working condition, so long as he can count on a hot shower at the end of the day. It is a simple but elegant pleasure that even the toughest of men enjoy.

The next morning I was full of enthusiasm as my sisters and I ran out to view the shoreline and exposed tidal beaches. We were not disappointed. This place was heaven. The bay was not deep where the camp was nestled into the shore. At low tide some of the camp floats nearer the shore were aground and so we could easily jump down to the beach. In addition, the part of the camp that remained floating had only seven to ten feet of water under it at the deepest point, so watching the bottom then was a cinch. I spent hours lying on my belly, arms in the water, with a pike pole held vertically a few inches off the bottom, waiting patiently for Mr. Dungeness Crab to walk under my pole, whereupon I would skewer him *à la* shish kabob. It's true, I did not get many crabs in this way, but I only wanted the monster crabs that never found their place in the crab trap resting close by.

Stovepipe

One day Pete Gazzola noticed me lying down peering into the water. He suggested to me that if I wanted to see the bottom really well, I should first get a length of stovepipe, whereupon he left and soon returned with one. Then he instructed me to sink the stovepipe vertically in the water, almost to the surface, and put my face into it looking at the bottom. I did as he suggested, while he stood casually, hands in pockets, waiting for my reaction. I was flabbergasted. The clarity was fantastic. It was as though I had been looking at the bottom previously through frosted glass. Now it was like I was standing on the bottom rather than looking down through ten feet of water. Pete saw how pleased I was from my excitement and with his understanding smirk he disappeared into a bunkhouse.

I can remember how gleeful I was at the prospect of disclosing state-of-the-art stovepipe technology to my sisters who understandably did not always share my enthusiasm for spending hours staring down into the murky depths. At last my sisters discovered me with the stovepipe, eyeballs scouring the bottom.

"What's that?" Audrey asked.

"What's what?" I replied.

"That thing you're looking in," she said.

"Oh, you mean this," I replied, "it's only a piece of stovepipe."

"What's it doing?" Cherie asked.

"Oh, nothing," I replied, "I'm just looking through it, is all."
Finally, Audrey could stand it no longer.

"Come on Jim, let me have a look."

"Okay," I said, getting painfully to my knees and rubbing my
chest, "but you better not drop it." After lying prone on a knotted
log for a half-hour or so, semipermanent indentures would form
on my chest; however, nine year olds seem to have a high threshold of pain. Soon Audrey was lying on the log in the required
position. I handed her the stovepipe, already down in the water.
She took it and putting her face into it, peered at the bottom.

"Wow, gee, wow, golly, Cherie, you should see this, gosh,
you won't believe it; gee, I can see everything. Look at that huge
crab. Cherie, you should see this, you will not believe it."

Cherie, standing resolutely by, her face in sort of a pout, said,
"Well, let me have a look then," and had to repeat it several times
before Audrey would relinquish the pipe. Cherie needless to say,
was impressed, but not nearly as vocal about it as Audrey, and
she too was reluctant to give up the pipe. They both wanted to
know how I got the stovepipe idea. Somehow they did not
believe that it was my idea, but I can't remember if I ever gave
Pete Gazzola the credit.

Besides stovepipe gazing, we spent many exciting hours jigging with hand lines and crabbing with ring nets. Most of our
fishing equipment came from friendly commercial fishermen
such as Olaf Slayback and Burt Shotbolt. They generously donated to us various hooks and lures and yards of commercial-grade
trolling line that we put to excellent use catching and hauling up
monsters of the deep.

With our stovepipe window on the bottom, it was no trouble
to spot a large Dungeness crab and lower a hook baited with a
generous chunk of raw beef right in front of his nose.
Immediately he would grab the bait with his pincer and we would
haul him up at our leisure, confident that the crab would not let
go. They never did. Many times in much deeper water, we inadvertently caught crabs in this manner when jigging for cod fish
with our lures on the bottom.

Bottom Fishing

When called for our lunch, we would secure our fish line to the float and leave. Often, upon returning, we would discover that our line was tight and headed off into the water at some obscure angle. If the line felt heavy as well as tight, hearts would start to pound faster; we would yell for each other to come and see what we had. Often, it took two of us to pull the creature up. If the line zigzagged as it neared the surface, our excitement grew more intense as our eyes strained for a first sight of the creature. Usually, we were not disappointed. All manner of goggle-eyed critters were hauled up with our lines, including dog fish, small shark, skate, eel, cod, small halibut, flounder and even ratfish. Ling cod up to three feet long, with heads as large as bowling balls and bodies tapering to a point, were among the most bizarre creatures from the deep. A three-foot-long wolf eel with its fanglike teeth was a close competitor for ugliness. Even a ratfish was pretty scary. It had a large goatlike head, small mouth and prominent ratlike teeth, long tapering body, smooth metallic brown skin and no scales. The ones we caught were eighteen to twenty-four inches, but they can get up to three feet long.

I used to think that we had caught everything that was down on the bottom until I would haul up some bizarre-looking creature that no one around us had ever seen before, and comments like, "My God, what is it?" would pop my chest out. Those were exciting times. Hauling up a crab trap never quite produced the adrenaline rush that hauling up a jerking fishline did. Fairly often though, we caught flounders, starfish, wolf eels, sea urchins, sea snails, octopus, jelly fish and other creatures besides crabs in our crab nets.

Clam Digging

Clam digging was interesting only because one could anticipate making a meal of them, but I could never call it exciting. Actually, it was hard work. Many trips were made between the particular location of the logging camp and Ocean Falls. It was not unusual to run into foul weather and have to put into a sheltered cove until the storm abated.

On one such occasion while the boat skipper, Roy Gadsden, prepared dinner for three of us, my friend Peter Gazzola and I decided to row ashore to dig for clams. In no time we found plenty of butter clams and littleneck clams, but also great quantities of "horse clams" (they look like giant butter clams and can be as big as a man's fist). I wanted to keep the horse clams, but Pete said they were poisonous and that I should never eat them. He then told me a story of being stormbound for days, years before, and for lack of food had dug up and eaten several horse clams. He said as a result he had developed a giant erection that was disconcerting, extremely painful and lasted for about three days. Seeing his point, I tossed the horse clams out of our bucket.

Years later, I related the story to my grandfather as the two of us were relaxing over a glass of beer. "By golly," he said, "I believe it, if Pete said so, then it was true." Grandfather continued with a smile, "I would like to have been there and seen that. Pete had a pecker as big around as a peavey handle when it was soft." Then laughing, "I wonder where he put it for those three days. That's something to think about."

Shark Bait

One day while still in the Hole-in-the-Wall, Gram and the girls had gone off picking berries and I was at loose ends looking for something to do. Taking Spunk, the camp dog, I decided to go for a row away from the camp and out into the bay.

It was a very hot and sultry summer's day. I had my shirt off and was about a quarter mile from the camp when I quit rowing and leaned on the oars while I contemplated a few momentous questions that lately were knocking around in my head. Questions like, why am I, who am I? How do I fit into the big picture of things? What is the big picture anyhow? If the Germans win the war, will I have to learn to speak German? While my mind was engaged in this day dreaming, a strange yet familiar splashing sound roused my senses. The surface of the water was like glass. Something had risen in the water behind me.

102

Adrenaline began shooting into my bloodstream, and suddenly I was in a cold sweat, never mind how hot it was. I could feel my scalp itching as the hairs began to stiffen on the back of my neck, yet I was scared spitless to turn around and look. Spunk had heard it and jumping to his feet with the hair on his back standing straight up he was looking past me at the "thing."

I turned slowly, stiffly, as if rigor mortis was all but complete in my body. My disbelieving eyes focused on a huge, shiny brown fin, motionless, about ten feet away and thrust at least twelve inches out of the water. Spunk went bananas, and acted like he was going to jump in and attack this thing. Gaping into the water surrounding the menacing fin, I could see the shadowy form of a brownish green mass fading away in all directions. It was flesh-creeping evidence of a very large, scary creature.

All of a sudden my mind and body snapped into unison and, grabbing the oars, I rowed hard for camp. Almost immediately to my horror, the nightmarish fin sank from sight. I now fantasized that it would either get ahead of me and block my path, or rise up directly under me, like a tale from Sinbad the Sailor, and capsize my boat. Also, I speculated, would it eat Spunk first and give me a chance to swim to shore or what? The bow wave from my rowboat must have been something to see. On reaching the safety of the float camp, still shaking, we both jumped out and I tried to find someone, anyone, to warn them of this huge thing with a fin on it. There was no one around that I thought would appreciate the seriousness and danger of my close encounter. Later on when my sisters, the berry pickers, returned, I excitedly related all the details of the incident, however, they did not seem impressed. It really did happen, honest.

Panning Gold

Naturally, I did not spend all of my time in the leisurely pursuits of boating, fishing and beach combing. Often I would accompany my grandfather on short hikes into the bush, usually when he wanted to make a quick check on timber nearby. As Granddad hiked around a hillside, I followed eating huckleberries and trying to figure out what he was up to. Occasionally he might ask

103

me a question or draw my attention to something he thought of interest. This particular afternoon I was beginning to lose interest in tramping up and down when Granddad stopped as he was fording a small stream. He squatted down and was peering into the bottom of a shallow pool of crystal clear water. "By golly, Jim," he says, "I think we may have struck gold." Soon he was swirling sand around in the bottom of a thermos bottle cup and collecting tiny gold flakes. It was slow, tedious work, but he kept at it for the most part of an hour. I was surprised at how involved and excited he got at the opportunity to pan gold. We came away with an amount of gold dust that would barely cover the bottom of Gram's sewing thimble. Granddad explained to me that the source of the gold was somewhere higher up on the mountain and that one needed a lot of time to locate it and then the total quantity may not be worth the search. This small occurrence showed me a side of my grandfather that I had rarely seen. He was more relaxed and he seemed to enjoy the opportunity to deviate from his normal activity.

As far back as I can remember, there were always great chunks of ore laying around under foot. Usually, it was very impressive looking stuff in that a lot of it looked like solid gold but wasn't; it was only low-grade copper and iron. Others, I remember, appeared to be large diamond crystals protruding from a mass of igneous rock. However, they were only water-clear quartz crystals, some as thick through and as long as a man's fingers.

One ten-pound chunk of quartz crystal was used by Grandmother as a door stop. For years it sat on the floor holding her kitchen door open. More than once I overheard Grandfather and others in conversation about where some of his ore specimens originated. Grandfather, I could tell, liked to talk about prospecting and the possibility of striking it rich, yet he always turned the conversation back to logging. I think he had chased a few golden rainbows unsuccessfully in his day and decided to stick with what he knew best. "We are loggers," he would say, "and not prospectors," or something to that effect. For this reason, I suppose, the source of many of those interesting old ore samples had long been forgotten.

In those days trout fishing was more important to me than looking for gold. I do remember where we found lakes and streams that were chock-full of trout, rainbows, cutthroat, dolly varden and brookies.

First Steelhead

I hooked my first steelhead trout in a stream in Moses Inlet. To be honest about it, I didn't have it on for long. Due to fortunate circumstances for the fish, it escaped.

I was fishing with Uncle Richard, casting a fly into a large dark pool, when I noticed several fish swimming out from beneath an old log jam near me that was straddling a large section of the river. The trout would dart out to take my fly as it drifted past. I caught a few keepers, but decided to investigate the jam itself. I crawled up on top of it and being small, only eight years old, I climbed down inside to where I was kneeling on the log directly above the water. The logs above shielded a lot of sunlight, hence I could see clearly, deep into the pool below. There looked to be hundreds of trout in all sizes, many of twelve inches and larger. Being so close to the fish and yet unseen by them, I felt like a sneak thief and wanted to hold my breath. Then I saw him—a giant trout. At first I thought it was a salmon, but on closer inspection realized that it was a large rainbow and most certainly a steelhead.

I did not have my rod. Space was limited. It lay on top of the log jam. I went out after it and leaving the rod on top of the jam, paid out enough line, I thought, to reach down inside where I would be crouched. I tied a small spinning lure on the line and crawled back inside the jam. He was still there so I carefully lowered my shiny little spinner with a red bead right beside him. He seemed disinterested. I jigged with the line and managed to hit him on the head with the lure—still no interest. Getting cramped and sore in the knees, I shifted position and must have jerked the lure just the way old steelheadie wanted, because he lunged and grabbed it good. I was unprepared. My heart ballooned into my throat and I totally forgot where I was. I bolted up in my claustrophobic space, bashing myself cuckoo on a log above me. Amazingly, I never lost the sense of the fish jerking on the line even though I was totally dysfunctional due to my scrambled brain. I never let go of the line. I don't know how I kept from falling into the water. When my head and vision finally cleared, I was holding an empty line. I remained there for a time depressed, not wanting to believe that the fish was gone.

McNair's Creek was too deep and swift in most places for an eight-year-old to negotiate. Richard, who was six feet two inches and husky, would hoist me onto his shoulders. With my legs hooked back of his arms, away he would go, leaping from rock to rock with me swaying around trying not to lose the string of pan-fry rainbows and cutthroats that swung wildly from my willow stick. All day long this scenario would be repeated, each time dropping me to the ground beside a deep dark pool or a perky rapid. We would try our luck awhile and then move on. It was my luck that Richard had been blessed with a strong pair of legs and that he loved trout fishing even more than I did. I never would have been able to cover so many good trout streams at an early age.

"Dirty Socks"

When I was young and impressionable, there was a picture hanging in a prominent spot in my grandfather's house. I spent many quiet moments studying that picture. It was enlarged to about twelve inches by twenty-four inches from an original postcard-sized photo.

The picture showed a man, a fellow hunter and friend of Granddad's, standing atop a rockpile, probably the site of an old rock slide, surrounded by five dead black bears. I stared at that picture of dead bears and tried to imagine how in the world it all came about.

The man standing amid the heap of dead bears holding the barrel of his rifle apparently had just shot all of them himself, one after the other. He was the man they called Dirty Socks. I wondered if the bears had attacked Dirty Socks en masse? Did he defend himself bravely after scrambling up that rock pile with the bears at his heels? Did he save his skin by downing all five bears rapid fire as they charged his mini-fortress? Or did he calmly draw a bead and plunk each one, as they in turn scrambled up the rocks after him?

Dirty Socks came by his name honestly. He was a tough, old Norwegian handlogger in his prime during the early 1920s, whose real name was Ed Anderson; however, his pseudonym and fame as a bear hunter lives on.

In those days and time, refrigeration was not common and meat spoiled easily. Thus, the men hunted for meat frequently, usually deer or goat. This particular day five men set out from camp, Dirty Socks among them. Dirty Socks, they said, nearly always chose to hunt alone and when in new territory he had a habit of tearing off a piece of his shirttail and attaching it to a tree trunk, as a beacon.

Evidently, that day, he approached the clearing caused by the old rock slide. Looking around he could see no game but sensed that he wasn't alone. Suddenly a large bear came into the small clearing and spotted Dirty Socks. The Norwegian's first impulse was survival and so he headed up the slide to higher ground. The bear, annoyingly, followed right on his heels, so Dirty Socks turned and shot the bear, just as another bear came into the clearing and headed up the rock slide toward him. Dirty Socks shot the second bear almost on top of the first, and then a third bear, and a fourth and fifth bear, practically on top of each other. His rifle was of small caliber and so it actually necessitated shooting an animal of that size at close range. He was also out of ammo after downing the last bear. My grandfather had written on the back of the picture of Dirty Socks and the five bears, "How about this for a bear story?"

If the preceding story didn't insure Dirty Socks' fame, there is a second story they told about him. On this occasion he was again alone, but hunting a large tidal flat where the swamp grass swayed like a field of hay and was taller than a man's head. The key to hunting an area such as this was to be vigilant for what one could not see as one wandered around in the maze of sloughs and gulches that crisscrossed the area.

Suddenly, Dirty Socks heard movement and turned to see the head of a large grizzly bear rise surreptitiously from a thicket of grass. He promptly took aim and shot. The head quickly disappeared then rose momentarily again, to look about. Dirty Socks shot a second time and again the head disappeared but rose again. He aimed and fired a third time and then took to his heels heading back to camp. He returned shortly with friends and more fire power. All, including Dirty Socks, were surprised to find three dead bears. To say the least, Dirty Socks had guaranteed the continuance of his bear-hunting fame.

Reportedly Ed Anderson lived to be 100 in a Swedish nursing home in Burnaby, B.C. and his famous small-caliber, bear-downing rifle resides in a museum at Gibson's Landing, B.C.

Hobbies

Being cooped up for several months in a logging camp with few recreational possibilities can have different effects on different people, but generally there tends to be an irritation threshold that gets lower and lower as the weeks go by. Some call this phenomenon "cabin fever."

There were always a few men in camp who developed an interest in hobbies. Keaton Gildersleeve had a small woodworking shop. He also built gas-powered model airplanes and boats, among other projects. A few other men made crossbows out of the springy yew wood that grows on the B.C. sidehills. Their craftsmanship was exceptional and the crossbows worked very well. Others took to challenging each other in one manner or another, to the point where one fellow almost blew himself up in a boat. Some others played cards regularly, such as poker, and seemed not to get terribly upset at the prospect of losing most of their hard-earned money, so long as their minds were kept busy during their leisure time.

Other men would turn to liquor in an attempt to relax their nerves, yet often it seemed to me that this had no beneficial effect at all. If anything, it exacerbated the situation, causing rough-housing and fist fights.

On one occasion, two young fellows after having too much to drink, got to pushing and shoving one another. Inevitably one of them took a haymaker on the jaw and went down like he was pole-axed, and he didn't move. He was out cold. They revived him with cold water but he fell asleep lying on the bunkhouse floor in a pool of water and started to snore. Soon it became evident that there was something pretty foul smelling in the room and everyone started checking their feet for you know what. Then they began to realize that the snoring individual on the floor had fouled his pants. The odor was so rank that they grabbed his arms and dragged him out of the bunkhouse onto the narrow board-walk and left him to lie snoring in the rain. That is the only time I can recall being present when a man really got the crap knocked out of him.

Speed Boat

In 1939 Frank Gildersleeve built himself a sixteen-foot speedboat out of yellow cedar. The construction design was yellow cedar strip planking over sawn frames with battens on the frames to secure the yellow cedar planks. Thousands of brass screws were employed in the fabrication process of that boat; I don't believe there was a single iron nail or screw in it.

He settled on a Gray Marine gas engine and it gave the boat a top speed of 30 mph. This meant that if anyone was in a real hurry, Ocean Falls was only three hours away (weather permitting), rather than ten with the camp tender, and Dawson's Landing was fifteen minutes away rather than one hour.

Frank's speedboat, I think, was intended strictly for pleasure and I'm sure it gave a lot of that. Naturally it could not sustain a cruising speed of say 20 mph, unless the seas were fairly calm with only small chop. Inside the bay at the Hole-in-the-Wall, where we were, the water was generally protected from strong winds and so it was an ideal place for Frank to make test runs with the boat as he tried out an engine or two and got a good grasp of the boat's performance and handling characteristics, i.e., on straight acceleration, tight turning, jumping small waves, etc.

In going for rides with Frank, I recall that once in a while, to demonstrate boat performance, he would head for the camp floats at full speed and then at the last moment swerve away to scare the pants off everyone watching, especially the passengers in the boat.

Self Esteem

As I think must be the case in any remote family-owned business, everyone, of necessity, learns to wear several hats. I can think of no better confidence builder for a young person than being able to perform several different tasks. As for building confidence and self esteem, it never happens overnight.

I remember Uncle Frank teaching himself to be a mechanic when he was eighteen to twenty. He would acquire used automotive engines and proceed to strip them to the block. He would then rebuild the engine from the ground up, cleaning and repairing each element or assembly, including ignition, timing and carburetion. I don't know if Frank ever used those engines for anything other than teaching devices. However, I'm sure that with each one rebuilt and running smoothly he also gradually built up his confidence in his mechanical abilities. In later years everyone knew him as a master mechanic.

The Curse

About that time, my grandmother gave me the everyday task of chopping kindling for her wood cookstove. That was my responsibility. After a few days I grew tired of this chore, even though it took me only a short time each day. Gram soon discovered that I was neglecting my duty and pronounced a sentence on me that has remained with me to this day. "Young man," she said, "one of these days you will love to work."

As I grew a little older and could rationalize the importance of her statement, chopping wood for Gram's stove took on artistic proportions. I began to relish creating heaps of uniformly split pieces of wood. Then I would pile it all neatly in long straight rows, taking extra care to box and crib the ends of the stacks to ensure stability as well as architectural aesthetics. Inhaling the earthy aroma of the wood also developed into a pleasant experience for me. My neatly stacked rows, however, did not last long. The monster cook stove, about eight feet long, lorded over by Grandmother, consumed enormous quantities of wood. In so doing, it destroyed whatever architectural integrity my rows had possessed.

I have often wondered if Gram's pronouncement that "one of these days you will love to work" acted like a workaholic curse on me, or did she know that the love for work was in my blood, and that with patience it would evolve. Whatever the truth is, she was right. I did grow up liking to work and came to appreciate the fulfillment and pleasure that demanding physical labor can bring.

Survival Lesson

Grandma was something else. Along with her many talents of culinary art, she had learned to find and identify special herbs and roots for their use in cooking, as well as their uses for medicinal purposes. If I had a cut that got infected, she would slap a poultice of some weird concoction on it and in no time it would draw out the poison. Mixtures of bread, mud or soap poultices, just to name a few, were frequently pressed on me.

One day when I was about nine, we went ashore and into the woods specifically to look for roots. She particularly favored a kind of licorice root. She would dry them out and grind them up (for what purpose I cannot remember). This particular day while we were foraging, we came across a large and very rotten fir log about three feet in diameter that had long since fallen to the ground. A bear or other large animal had been digging and tearing at the log and had removed large chunks. Grandma got interested in this rotten log and began pulling large chunks from it, showing me the large grub worms that were living in the rotten wood. The grubs were white, about one inch long and one-quarter inch in diameter, soft and fat like a hairless caterpillar, only quite pointed at both ends. She took one of these grubs in the palm of her hand and popped it in her mouth, swallowing it. She instructed me to do the same. "Pop him to the back of your throat and just swallow him down like a pill," she said. "Don't bite him." I did as instructed, reluctantly. That was my first and last grub worm. She said "In an emergency these grubs can keep you from starving." She allowed that a handful of those grubs had as much food value as a regular small meal. "The bears sure like them," she said, and "they chew them so they must taste pretty good." Pure protein, no doubt. She was probably right, but I was very well fed then and otherwise never had the dubious opportunity of testing her theory.

Peter Gazzola

Grandfather Gildersleeve had a nucleus of longtime employees. First of all there were his three sons, Richard, Frank and Keaton. Then there were Andy Torkelson, Pete Gazzola, Charlie Rippington and Roy Gadsden, to name the best of the extended family. Roy Gadsden became Granddad's son-in-law and my stepfather. All of these men, in one way or another, I feel, had some significant influence on me while I grew up.

Peter Gazzola was born in 1898 in Bessica Loria, Italy, in the province of Teriso. He emigrated to Montreal in 1919–20 at about the age of twenty-one. His first work in Canada was in the eastern steel mills and farms. Later, as he put it, he worked his way west with a salami and a suitcase. His first jobs in the West were at Grant Island, B.C., quarrying stone and at another location where dynamite was made.

Later he went to Ocean Falls, initially to cut cord wood, and wound up working with Jack Clozza Logging on Link Lake. Peter was a man of very even temperament, had a great sense of humor and I felt that he liked us kids. In 1938 when I was seven, Pete was thirty-nine. He was about five feet ten inches tall with very broad muscular shoulders and neck, deeply defined chest muscles, narrow flat waist, thick arms and legs, with a lot of muscle definition all over his body. Except for his tanned face, hands and wrists and the V extending from throat to chest, his skin was alabaster white and actually seemed to glow like ivory. He was "a man among men." When Pete stripped out of his sweat-stained longjohns in the bunkhouse after work, the other men, most of whom were also heavily muscled, would stare at the wonder of Pete's beautifully proportioned physique. He looked for all the world like one of Michelangelo's marble statues.

With a physique like his, Peter was also a powerful man. On many occasions, when necessary, he carried a 400-pound drum of gasoline on his back for short distances. At one particular time he carried a complete 450-pound cook stove from the steamship where it was off-loaded up a narrow plank walkway across the log floats to its place in the cookhouse, about 150 yards' distant.

Pete was a man who could do most tasks around a logging camp well. He was self motivated, needed no supervision and was always enthusiastic and cheerful. Pete was a major entity in Grandfather's extended family.

Being young and impressionable, I was astonished by Pete's ability to smoke a cigar backwards—the lit end in his mouth. In those days, little boys were supposed to be seen and not heard. Fortunately for me, I ignored this peculiar social injustice and managed not to grow up a complete clod. Under my skillful interrogation Pete disclosed to me that because cigars cost so much, he had learned when he was on a railway gang how to keep the burning end of the cigar moist. Turning it around once in a while moistened the tip, thus it took a lot longer to burn down. When pouring gasoline Pete would rotate the cigar so that the lit end was in his mouth till he was finished. When asked how he could hold a glowing cigar in his mouth, he replied, "Just keep your tongue out of the way." When the cigar finally was too short to hold between his lips, he would cut it up, tamp it into his pipe and smoke it. The last procedure was to scrape the leavings from the pipe, moisten it with a little spit in the palm of his hand and pop it under his lip for the final recycling of the tobacco. All in the name of economy. Remember this was the twenties and thirties and cheap cigars were "only" a nickel. Pete was a survivor.

As I mentioned, Pete could do any job well, but basically in those days he was a faller—a falling ax, misery-whip, crosscut faller. A device called a springboard was used by fallers in those days, and most made their own. The springboard was a plank of wood five to six feet long by eight inches wide by three inches thick, with a metal shoe or toe plate fitted to the butt end of the board. To use the springboard, a notch was cut into the trunk of the tree about one half the faller's height below where he intended to chop his undercut. After jamming the metal toe plate of the springboard into the notch and climbing onto it, the faller could, using body language, change the angle of the board to the tree by pivoting it on the toe plate. This procedure enabled him to access the most comfortable angle as he got set to swing his ax. Once the undercut was finished, another notch was necessary to put the springboard in the proper position to work the crosscut saw on the back cut. It was not unusual on a steep sidehill for the fallers to be working from their springboards many feet off the ground, and for this reason they were very careful to ensure that their springboards felt and worked to their satisfaction.

Lesson with Sharp Tools

One day Pete selected a piece of yellow cedar with which to fashion himself a new springboard. Yellow cedar is a wood that is quite soft and is very easy to work with carpenter's tools. Not the least important, it has a wonderful aroma. Taking the slab of yellow cedar and the tools he needed out to the wood yard between bunkhouses, Pete proceeded with a razor-sharp draw knife to develop the shape he wanted for his springboard. His other tools were a large rasp, hand saw and brace with bits. I watched as Pete expertly drew the knife to himself producing long, tight silky curls of yellow cedar. Presently, Pete put the draw knife aside and was continuing the shaping with the large rasp. Bursting with youthful enthusiasm, I grabbed the draw knife and was hurriedly producing curly shavings from a chest-high block of red cedar laying nearby. Pete immediately warned me to put the draw knife down as it was too dangerous a tool for me to fool with. I ignored him and he warned me again saying that if I hurt myself I would get no sympathy from him.

A few moments later I sank the draw knife deeply into the soft-grained cedar and raised my foot waist-high against the

114

block to increase pulling power with my arms. Instantly, from too much force, the draw knife broke loose, shot forward and plunged deep into my shin bone three inches below my knee cap. It happened so fast the shock stunned me. I felt the razor edge of the blade bite deep and heard the crunch of bone. The pain took my breath away, but I said nothing. I lowered my leg and tried to act as if nothing was wrong. Amazingly, there was not much blood at first, yet I could feel a trickle moving down my leg. I was afraid to raise my pantleg to see what horrible damage I might have done. Pete, naturally, had seen the whole thing and just stared at me with an angry look, but said nothing. At last, I raised my pant leg to expose a terrible gash, which had begun to throb. Pete took a good look and without his customary humor or indication of sympathy, he shook his head allowing that it looked pretty bad and "hoped that I would not lose my leg." After all, he said, he had warned me and could not feel a bit sorry for me as I hadn't listened to him. "Now," he said, "you are going to suffer." And did I suffer—my leg swelled up to the size of a small stovepipe. I sobbed (in private) and felt sorry for myself for days with the pain. What I needed to do was stay off it and let it heal, but small boys cannot sit still and I was no exception.

I saw Pete every day, sometimes more than once, and often I would be holding my swollen leg in pain, having collided with some protrusion or other. Pete would appear as if from nowhere. He never offered any words of comfort, such as, "Wow, that was a good whack, does it hurt pretty bad?" or "How do you stand the pain for someone so young?" Pete would only narrow his eyes and shrug his shoulders knowingly. He must have spread the word, for as I recall, I never did get much sympathy from anyone during that disastrous episode. It took a month or more, but gradually my leg healed and, luckily, I never had any more problems with it. On many occasions in the months and years that followed, when Pete wanted to warn me about something, he had only to raise his index finger and give me that knowing look. He would then turn his head away with a large smile and we both knew what that meant.

Pete's Shack

Not very long after my leg-chopping fiasco in 1940, Uncle Richard and Pete Gazzola established a falling camp a few miles up Johnston Creek. They built themselves a shack out of poles with split cedar shakes for covering. Up to that time I had never been to their shack but had heard about it and the wild animals that they claimed were a nuisance and sometimes kept them awake at night. I wanted to know what it would be like to spend time in the woods with only a small pole shack for protection. As chance would have it, Richard came down with an attack of appendicitis and had gone off to Ocean Falls to have his appendix removed. The following weekend Pete asked me if I wanted to accompany him to the falling shack for a few days as he had some repairs to make to the structure, and wouldn't mind having me along for company. Also, I might assist him in packing-in needed supplies.

On the trail I alternately skipped and jogged along behind Pete, who kept a steady pace, secure in my belief that Pete could handle anything singlehanded short of a grizzly bear. All was well with the world. After what seemed quite a long time, we arrived at a small clearing, and I could see the cabin on a rise about fifty yards away. Nearing the cabin, we passed by a large animal skull that had been poised skillfully on the end of a vertical pole about four feet off the ground. Pete said that it was a warning. It was a wolf's skull, one that Pete had shot and beheaded. He hoped that wolves, being clever, would know that the skull had belonged to one of their brothers and would stay away.

I was surprised at how large and roomy the cabin seemed inside, with windows on two sides for light. As I stood inside the shack of poles and shakes, it seemed that daylight was entering from everywhere not just the windows. There were two large bunks, one near the door and one at the far end of the cabin. The one I was to use was by the door and was constructed out of log slabs. Window glass, stove and stovepipe had been hauled there via packboard.

Pete set to work on the cabin and had me opening cans and mixing the contents into a pot. That was to be our first meal in camp. We were having corn niblets, pork and beans and Spam plus chopped onions, all in the same pot. Spuds were in another pot. When Pete came in to finalize the cooking, he gave his approval, grinning. Then, he began brief instructions on the use of herbs and spices and proceeded to put copious amounts into the slumgullion pot along with a dash of olive oil and a large handful of chopped garlic.

Being alone out there in the wilds with Pete was a great adventure for me. That first meal, I thought, was wonderfully delicious, but of course my appetite may have swayed my judgment just a little bit.

Ax Handling

After dinner I went outside with Pete to chop kindling for the morning fire. Pete gave me a few pointers about handling an ax, mostly about safety, and this time I was listening. The first thing, he instructed, was to look around and especially above one's head before swinging your ax. He pointed out that if one's ax hooked an overhead branch in the middle of a swing, likely as not it would be jerked out of one's hands and might then descend on one's head, back or leg, causing a very serious wound. The same precaution goes for bushes on either side. If the bushes are thick and dense where one wishes to chop, then first of all, the offending brush must be cleared. Suffice it to say that once or twice not long after this lesson in axmanship, I failed to take the proper safety precautions and came very close to regretting it. Even today as I lift an ax to use it, I instinctively look up and around, remembering Pete. He taught me well.

Dry Socks

Before lights out, which was about eight or nine o'clock, we had been talking about the things woodsmen must know for comfort in the bush. Besides good food, Pete warned me, to maintain strength a man also needs to stay warm. I was full of questions and Pete had most of the answers. In particular, I recall him telling me, quite seriously, never to crawl into bed on the trail with damp socks. Always carry two pairs of heavy wool socks and put the dry pair on when sleeping. Take the damp pair into your bedroll with you so that they might dry out. Switch socks again in the morning, always keeping one pair dry. According to Pete, such simple wisdom will prevent many potential problems such as loss of energy due to cold shivery nights, sore feet, possible colds, etc.

Wolves

Long before the Coleman lamp died, we could hear the wolves howling nearby. One old wolf, according to Pete, was badgering him for shooting and beheading his brother wolf and would come and howl near the cabin. So much for Pete's warning skull. I thought of the wolves peering through large cracks in the cabin where daylight had streamed in. It was early October and I noticed that a cold breeze came in just as easily as did the sounds of critters outside. Pack rats, martin, porcupine, and what-have-you were all scurrying about gnawing on this or that, including parts of the cabin. It sounded like they all had hammers and saws from the noise they were making.

Soon I heard the thumpety-thump of padded feet bounding around the cabin. Then, loud howling began very close by and again I thought of the large cracks in the cabin walls. I imagined myself in the wilds surrounded by hungry wolves and protected by nothing more than a picket fence.

Pete's loaded .30-30 leaned against the shakes by the door and I wondered how much protection it would be if the wolves burst through the walls en masse. The howling got louder, so Pete got up and went to the door in the dark and stood silently in his long underwear while he peered out the window. Suddenly, he jerked the door open and emitted a tremendously loud bellow that stiffened me. The wolves stopped howling immediately and scattered into the brush. Pete was laughing loudly as he groped his way back to his bunk, saying, "That ought to put the fear into them pretty bad." Soon Pete was snoring loudly, but I could hear that the wolves with their padded feet were back. I figured they knew it was the beginning of a very long night for me.

Expletives

Pete Gazzola was a man not given to wild outbursts of emotion. He was thoughtful and reflective and seemed in total control of himself, always. However, unlike Charlie Rippington, Pete was able to call upon his knowledge of some pretty strong language when he felt it was appropriate.

One day as I was passing by the open door of the blacksmith's shop, I happened to see Pete and other men working at something on one of the benches. I ran in to have a look and found them bending a piece of metal rod. Suddenly, one of the men swinging a three-pound hammer about as hard as he could, accidentally whacked Pete on the back of his hand. They all gasped, looking at Pete in dismay, as if waiting for his hand to drop off, or at least hear a cry of rage and pain. But Pete was silent. He was bent over with his arm between his legs, teeth clenched, the muscles in his neck standing out like lengths of rope. His face was frozen into a mask of pain. Slowly, he straightened up, managing an agonized grin and said, simply, "curses." Wonderful, I thought, perhaps he had learned it from old Charlie Rippington. I felt then, that "curses" said it all in a gentlemanly way. From then on, when scraping my leg on a rusty cable, getting poked in the eye with a tree branch, or stabbing my hand with a cod fish hook I need not complicate the issue with "God-damned shit," "Son-of-a-bitch" or "Holy MacKinaw Moses," just simply, "curses." It seemed like pure genius. Soon after, especially if anyone was close enough to hear, I would salve some irritating situation with a resounding "curses." Even today, it still works pretty well on the right occasion.

When Pete was forty-nine, a young lady of twenty-four arrived in camp to help out in the cookhouse. Her name was Mary Leavy. Coincidentally, at that time many of the men in camp were suffering from dysentery due to having eaten rotten meat. Pete took it upon himself to escort Mary to the bunkhouses, where she administered warm milk to the suffering loggers. Mary in her own right was no shrinking violet, being about six feet tall and weighing well over 200 pounds. She had worked during WW II in the Vancouver shipyards and near war's end had injured her forearm severely. Lighter work for her was required and thus the position at Grandfather's camp.

After a brief courtship Peter, at fifty, married Mary who was then twenty-five. They had four children: Judy, born 1946; Peter, born 1948; Michael, born 1953; Edith, born 1959. Pete and Mary moved to Yale, B.C., in 1964 to work for Viv Williams at his Spuzzum logging operation.

Peter Gazzola passed away in 1979, age eighty-one, of liver cancer. Mary Gazzola, at this writing, lives at Hope, B.C.

Bonded to Grandfather

When Uncle Frank was twenty, I was eight years old and solidly bonded to my grandfather as a father figure. Whether Granddad was aware of this, I do not know. As long as I was allowed, I followed him like his shadow and often tagged along on short journeys into the woods while he viewed the progress of his logging operations. He also took me with him if he was going to "cruise" timber or in general explore the forest territories around the camp. At these times we might be gone during the lunch hour, so I would carry a packed lunch for two. Granddad would carry either his .270 rifle or a falling ax.

Gildersleeve logging activities, in those days, consisted of a wooden spar tree and a yarding machine of some type for cold-decking logs. Finally, the A-frame and steam donkey on a log float would "swing" the cold-decked logs to the chuck. To me, all of the equipment used then was massive and seemed very complicated looking. At eight years old, the machines scared me. They always seemed to be going flat out and generating an unbearable amount of noise. Often Frank was running the yarder and he impressed me no end with his dancing on levers or pulling others, shifting gears and razzing the throttle, all at the same time it seemed. The howling machine noise, the slapping and screeching together of steel cables, the rattling of the rigging chain and shackles, all combined, plus the mixed smells of the forest and freshly exhumed earth had me spellbound, wide eyed and dry mouthed with silent admiration, as the "turn" of logs twisted and smashed through virtually everything left standing in their path. The experience was always both riveting and scary.

Torkelson

Andy Torkelson was the woods boss and also the head rigger at Gildersleeve Logging. He had worked for Granddad longer than I can remember and was one of the company's key men. Andy was five feet eleven inches, completely bald, no neck, heavy shouldered with a barrel-like chest, no belly, no rear and skinny legs. With no buttocks, he was constantly hitching his pants up (strangely, Andy rarely wore suspenders). Due to his Scandinavian origins, Andy could not pronounce Jimmy, so he called me "Yimmy." He went at most tasks full speed, necessary or not. In putting a line ashore from a boat, for example, he never expected to step onto dry land or at best, knee-deep water. Andy, anxious to get going, would leap from the bow of the boat into chilling waist-deep water, dragging the line after him as if there was nothing unusual about it. Often, however, it was damn cold and raining and he might be facing a long day in wet clothing. With belt and spurs, ax and saw, he attacked the proposed spar tree to be limbed and topped as if it were an adversary, but always with a grin on his face.

One day Andy came roaring into camp alone in one of the crew boats with blood gushing from a large split in the crown of his bald scalp. He dashed over to the cookhouse and in a few moments returned, hurrying back to work, looking grotesque. He had splashed flour onto the top of his head and shoulders and later told me that it was a good quick remedy for coagulating blood to stop bleeding. "You remember that," he said. I did remember, too, as you can see; luckily, however, I have yet to put this special knowledge to any good use.

Later, in his golden years, Andy had a live-in girl friend who, it was said, had been a hooker when she and Andy were a lot younger and times were tough. In those lean years, the special rate for longtime customers was two dollars a pop.

Andy allowed this lady to handle their finances, not only because she had saved quite a nest egg over the years, but also because she, as it turned out, was somewhat of a financial wizard.

Periodically, old friends stopped by to visit the pair and to obtain small loans to bridge them over a financial dead spot. It was said that she doled money out from a seemingly bottomless supply of two-dollar bills. Whispers were that she still charged Andy.

What's a Konk Knot?

Granddad's deafness presented a challenge for me. One had to shout into his good ear to be understood. This state of affairs made it quite difficult for me to carry on any conversation with him, yet he would make me aware of whatever he thought was important and that I should know. Because my young mind was full of questions that often I could not ask, I learned to assimilate the goings on around me in an effort to answer my own questions as best I could.

One day Granddad and I stood at the foot of a huge spruce tree that must have been six feet in diameter. It looked to me as I gazed upward, that the top reached into the clouds. Granddad walked around the tree slowly, shading his eyes with his battered old Stetson. I watched him intently and was itching to ask him what he was looking for. In my enthusiasm I felt that I could probably spot it in a twinkle. Finally, he looked at me with a grin, and asked, "Do you see any konk knots?" The question stunned me. Finally, my big chance to show my knowledge had come and I had no idea of the answer. I could tell from the tone of his question that he expected me to know what a konk knot was. Rather than fake it, I blurted out in his ear, "What's a konk knot?" The grin slowly sank from his face. I remember the look of dismay in his eyes at my ignorance. I was disgusted with myself. How in the world could I not know what a konk knot was? The dictionary says "any of various diseases of trees characterized by the formation of an excrescence, knob or gnarl" (or in simple language, rot).

The question was indeed significant as Granddad needed to select a tree in this area for a spar tree. The tree after being topped would be "rigged" with guy wires for increased stability. A ground yarding machine would then be able to use the height of the spar tree to reach out in a large arc to the surrounding area and haul the fallen and bucked logs into what was called a cold deck pile. The spar tree indeed needed to be a healthy tree, devoid of all cracks, splits and especially rot, such as characterized by a konk knot.

In this case, Grandfather decided by himself the tree was solid with no konk knots or other forms of rot, and he cut a large X through the shallow spruce bark. This was a sign to the fallers, who had not yet entered this area, to leave this tree standing.

Once the timber in the area of the spar tree was felled, then the rigging of the tree would begin. First of all, the tree would be cleared of branches by the high rigger as he climbed up with belt and spurs. At the appropriate height he would saw the top out of it. The tree would then be ready for rigging.

The Pump Handle

Near the end of the summer of 1940, when Rivers Inlet was still thick with gillnet boats, one unfortunate fisherman committed suicide. The Provincial Police towed the fisherman's boat from Wadhams Cannery over to our camp at the Hole-in-the-Wall and, with Granddad's permission, tied it up and left. Granddad then gave me the job of keeping the boat pumped out. I recall being a little miffed at this added responsibility. I had about all I could handle, with chopping wood, beach combing with my sisters, and being a gofer for anyone needing anything.

It turned out that the boat leaked a whole lot. The manual suction pump on the back deck worked much like an old butter churn. A few quick up and down motions would prime the pump. Pull the handle up and water would flow out into a trough and over the side; push the handle down and a diaphragm valve would open allowing the plunger to descend quickly through water, to the bottom of the pump housing. Pull the handle up again and the valve closed, trapping the head of water. I was familiar with this type of plunger pump as nearly all small boats in camp had one. They differed only in size, shape and manner of construction.

To make matters worse, it began to rain hard and continued for days. I was now spending a lot of time pumping that boat. I noticed, however, that the pump worked very well and seemed more efficient than similar pumps in the camp boats. Curiosity got the best of me one day as I completed pumping out the fisherman's boat. I removed the pump plunger from its housing and was admiring the way it was made, noticing that it was more elaborate in design and construction detail than our other pump plungers.

Inexplicably, the plunger fell from my grasp. Like a drunk with no coordination, I was all over the deck trying to grab the plunger. I felt it hit the back of my hand, then my fingers touched it. I lunged again, but in seconds it was overboard and had slipped beneath the surface of the water. I could see its refraction distorted brown shape sinking out of sight with a snakelike pendulum movement. It was lost forever. I stood up and looked around incredulously, hoping that some silent witness to this bizarre occurrence would console me by pointing out that, after all, this was not real. It was just a dream.

In retrospect, I must have intuitively thought that the plunger would float since it was constructed of wood. In any case, I did not know of Lignum Vitae, or gum wood. These were nonfloating woods used in boat building in those days. The pump plunger handle was heavy and probably was one such wood.

After I regained my composure, which was slightly under the threshold of panic, I dashed around to the other boats with similar bilge pumps and inspected their plungers. I even took one or two that looked like they might fit and tried them out, but nothing worked. Nothing I could think of or tried did any good. Those were dark moments for me at nine, going on ten. Facing the music and telling Grandfather of my stupidity and carelessness was one thing, but that did not solve the problem. Men were already in short supply in camp. World War II had begun. Uncles Frank and Keaton were temporarily away from camp. My friend,

Pete Gazzola was considered an alien of a belligerent power (Italy) and was absent from camp for a time until his credentials were cleared by the authorities. To make matters much worse in the days that followed, it started raining more heavily. A few more days went by while I tried to figure what to do. Meanwhile, the fish boat was sinking by the bow. Still, no one seemed to notice.

One day in desperation, I told Uncle Richard what had happened to the pump and even though he was busy wearing several hats, he came over to inspect the situation. He asked me if I had tried parts from the other pumps. When I told him yes, but nothing fit, he slapped his thigh and said matter of factly to me, "Well then, I guess that you are just going to have to make one," and he walked off.

Uncle Richard's solution to my problem floored me. I felt nauseated and could feel the panic coming back. After I calmed down some, I began to think about the possibility of actually making a valve and plunger handle. I tried to recall how the handle and valve had been constructed, but gradually realized that how it had functioned was more important for now. Having got that far with my thinking, I made another inspection of the other similar pumps to get ideas. For a valve design I chose one that looked functionally simple and it was also one that I thought with minor changes I would be able to duplicate. One important requirement, I realized, was that it had to fit snugly in the pump housing. I was also aware that the apparatus needed to be rugged and reliable.

With these specifications in mind, I set out to locate a stout handle that might already be available and would obviate the act of having to make one. I had in mind a length of wooden pike pole because there were a number of ten-foot poles around and I hoped no one would notice if one of them disappeared. Over the next several days in the blacksmith's shop my energies were consumed with the effort and many abortive attempts at fabricating the diaphragm valve head. Basically it consisted of a flat piece of wood approximately one inch by four inches by four inches square with a one and one-half inch hole through the center of the four inches by four inches surface. Over the hole was placed a piece of flexible rubberlike gasket material that would function as the valve. Once all the pieces were made and I was sure that my valve fit snugly into the pump housing, I still had the major problem of final assembly.

The main assembly problem was attaching the handle securely to the valve head. I could not see how to assemble it so that it would be strong. The tools I had were crude—a crosscut carpenter's saw, draw knife, hack saw, jack knife, some chisels, hammer and nails. I also had a brace and bits. My first attempts at joining the handle to the valve head ended in failure. Further attempts caused split handles as I tried nailing the two parts together and soon, handles became a scarce commodity. Disaster struck again when I split my valve head and rendered it useless. I had to spend the next few days remaking it. This time I could see how a simple change in design would help in the final assembly process. Meanwhile, the fish boat was sinking. I had to remove the hatch covers from the fish hold and bail the boat with a bucket by throwing the water on deck where it drained out through the scuppers. It was exhausting work but I did not mind because by now I was confident that I was going to solve this problem.

Back in the shop I managed to drill several small holes with a hand awl in both valve head and handle. I then found nails that would fit snugly into the holes. I would pin the parts together. The idea worked well without, for the first time, splitting any of the parts, and it felt strong. Now came the moment of truth, would it work?

During this whole period, I don't believe that anyone in particular was interested in what I was doing. I don't recall asking anyone's advice on any part of what I was trying to do. I don't think it occurred to me to ask. It was clear what needed to be done and it was my responsibility.

Taking the new valve pump handle in hand, I proceeded over to the boat where it was again beginning to look heavy with water. Nervously I inserted the valve head and pump handle into the pump housing and let it drop. The valve end slipped rapidly down where it splashed into the water of the flooded bilge.

Grasping the handle firmly, a few quick up and down strokes produced the unmistakable sucking sounds of the flapper valve working perfectly. Soon the water was welling up the pump housing and onto the deck where it ran over the side. In no time at all the boat was pumped out. I had done it. It seemed so improbable to me then, but there it was. My joy was overwhelming. I believe that it was the high point in my entire life up to that time, and possibly for all time. I realized that it was not practical to share my good fortune and feelings of euphoria with anyone since I had no pals my age except my sisters, aged eight and eleven, who I felt probably would not care about such momentous stuff. So I just stood around looking at the pump and feeling it, not wanting to leave the scene of my glory. I was indeed basking in my success.

A while later I decided that Richard should be notified that a major problem in camp had been solved. When I asked him to come and inspect my work I had the distinct feeling that he had forgotten all about it. After some persuasion, he arrived at the boat, tried the pump and saw that it worked fine. He then withdrew the pump handle and gave the valve end a closer inspection. Without looking at me, he reinserted the pump handle and commented, "Well I'll be goddamned," and left. My spirits were not dampened. I still felt great. I had learned earlier not to expect a whole lot of congratulations just for meeting one's day-to-day responsibilities. My uncle's reaction told me that I had impressed him and that was all the comment I needed.

Years later, as a successful product design consultant, I never achieved the exhilaration I felt that day as a nine-year-old, having fabricated that simple valve that kept the fish boat from sinking. That was my whole world then, and I alone had saved it.

Kinky Kid I

One sunny afternoon in the fall of 1939, a commercial fish troller named the *Kinky Kid* quietly slipped into a berth at one of our floats and tied up. My sense at the time was that the fellow who owned the *Kinky Kid* was a friend of my Uncle Frank. Not long after the boat arrived, the owner had his engine hatch removed and was down, taking things apart.

As usual, I was hanging around asking him questions about where he was from, why he was here and where he was going. One must realize that I thought our camp was a pretty important place and not just anyone should be allowed to come and tie up, just like that. My granddad should know that this fellow with his boat was tied up at the end of the camp, where otherwise he might go unnoticed. Of course, I noticed almost everything and made sure that certain people in camp were informed as well. That meant, of course, nearly everyone.

Later on, after dinner that day, I saw the *Kinky Kid* owner strolling back to his boat picking his teeth with a toothpick, looking quite satisfied with himself. The fact that he had eaten in the cookhouse was not in itself so significant, because all visitors to camp, as a general rule, were invited to take their meals there. At the very least, however, I figured that he owed somebody at Gildersleeve's something. As far as I was concerned, that somebody could just as easy be me. Anyhow, I felt that he might as well realize that I was looking after things for the camp and so I made myself prominent hanging around watching him.

The last afternoon he was in camp, he was finishing his engine repairs. I was helpful in showing him that I knew what a crescent wrench was, as I handed him tools when he needed them.

Eventually the job was complete and looking up he asked me the time of day. Reading his large alarm clock near the steering console I said "the big hand is at five and the little hand is on the four." Raising his eyebrows slightly, he asked, "Don't you know how to tell time yet? How old are you anyhow?" I told him that I was nine but I never learned because no one ever wanted to know the time from me. Right on the spot, I got my first lesson on telling time by the clock.

After breakfast the following morning, I was present when he started up the *Kinky Kid*'s engine and was getting ready to leave camp. In pulling away from the float, he said, "I'll be back next year, so you be sure, by then, that you can tell the time properly."

Kinky Kid II

The following spring, the *Kinky Kid* did arrive back in camp. Soon, I was on board to show my friend that I could tell time. "It was easy," I told him, and proved that I could do it. What I did not say was that my Aunt Phil had spent a lot of time coaching me, thinking that I would never get the hang of it.

A little later, I followed him down into the forecastle of the *Kinky Kid* where there were two bunks. Upon one of the bunks lay some articles of clothing, including a brown Stetson hat. For no reason at all I plopped the Stetson on my head, finding it much too large for me. The boat owner watching me, looked startled, shook his head and said I should not have done that. He explained that he had just come from transporting a crazy man up Rivers Inlet to the hospital and that these articles of clothing, hat, pants, etc., were his and had been left by mistake on board the boat. The worst of it was, he said, this crazy person had a scalp disease, which as far as anyone knew was incurable and may have been what drove the man crazy. Right off, I saw through this charade and said that I thought his story was a lot of bunk. However, as I nervously ran my fingers through my hair, I did sense a slight tingling sensation not noticed before.

I left the boat soon thereafter and headed for the wash house. The loggers had personal wash basins and bars of soap, all laying neatly in a long wooden trough below a long line of hot and cold water faucets. There was plenty of soap to choose from, Fels Naphtha, Lifebuoy, Ivory and others. I did not believe the scalp disease story, but why take chances. Play it safe, I thought. I scrubbed my head and scalp with every kind of soap that I could find. I was in there over an hour. Later on in the day I felt more itching in my scalp and it worried me so I went back and scrubbed it again, I think for an even longer time. My scalp was so squeaky clean that all hairs were standing up and waving like a field of swamp grass. Hardly anyone noticed except my Aunt Phil who wondered out loud that evening, "what had happened to Jim's hair," that, "it was all so flat and shiny." In panic at the waving grass effect, I had doused my head with some of my Grandfather's Vitalis hair tonic and slicked it down. Of course no disease ever developed, but who knows, maybe all that soap mixture was the cure.

Third Grade

In the fall of 1939–40, when World War II in Europe was not going well, I was starting the third grade. My sisters and I, it was decided, would not go into Ocean Falls to school. Instead we would stay in camp and take correspondence lessons distributed by the Canadian government. Aunt Phil, our stepfather's sister, was going to be our teacher. When I learned that I would have to do lessons only in the mornings I was greatly relieved. It meant that my main interest of knowing what was going on around camp would not be unduly interrupted. At this same time Uncle Keaton was starting the ninth grade, also by correspondence. Aunt Pearl went into Ocean Falls to enter grade twelve. She boarded with the Williams family.

That winter and school year passed without much excitement for us three kids. However, every once in a while, about noon, just as our morning lessons were winding down, Uncle Richard would come to see Aunt Phil (actually she was to become Aunt Phil), who he was sweet on. Later they would marry. Uncle Richard's interest was in obtaining a few sly hugs, but Aunt Phil kept her cool and showed much more restraint. Once after some hugs and squeezes, pokes, tickles and jabs and a cry from Aunt Phil of "Richard behave, the kids are here," the two of them wound up on the floor in a tangle of arms and legs and uproarious laughter. Scrambling to their feet Richard excused himself and left quickly with a huge grin on his face. Aunt Phil being more sophisticated and reserved, kept a straight face; yet, I knew, that she was grinning inside just the same. With the concurrence of the Provincial Government Correspondence Schools, I was promoted into the fourth grade and let go for the summer.

Mug-Up

"Mug-up," was a nightly affair, especially during the warm summer months. About 9:00 P.M. the loggers would gravitate to the cookhouse for an evening cup of tea or coffee, plus pie, cake or cookies set out for them. One evening when I entered the cookhouse for my usual piece of pie, I noticed that the cook stove fire was almost out. The coffee pots were lukewarm, at best. I opened the firebox door and sure enough, only a few glowing embers remained—someone forgot to stoke the fire. I stacked in a few pieces of kindling wood and then a few larger pieces of stove wood. The embers were too small and cool, and blowing on them did no good. I found the coal oil can and after tossing in a shot of the liquid, closed the fire box door. Munching my raisin pie I waited for the fire to ignite before I left. Nothing was happening so I, again, opened the firebox door and squatting, in front, with my face squarely in the opening, blew solidly onto the smoldering mass once or twice. All of a sudden there was a terrible roar as the coal oil exploded, enveloping my face and head in flame. The next thing I realized was that I was laying on my back about four feet away on the floor. My face felt flushed. I quickly got up and closed the firebox door, satisfied that the cook stove would now heat up.

I left and headed for my Aunt Phil's where the evening family mug-up would be in full swing. When I walked in the door, perceptive Aunt Phil again noticed a difference about me. She exclaimed, "Look, Jim's been smoking again." My eyebrows, it seems, along with my eyelashes were streaks of fuzzy white ash. The hair normally hanging over my forehead was burned away and my face was slightly flushed. I let them all have their little joke and laugh at my expense. If they had known what really happened I would have had my ass kicked good and hard. I often wondered, though, what the devil did they think I was using for matches, a blow torch? To my amazement no one ever asked.

Sitting on the Ax

One hot summer afternoon the camp ladies had gathered at my mother's house for tea and cookies, a commonplace ritual. They shared this important social responsibility on a rotational basis.

In a microcosm community such as ours was, one wonders what the ladies found to discuss the hour or so the gathering lasted. I know that at least one member belonged to the Book of the Month Club. She no doubt had the literary advantage and could regale the others with the latest chapters in her current book. I confess that I really have no idea what they discussed in general, but whatever the subject, their voices were mixed with many outbursts of laughter.

On this particular afternoon in front of my mother's house, I was engaged in one of my daily responsibilities of chopping kindling for the wood-burning heaters. My friend Pete Gazzola had shortened the handle of a standard double-bitted falling ax for me, so that at nine years of age I was wielding the ax in one hand like a small hatchet. I was only subconsciously aware of the chatter coming from the house while I was rapidly producing large piles of cedar kindling around my feet. Soon it became difficult for me to move my feet without stumbling over piles of sticks. With a single motion and without moving my feet, I turned my torso toward the rear and stuck the ax in the boardwalk directly in back of me. Bending over from the waist, I proceeded to gather the kindling into a neatly stacked pile alongside the boardwalk. Absentmindedly, as I concentrated on this task, I apparently must have altered my position, because, bouncing down to reach a few stray sticks, I sat squarely on the ax head.

The recollection of squatting to my knees and embedding the razor edge of that ax in my buttock close to my genitals is not one of pain. The ax was so sharp that there was no pain, as such. It was more like a hot burning sensation. Instantly, I realized my mistake and clamped my hand under my rump feeling the hot sticky gush of blood. Observing a pool of blood in my cupped hand, I panicked and without thinking, ran into the house where the ladies were winding down their tea party. When the women saw the blood on my hands and I announced that my rear end was wounded, they all jumped me at once.

Before I could prevent it, my bib overalls were down to my ankles and I was stretched bum up over someone's lap like a sack of potatoes. No one seemed to care that I wore no underwear, except me. My embarrassment was total. I've no doubt my face was redder than the wound on my rear. Everyone, however, seemed to be involved in how to keep me from bleeding to death. The gash was a couple of inches long and I don't know how deep, but blood was gushing out. I remember comments like, "Wow, would you look at that" and "My goodness gracious, my, my." I suppose they were referring to the size of the ax gash, but due partly to my embarrassment I was highly suspect of their real interest.

When the initial shock of my bloody bare buttocks staring up at them wore off, some applied absorbent gauze while others taped the gash closed as best they could. The wound bled profusely for the next hour or so but finally clotted over and stopped bleeding so long as I laid still on my bed. I wasn't very active the next few days as the cut would open up and begin bleeding again. I walked around slowly like I had dropped a load in my pants and those who relished dark humor made bad jokes at my expense.

The Pensioner

When not traveling with my stepfather aboard the camp tender *Crusader I* that summer, I was fishing and exploring the shore with my sisters in one of several row boats that were at our disposal. Grandmother and the girls had discovered a new place to pick salal berries, not far from the camp, in a small cove where an old pensioner lived alone. It was said that he was gassed during the Great War (WWI) and had come to the B.C. coast to live as a recluse. It seemed back then that there were a number of single men living in small coves along the coast, close to canneries where they could row for supplies. I accompanied the berry pickers this particular morning and was surprised when the old fellow came out to greet us. He showed Grandmother where the best berries usually ripened and she and the girls were soon filling their buckets.

The old fellow, who seemed pretty spry and showed no symptoms of being gassed that I could see, asked me into his cabin. It was a boxlike structure about twelve feet by twelve feet, built of poles and covered over with long four- to five-foot cedar shakes. The roof was flat with a good slope to it. The inside of the cabin was one room. The poles were covered with cardboard material, which in turn was covered with tarpaper and over that newspaper. It was 1939, but the newspapers on the walls were of 1920s vintage and yellowed, with pieces torn away in spots to expose the tarpaper. There might have been some form of insulation inside the walls next to the poles, but I could not tell. The temperature got down close to zero during the winter and he lived there the year around.

His stove, a cast-iron heater with a flat top, stood against a side wall of the cabin. I remember thinking how small it looked compared to the huge cook stove that Grandmother cooked on, yet this was a small cabin and no doubt was easily heated. The stove had no regular feet. It stood on four empty Pacific Milk cans, one in each corner, the labels still on the cans. We sat and chatted for quite a spell until I suggested that I better go help my Grandmother. That was a fib because I hated picking berries. I just wanted to get out into the fresh air.

A week or two later it was Thanksgiving. Uncle Keaton and I had to row over to Wadhams Cannery for some reason, probably to take outgoing mail. Grandmother, who was always "remembering" people at celebration times, gave Keaton and me a large roaster full of Thanksgiving turkey dinner with cranberry sauce and all the trimmings. It was to be dropped off at the old pensioner's as we rowed past his shack on our way to the Cannery, two miles hence.

Thinking himself very clever, Keaton managed to sneak a small amount of port wine out of Grandfather's jug. He returned the wine to its original level with an equal amount of water. I remember that it was just getting to be dusk when we left camp. We rowed with gusto sipping our filched wine. By the time we reached the old pensioner's place we were laughing and cackling like a pair of roosters. We told the old guy that we would be back in a day or two for the roasting pan and left. For equipment, besides oars, we had a flashlight and a 12-gauge shotgun of ancient vintage. The breech of the shotgun locked (closed) loose, probably showing daylight and then some. Somehow we got to Wadhams with no problem and left soon after we conducted our business. On the return trip we were rationing our wine, anticipating increasingly tired muscles. I had rowed going out and Keaton was rowing back. However, due to our merry making, he was not doing a great job. We were zigzagging a lot, making the journey longer. By now it was almost dark.

We thought we were in deep water away from shore when without warning we came to a sudden barnacle crunching halt. I froze stiff with fright. Keaton also was speechless, at first. I believe his less-than-intelligent comment was, "What the heck." We sat there in silence, in the dark, confused. Had we rowed atop the barnacled back of a sleeping whale, or what? Eventually, I found our flashlight and nervously shone it into the water near the boat. We had grounded on an immense bald rock fairly well out into the channel. Normally this rock was hidden from view except at very low water when masses of flat, brown kelp and a slimy barnacled dome appeared. Peering into that dark abyss at the encrusted mass illuminated by the flashlight and observing the undulating forms disappearing all around us into the spooky depths was more terrifying than being in the dark. I doused the light. The tide was still falling. We were stuck solid. Arguing briefly about who should get out and push off, you might well imagine, I lost. Stepping out of the boat in my worn-out sneakers, onto that smelly, snakelike tangle of kelp and barnacles was no picnic. I wasted no time in propelling the boat off the reef.

Once again we were headed for camp with one mile to go. The moon was rising and it illuminated our path. Soon, we spotted some ducks that appeared to be sleeping on the water. We rowed quietly toward them. Keaton then shipped his oars and loaded his single-shot twelve gauge. It had an extremely long barrel that looked to me like a piece of galvanized water pipe. The plan was simple. On cue, I would shine the flashlight beam on the ducks and he would begin blasting. Everything went well until he fired. Flame appeared to burst from both ends of the gun. The flash from the breech of the shotgun, it seemed, was as great as that from the muzzle. The noise nearly blew out my ear drums. The concussion to his shoulder, together with raw flame jetting past his nose startled Keaton badly. He lost his balance and fell backwards into the boat, wrenching his arm in the process. The ducks got away. We surmised that they were probably no-good fishy sawbills. I don't think Keaton ever fired that gun again. Come to think of it, I never saw it again after that night. In his good judgment he may have donated it to Davey Jones.

Where are We?

Many adults in camp were friendly with the Wadhams Cannery manager, his family and others of the cannery crew. After dinner one evening Aunt Phil, Uncle Dick, my mother Elsie and Roy Gadsden, took the camp tender, *Crusader I*, over to Wadhams. It was only a fifteen-minute trip.

The reason for going that evening seemed to be to attend some sort of celebration. It wasn't at all unusual at celebrations, even minor ones, to do a little partying with demon rum. At any rate, quite late that night, or was it morning, while it was still black as pitch, the partying members decided to head back to camp.

They all piled aboard the *Crusader I* and Roy, the skipper, who was in a very jovial state of mind, started up the engine. Someone untied the mooring lines and hollered: "She's all clear, Roy." Roy responded by advancing the throttle gradually to a cruising speed and amid the loud chatter and laughter, he headed her out into the bay, toward home.

A short time later Aunt Phil remarked to her brother Roy that "we should be getting close to home, Roy. Where exactly are we?" Roy, who knew the way back to camp blindfolded on any ordinary occasion wasn't a bit perturbed by the question, as he was, like all the others, feeling no pain at all. Good naturedly he remarked to his sister that he wasn't sure exactly where they were; however, he offered to turn on the overhead searchlight to verify that he thought they should be getting pretty close to home.

Snapping on the searchlight brought gasps from everyone. "Holy shit," Roy cried out, "we're still here," as the searchlight beam picked up the cannery dock and floats that they had been tied to. They had floated only a few yards away. Roy, in his some-what inebriated state, had somehow failed to throw in the motor clutch and no one else was sober enough at the time to notice. A

136

short while later they arrived safely at their home dock, all happily amused at the joke on themselves.

Dawson's Landing

In the fall of 1940 our mother informed us three kids that we were moving to Dawson's Landing in Rivers Inlet to school. In the community around Dawson's there were several potential young students who also needed schooling. Apparently all the parents had decided to pool their resources and hire a school master. His job would be to supervise and tutor each one of us at our separate grade levels using government-sponsored correspondence courses. Audrey was in the fifth grade, I was in the fourth and Cherie was in the third grade. The other students came from two families, the Hendricks and the Everetts.

Dawson's Landing in 1940 was a general store and fuel station owned and run by Jimmy and Jean Dawson. It was situated just off Rivers Inlet at the entrance to what was then called Schooner Pass, now renamed Darby Channel.

Dawson's store was serviced once a week from Vancouver by one of the Union Steamship boats, bringing all kinds of supplies and mail to the Dawson's store and others in the community. The *Venture*, *Cardena*, *Camosun* and the *Catala* were only four of the many Union ships that made the trip up the coast to Rivers Inlet to service communities like Dawson's Landing and all of the fish canneries in the area. Records indicate that at one time the Union Steamship boats coming up the coast made sixty-five stops prior to reaching Rivers Inlet. They then proceeded further north to Bella Bella, Bella Coola, Ocean Falls and beyond. They returned on the southbound journey to load cases of canned fish, especially at Wadhams and Namu, two canneries that were still operating in 1939–41.

To a ten-year-old youngster, the store at Dawson's was a fascinating emporium. It was an old country store, and much more, as if resurrected from the 1850s and brought forth into the early 1940s. Even the cracker barrel was there, except it was not a barrel. It was a heavy wire stand with large, square tin containers holding bulk quantities of Arrowroot cookies and crackers of every kind and description. Big Ben pocket watches were stapled to cardboard point of sale displays, $1.50 each. All sorts of jack knives were similarly displayed, only $1.75 for a real toad stabber with stag handles. My mouth watered at the prospect of owning such wonderful things.

There seemed as much merchandise hanging from the ceiling of the Dawson's store as there was stacked on the shelves and counters. My sisters and me, along with some of the Indian children, would wander around, a cream soda in hand, heads thrown back on our shoulders gazing up in wonder at the mass of hanging stuff. We scarcely recognized most of what we were looking at. The smell of the place was awesome. Chandlery odors of rope, linseed oil and hardware mingled with the bouquet of coffee, cabbages, flour and dry goods. Blended together, the various aromas revealed an olfactory experience for young and old alike that provided a shoulder-squaring attitude while inside the store.

Harry Furnace

I enjoyed knowing many of the older citizens who it seemed were usually in good humor. For instance, there was Harry Furnace, about fifty, an all-around mechanic who worked for Jimmy Dawson. He was in charge of the electrical light plant as well as the fuel sales to loggers, fishermen and the like. Harry was a fine person. He had sailed on the old windjammers as a boy. He liked kids and was a wonderful teller of stories. Many times of an evening he mesmerized my sisters and me with wild and scary tales from the South Seas.

Harvey Fulton

Harvey Fulton, a toothless sixty-five year old, was another of my favorites. He always wore a pair of heavy wool fishermen's pants with Stanfields underneath, no matter winter or summer. The Stanfields were disclosed by virtue of the visible loops that hung on his suspender tabs at the beltline of his trousers. Sometimes Harvey's fly would be unbuttoned. If anyone pointed this out to him, his standard reply through grinning, toothless lips was,

"Well, by golly, it pays to advertise." Then, he would laugh. One day in Dawson's store as Harvey was conversing with some of his peers and telling a few jokes with me hanging around the Arrowroot containers, he asked me the question. "Say son, do you know why women have fur trim around the bottom of their night shirts?" Winking at me, he says, "To keep their necks warm, of course." Then he laughed harder than everyone else, including me. (I did, however, get the joke.)

Burt Shotbolt

Then there was Burt Shotbolt. What a character. It was said that he had inherited $40,000 (1940) and kept it in two Empress jam tins on his gas boat. He didn't trust banks. Apparently, though, he did trust his friends. They said that he had been very well educated and came from a prominent family. When I knew him, he was about fifty-five and wore those same stiff, heavy brown wool pants that most of the fishermen wore. I felt sure that he could have removed them and stood them up anywhere. Burt was good to me, giving me all kinds of fish hooks and trolling spoons that he no longer wanted. He often had a cake he had baked stowed on the deck of his gillnet boat outside the cabin door. His cakes always had a beautiful golden brown color and looked delicious. Over a period of time he had offered and I had eaten many pieces of his cakes. He always said "I have plenty, you just help yourself." The problem was that, even though they looked very good, they tasted awful. They were absolutely flavorless. It was like eating finely ground up wood dust, bound together with a tasteless glue. Somehow, I always managed to choke down a huge piece that he would cut out and hand to me with a great smile. He was such a humorous, likable person and he did not seem to mind me hanging around. I ate and endured his terrible cake, and with a smile said, "Thank you, Mr. Shotbolt."

Mrs. Everett

Mrs. Everett was another storybook figure. She could have been a character straight out of Charles Dickens. I thought she was elegant, mysterious and a wonderful soul. She wore dark clothing beneath a tweedy-looking outer cloak. A long-strapped black handbag completed her attire.

One day her eyes caught me red-handed snitching a cookie out of one of the Arrowroot containers in Dawson's store. With a glance that pierced my gizzard, she recorded my crime. She never told on me, knowing from my embarrassed expression that her evil eye had my guilty juices in turmoil.

Mrs. Everett, about fifty, was small of stature, with a thin, well-lined caring visage that most of the time was serious but could produce a great grin that lit up her whole face. I liked the way she referred to the male population, in general, as men folk. I think that she quietly and secretly understood that we males have a singularly tedious cross to bear in our earthly journey. I liked her a lot. It was said that she was the local bootlegger. If this accusation was true, and I suspect that it was, then no doubt she contributed greatly to the comfort and well being of the handful of local residents, especially during the cold, wet winters when flu, grippe and rheumatism struck hard at the small population of men folk. Sloan's Liniment and Absorbine Junior were fine for exterior aches and pains, but a hot toddy of Scotch Whiskey or Navy Rum could not be beat for internal medicinal purposes. With no liquor store within 100 miles, Mrs. Everett's services must have been a godsend.

School Taxi

Every school day Mrs. Everett or her son Miles, a ninth-grade student, arrived at the government dock at Dawson's in their inboard open boat to transport my sisters and me to school. Our teacher, a Mr. Sterling, had come reluctantly on short notice to Dawson's Landing that winter to teach the students the three Rs. There were at least seven of us. Our grade levels ranged from third grade to the ninth grade. I was in the fourth.

The school house was more than a mile across the bay from Dawson's store. The Hendricks family owned the floating wharves and houses that included the school house. Their three younger kids attended classes along with Miles Everett, myself and my two sisters. The three of us would pile into the boat, about twenty feet in length, and Miles would head her out across the channel for the school house. The little boat came for us, every day, all winter long, rain or shine, snow or sleet, picked us up and returned us home again. Often it was very windy, with white caps kicking up on the channel along with freezing rain or snow. A few times Mrs. Everett came alone to get us because, as she put it, "the men folk are all down with the flu."

That winter I missed the logging camp and the subsequent interaction with the men. A few would remain in camp most of the winter due partly to the fact that they had no other family to be with or they may have been broke having lost all their wages gambling. It was normal for my sisters and me to have only each other to relate to once we left school in the late afternoon. We did not see other children again until the following day.

Winter in Rivers Inlet

The days and months over that winter at Dawson's must have been very lonely for our mother, as she was alone every day and had no adult conversation to stimulate her thinking. She saw my stepfather only on weekends and then sometimes only for a few hours. The logging camp was still at Hole-in-the-Wall, about six miles away. It was a forty-five-minute trip on a calm day in the camp tender *Crusader II*, traveling at eight miles per hour. Often during the winter that short run up Rivers Inlet to Dawson's was a trip to be reckoned with. The whole channel could be "smoking" as the wind tore the tops off the six- or eight-foot whitecaps and turned the surface of the water to a misty fog. If it was freezing weather, the wind hit your face like a frozen gunny sack, leaving your nose and ears raw in minutes. The leaping, plunging, rolling action of the boat as it plowed its way along was a sickening, if not frightening, experience. People ventured out in weather like that only when they had extremely good reasons.

There is a story about two inebriated fishermen who were about to depart Dawson's Landing headed for Wadhams Cannery about four miles down Rivers Inlet. They were both so drunk that one of them could not get into their gas boat, so his partner thoughtfully rolled him into the dingy they towed behind. Off they went into the wind and freezing cold heading down the Inlet. In that wind and heavy seas it probably took them a couple of hours to reach Wadhams. Arriving with a clearer head, but confused as to the whereabouts of his partner, the boat operator finally found him in the rowboat frozen stiff and quite dead.

Come spring, after school was out, the camp tender arrived at Dawson's to tow our float house back to Hole-in-the-Wall to join the rest at the logging camp. It was a great feeling to be back among the family with Grandmother and Grandfather, plus the extended family including Pete Gazzola, Charlie Rippington, Andy Torkelson and others.

Deck Hand

Being almost eleven, I was included now little by little into the routine of daily work activities. My stepfather, Roy Gadsden, began taking me along with him on the camp tender as he went about his many duties that required use of the boat. I was the deck hand. Bag booms of logs were relocated to a place where boom men could stow them into flat rafts. The flat rafts sometimes were moved to a place secure from sudden storms for later, when the quantity justified a large tow into Ocean Falls.

I was eager to learn how to handle the heavy manila tow rope used for pulling the booms of logs from place to place. A large iron hook, made in our blacksmith's shop, hung in an eye splice at the business end of the towline. Once a boom of logs was cut loose, the skipper would cruise alongside and, using the hook, I would attempt to "snag" the boomchain ring "on the fly." At first I was not good at it and my poor performance produced much scowling from the wheel house and often colorful language, especially when a second and even a third pass was necessary. Once the towline hook was secured, I quickly "threw" a couple of half hitches around the towing bit and the skipper eased into the tow before increasing power.

As time progressed I was shown how to ready the steel straps (braided cable) with eye splices and shackles in either end in preparation for securing the booms at the new location. I was still

142

too young to possess a pair of caulk shoes, but I was very much at home on boomsticks. With a steel strap over my shoulder and pike pole in hand I would race across the boom in tennis shoes, "choke" a standing boom stick with the strap and shackle the eye to a chain ring, then repeat the process at the other end of the raft.

Once a week the short two-mile trip to Wadhams Cannery was made via the camp tender for mail, groceries or to get parts fixed, e.g., brazed or welded brake bands for the "donkey." Occasionally a daytime or moonlight run to Ocean Falls was needed to pick up a string of boom sticks, a load of boom chains, machinery parts, steel cable, rope or even dynamite. If it was dynamite, we had to leave the harbor forthwith. They would not allow us to remain overnight. Sickness or accidents were irregular happenings. It took us ten long hours to run from the head of Rivers Inlet to the hospital at Ocean Falls.

At the Helm

Gradually I became reliable at relieving Roy at the wheel while he saw to maintenance of the diesel engine, prepared meals or just relaxed in a bunk to read. I was made to understand basic use of the compass and taught to steer a specific heading. Channel navigation consisted mainly in maintaining a heading from point to point avoiding any large flotsam such as deadheads and other floating debris. A few trips were all I needed to know the directions to a certain place. Confusion concerning our direction would occur only rarely, when fog or heavy rain squalls would obscure vision and cause us to slow down or even heave to.

Fog

One day when I was twelve we were groping our way in fog along a channel in search of a tow of logs that we had previously tied to the beach. I had never been in fog so thick and it was very disorienting, to say the least. Stationed on the bow of the boat and looking aft toward the wheel house not more than ten feet away I could hardly see Roy, with his head and shoulders hanging out the window for better vision.

I was supposed to be the lookout as we slowly approached the shore, keeping an eye out for shallow water and dangerous rocks. This area of coastal shoreline was mostly straight up and down, thus we did not expect shallow water even close to the beach. I could tell that we were getting close to shore because a familiar stillness had set in. On my face I sensed a cool temperature drop, reflected I thought, from the thick damp evergreen growth along the shore, yet I could see nothing at all. It was as if we were miles from anywhere. Roy skillfully edged closer, a few feet at a time and still nothing. In a situation like this, I should point out that maintaining a perpendicular position with respect to the shoreline is no simple task. Familiarity with local charts and the shoreline is mandatory when using the compass to maintain the necessary angle with the beach. We crept closer. In those days there were no depth sounders or radar. The skipper was uneasy too, being able to see nothing. With a twelve-year-old boy calling signals from the bow, he had a right to be nervous. We slid even closer. Without warning, a glistening appendage shaped like a massive mastodon tusk rammed out of the dense fog, striking me from above. I remember that monstrous sopping evergreen limb clubbing me on the side of the head, sending quarts of chilled water cascading over my face and neck. I screeched with terror, as it scared the daylights out of me. The skipper, showing tight lips, went into slow reverse. Nervously I lay on the deck and peered over the side. Sure enough, the rocky beach was there and the skipper had hit it at the right angle and almost precisely where we wanted to be.

Hanging feet first over the bow, I swung myself to the rocks below. Removing a shackled steel strap from around a tree, I brought it back with me to the boat as I had been instructed to do. This I managed with some difficulty, as I needed the boat to push on the log boom, relaxing the tension on the shoreline strap. Communication was poor at best since visibility was zero. However, the skipper knew what my needs were. While accomplishing the above, I had time to notice that a very large old growth cedar tree hung out over the water where the boat had "nosed" in. A few of its enormous pendulumlike branches swept down and far out over the water. These were the fog shrouded "tusks" that had "spooked" me. Once back aboard the boat and underway with our tow, I felt pretty good about our accomplishment that morning.

Fish Cannery

Oftentimes at Wadhams Cannery, Roy Gadsden, with me following, would enter the cannery buildings and seemingly wander among the equipment and cannery workers, mostly women, and exit some distance later. I presume that the route we took was some sort of shortcut. I did not mind because the journey was always interesting as well as educational. Almost always we would pass the "Iron Chink." Roy, knowing that it interested me, would let me stand and study it for a moment or two. It had to be the most fascinating and unusual-looking contraption that I had ever witnessed in operation.

The Iron Chink, a large steam-operated machine originally invented by E. A. Smith, circa 1900, stood near the beginning of the fish canning process. Whole fish were fed into the iron monster, heads, tails, guts, etc., and came out *sans* the above, with the fish flesh all whacked up into pieces that would nest easily into the empty cans that were racing down and around from above to various filling stations. Long lines of white-clothed women picked the fish chunks from the conveyer, sometimes trimming them with a knife, stuffing empty cans and returning the cans to a conveyor where salt was added and lids attached. Pallets of stacked canned fish then were wheeled into large steam-pressure vessels and cooked under carefully controlled heat pressure and time specifications. Watching the canning process was always thought provoking. Everyone seemed to be working at fever pitch. Nauseating fish odors, screeching cans, combined with the high pressure whine of water pumps forcing endless gallons of water to jet from many hoses, often caused me to return to the fresh air and sunlight with clenched teeth.

Sometimes at the cannery, my stepfather went alone on an errand, leaving me to look after the boat. On such occasions I sat on the dock to watch the unloading of fish packers laden with fish collected from gillnet boats. Back then, they did not have any of the high technology fish-handling equipment that exists now. Each fish was speared with a single-pronged fork and lifted one at a time to a weighing scale bucket. When full, it was dumped onto a conveyor going directly to the Iron Chink.

There had been at least ten (one source says nineteen) operating canneries in Rivers Inlet. They were: McTavish, Kildala, Brunswick, Good Hope, Strathcona, Beaver, Provincial, Goose Bay, Wadhams and the RIC (Rivers Inlet Cannery). Only Goose Bay and Wadhams, as I recall, were canning fish in 1940. The rest were either derelict or served as net lofts for the fishermen.

In 1940 canneries still employed the use of large, wooden, dorylike skiffs for gillnetting fish. The dories were about twenty-two feet long and had a lean-to shelter at the bow end. Large sweeps (oars) were used to maneuver the dory away from shore or other short distances. A fish packer would tow a string of dories and their crews out to the fishing grounds Sunday afternoon and then back Friday afternoons for five days and nights of fishing per week. I have witnessed whole families, father, mother and small kids aboard those dories, huddled for warmth and shelter under the lean-to, with their gillnets strung out from the stern like a knobby, black undulating snake. In those days, traveling anywhere in Rivers Inlet during fishing season meant a slow, cautious trip. Trying to dodge gillnets when the boats were packed hundreds deep in a fairly narrow channel was a chancy business. Many a skipper, especially at night, has run over a gillnet and got it wrapped tightly around his propeller. Sometimes the net would be wrapped so tightly that the boat would need to be towed in and hauled out in order to remove the net (usually cut with a knife) from the propeller shaft.

Some gillnet fishermen before World War II did have boats with power. The motors were often one-, two- or three-cylinder Easthope, Vivian or Palmer gas engines, to name only three manufacturers. They were very reliable engines that turned propeller shafts at fairly low rpm. The boat hulls, mainly, were displacement type hulls so that the boats and engines were a good match. In a year or two, high-speed engines were introduced into small fishing boats, e.g., Gray Marine engines (Chrysler Crown). With a lot more power, the boats went only a little faster due to improper hull design.

Leyton Evans and the Loud Engine

A frequent caller at camp in 1940 was a fellow who was to marry Aunt Pearl. His name was Leyton Evans and he was employed by Pacific Mills Company Limited as a skipper of one of their camp tenders, the *Yuklataw*.

This motor vessel was fitted with an old-time four-cylinder diesel engine that required heated cylinder heads to start it up when cold. A blow torch system mounted on the exterior of each cylinder head was there for this purpose. If the engine was hot due to running for long periods, as was the case this particular day, no further heating via the cylinder blow torches was required.

Always eager to make myself useful, with Leyton's permission I had gone down into the engine room of this vessel where the large wing pump for the bilge was located and proceeded, as I had done on several previous occasions, to pump the bilge. I had been at this task for about ten minutes when, unknown to me, Leyton was cautioning everyone on the wharf that he was about to fire up the *Yuklataw*'s engine. It was necessary to warn people in this manner because the atrocious noise produced by this engine on start up was shocking in the extreme. Thus, the folks outside on the wharf were being prepared for an outrageous din. The experienced docksiders opened their mouths and stuck fingers in their ears as if expecting an artillery blast. Inside the boat, standing innocently alongside the mammoth machine, I dutifully remained pumping the bilge.

When the engine exploded to life, the scream of wrenching steel all but petrified my auditory canals. The massive injection of adrenaline to the audio centers of my brain skewed my thinking. All senses flashed blood red. I distinctly recall a sensation of levitation. It was as if I was floating while some inner clock was malfunctioning on slow motion. For the next several seconds, which actually seemed much longer, I was borne magically from

147

behind that monstrous, rattling, machine along a very narrow passageway designed only for small monkeys. All manner of pipes, valves and hoses interrupted the way out. Lastly, through a confined ship's galley where numerous obstacles of furniture blocked my way, I climbed a near-vertical stairwell and out through a sliding door to the safety of the after deck.

My future uncle, who still had his hand on the ignition lanyard was flabbergasted to see me pop out of the hatchway. Instantly he remembered that I had asked permission to pump the bilge and had forgotten about me. Immediately he came to see if I was okay. Years later he remembered that "I had looked pretty dazed." The craziest thing about that whole episode was that over the next few days I was stiff in every part of my body. All my muscles ached, my knees, hips and elbows were sore as if they were bruised. As I have implied, my mind went blank and my sensation of getting out of there was one of floating out. I must have been running flat out and probably caromed off every obstacle in my path. It was what one might call a crudely instigated mind-altering experience—*sans* drugs.

Mr. Thomas

The fall of 1942 both Uncles Keaton and Frank left camp to join the Royal Canadian Airforce. I was told that I could not remain in camp that fall to take my school lessons there. My mother had arranged to board us three kids, myself, Audrey and Cherie, out to three different families in Ocean Falls. Her reasoning was that we would get a better education there.

The family I went to stay with, the Vic Bonds, had two boys, both younger than myself. Vic Bond was a policeman with the Provincial Police. As I got to know him, he seemed personable with a good sense of humor. Bond was a big solid man, a six-footer, thick of shoulders and chest and carried himself with a no-nonsense air, yet he was quick to smile when approached. Mrs. Bond was about five-foot-seven, a husky woman, not overweight, but with muscular shoulders, broad chest and thick of thigh. I heard it said that she had once been a long-distance swimmer. She did not have her husband's sense of humor nor his quick, engaging smile. She tended to be somewhat withdrawn, even sullen at times. I had the definite feeling that she was not happy. In retrospect, from later events, I also feel that she was not a good mother.

Earlier that summer Mrs. Bond turned up at the logging camp, presumably for a week of relaxation. It now seems possible that my mother may have been testing Mrs. Bond to determine if she was able to tolerate the likes of me.

One afternoon it was arranged that I would take Mrs. Bond for a rowboat ride to view the shoreline around the camp. The rowboat I normally used was not particularly large, about twelve feet long; however, many times I had hauled my grandmother and two sisters in it on berry-picking expeditions.

On this occasion naiveté was our undoing, Mrs. Bond's and my own. I assumed, quite wrongly, that everyone knew how to get into a rowboat. I maneuvered the transom of the boat to the low boardwalk on the float where Mrs. Bond was standing and sculled the oars in reverse to maintain that position. To my horror, Mrs. Bond innocently stepped from the float placing one foot well off center on the transom seat as if she were out for a Sunday stroll. Immediately under her considerable weight the rowboat scooted forward, my stalwart efforts to keep the transom tight to the float notwithstanding. A weird form of the "splits" was awkwardly performed by Mrs. Bond prior to an unusually frantic burst of screaming and a dramatically executed cannon ball dive into the salt chuck, creating a huge geyser of water and foaming bubbles that rose several feet high before drenching me as well as the boat.

I was speechless with disbelief. I had never seen anything as fantastically performed. Mrs. Bond's head and shoulders finally appeared in the froth alongside my boat. With her hair over her eyes, she was already shouting insults at me for my stupidity and carelessness. The bullcook had watched the whole thing in utter astonishment. He rushed over and offered her his hand in order to heave her, like some disoriented sea mammal, up onto the float. This done she resumed shouting at me and declared that I had dumped her on purpose. My mother did not appear on the scene.

Grandmother came to my rescue and declared on the spot that Mrs. Bond must be crazy. Much later on, however, Mrs. Bond may have had her ultimate revenge.

In spite of this bizarre beginning, unfortunately I did have to go to live with the Bonds and their two boys in Ocean Falls in order to be enrolled in the fifth grade fall and winter school term. You can take it from me, the sacrifice that some people have had to make to get a regular education is enormous. My sisters, too, had to make such sacrifices. However, they apparently faired no worse than I, as they seemed to have suffered no long-lasting ill effects.

Victor, the oldest Bond boy, was a year or two younger than I. Melvin Bond was a year or two younger than Victor. All three of us slept in the same room, Victor and I in the same bed.

The very first night that I slept with Victor I discovered that he had a problem. It would plague both of us, but especially me, for the duration of my stay with the Bonds. Victor wet the bed, not on occasion, but every single night. At first I was dumbfounded and expected everyone else to be, also. When nothing was said, even though the smell of urine was vile in that little room, I decided to go slow on the matter and pretend, like everyone else, that it had not happened. The mattress was not aired, the sheets were not changed and the following night I crawled in, with nose curling and body recoiling at the prospect of damp, soiled, smelly linens. I eventually fell asleep and was awakened later with the warm gurgling rush of urine squirting against my leg. I yelped and sprang up, throwing covers in all directions, lifting my sopping pajamas off my thigh. Victor had not moved and slept on. Gradually, I forced myself to lie back down, pulling covers over me as far away from the soggy bed clothing as I could get. I was hanging over the edge of the bed against the wall.

The following morning I announced to Mrs. Bond that Victor had wet the bed again. She took the information with a blank look as if she had not heard. I had the feeling that she did not believe me, even though she could have chinned herself on the urine cloud in our bedroom. At her nonresponse, I quickly determined that I had a problem that was not going to get better soon. At times like this I had learned to adopt a stoic attitude. I realized that help was not coming from any quarter and I would have to deal with the problem myself.

By now it was the end of September and school had been underway since Labor Day. I showed up at the fifth grade classroom with my package of pencils, scribblers and textbooks wrapped in the proverbial brown wrapping paper that I felt made me stand out like a rube.

My teacher was to be a man named Mr. Thomas. He was tall and sparse with a large Roman nose and balding scalp. He was immaculate in his dress, from his stiff white starched collar to his Victorian vest and trousers. He wore a beautiful, dark gray Homburg hat, carried an umbrella over his arm and wore spats, no matter what the weather. He was every bit the English gentleman and schoolmaster. Mr. Thomas seemed a nervous individual and, combined with his fastidious nature, it tended to make one think that he was effeminate.

Since my academic credentials were pretty meager, he explained that he would test me to see where I might fit in the fifth-grade curriculum. The tests were devastating to me. One afternoon he drew me aside when the others had gone and told me that he would allow me to remain in the fifth grade only because there wasn't room in the fourth-grade classroom. To say the very least, I was upset and embarrassed at his words and the serious manner of his telling me. This was a deadly blow to my ego, at a time when I was having some difficulty keeping my balance at the Bonds.

Mr. Thomas, however, did not turn me out that afternoon without some words of advice and encouragement. He said that if I was willing to work he was willing to work with me in an attempt to catch up to the other students by the end of the school term. He told me that it would be difficult for me and would take much of my time, every day, after normal classes. He suggested I think about it and talk it over with my guardian, Mrs. Bond, and report to him the following day.

I had already decided that talking to Mrs. Bond about anything was out of the question, so I said nothing to her about it. I would have talked to Mr. Bond, but could not, at this time, because he was away on police business. Anyway, the decision seemed clear. What were my options, besides rolling up my sleeves and getting to work? None that I could see. Failure was not an option I could accept.

The following afternoon I told Mr. Thomas that I wanted the extra work and that I was prepared to study as required to get it all done. And so every day he had material prepared which we would go over briefly. I would sit in the classroom and work on the lessons until he closed the school; then I went home to work.

All fall and winter, every day and evening, with few exceptions, I kept at it. Mr. Thomas graded my work, showed me where I needed to improve and gave me encouragement. I felt that I was making progress. I had long division, spelling, composition and grammar coming out my ears. By spring Mr. Thomas told me that I was catching up with the rest of his group but that we should not let up, and so we kept on.

The winter at the Bonds was not entirely without humor. When Mr. Bond was home, everyone seemed to shape up, including Mrs. Bond. I think that she missed him a lot and was lonely when he was gone. She needed people that stimulated her and the three of us boys did not fill that bill; we were, I think, a headache to her.

The war had provoked blackouts in Ocean Falls. Pulp and paper was considered a necessary wartime material and since the Japanese had entered the war on the side of the Axis Powers, there were fears that we might be attacked via submarine from the bay below the town.

All apartment buildings and many of the houses in the town had had their windows painted black. No street lights of any kind were visible after dark. The town, at night, situated as it was at the base of tall mountains, became the proverbial black hole. Out of doors after dark one could not see one's hand in front of one's nose. It was perfect for us kids.

One afternoon there was a dubious report that someone had seen a periscope rise out in the bay. This, of course, raised considerable consternation among the town officers. The rumor was that a submarine could rise during the night and shell the concrete dam that was in plain view of the bay. Without the nineteen miles of water supply behind the dam, the powerhouse and pulp mill would have been kaput. Paper making requires a lot of water, not only in the paper making process, but also for the power generation requirements.

A decision was made by the town officers that the dam should be guarded. They conscripted a lone sentry to stand guard duty at night atop the dam. I don't recall how long this lasted, possibly only a short time. One night a few of us boys decided to visit the guard, whom one of our number knew intimately. I don't recall what we thought we were doing, but we decided to sneak up on him and get as close as we could.

At one end of the dam we were crouched in some salal and dormant huckleberry bushes next to the cyclone fencing that terminated the guard's march in our direction, whence he would pivot and march back the other way, returning in a few minutes. There was plenty of time, if anyone wanted to climb over the fence, lower a bomb or two into the water next to the dam and leave the same way undetected. Presently, the guard came. It was difficult even for twelve-year-old kids to believe what we saw.

The middle-aged sentry was dressed in the full British infantry battle dress uniform of World War I vintage, including the dog bowl helmet, and heavy boots with gaiters. Over his shoulder he had a World War I Lee Enfield bolt-action rifle with a two-foot-long bayonet. There were no electric lights anywhere, only moonlight; however, it was easy to see around the area, since we were high up on the side of a hill. We had gathered a few pebbles and now lobbed them over the fence at the guard, who to our surprise and annoyance, paid little attention. I suppose we expected him to go into a crouch shouting, "Stop! Who goes there?" The lad who knew him by name called out to him quietly, as we all snickered. The sentry's reply was terse: "All right you kids, quit screwing around and bugger off or I'll come over there and kick your asses, and tell your mothers besides." It was "the mother" thing that scared us and we retreated rapidly. Of course, the next day at school our story had a lot more macho ring to it.

Living with the Bonds, I had no money given me and so I had to scrounge for pocket change. I have always had a resourceful attitude and on weekends when I was not doing lessons I started to collect beer bottles. I went through all the apartments knocking on doors asking for bottles. Soon I had built up a regular clientele. I was reliable and they began to save bottles for me, even if others called to collect. It was not long before I had more money than I needed, even though I got only one cent a bottle from the local dealer. The dealer got two cents a bottle.

Soon I realized that my turf had to be protected. Other boys, sensing my prosperity, tried to woo some of my customers, but with only moderate success. One weekend I came across the enemy in one of the apartments where some of my good customers were. The resultant name calling precipitated into a sprawling fist fight and wrestling match. The noise drew several tenants to the hall to see what the commotion was about, whereupon my competition took to his heels. I was not hurt, only a few scratches, and I guessed that my turf would be safe for a while.

Victor Bond seemed always to be asking his father for pocket money. One day, a little aggravated, he said to Victor, "Why can't you be more resourceful, like Jim, and collect bottles or something?" I remember being pleased that Mr. Bond noticed my entrepreneurship. Even so, I felt that his comments did not help Victor any. By now, I wondered if his bed wetting was at least partly due to his mother's influence over him. She was stern, snappish and not loving. My early anger at Victor gradually turned to sympathy, but I was in no position, I thought, to help him.

By now it was well into spring and I had received information from my mother that she and Roy would be in to Ocean Falls soon to collect my sisters and me, returning us to the logging camp.

I passed this information to Mr. Thomas. Since he had not yet prepared final examination papers for his class, he hurriedly made up some tests and gave them to me over the next week or

154

so. A few days before I was to leave he asked me to meet with him after school. He said he wanted to discuss my exam results. I will never forget that meeting. Mr. Thomas seemed more nervous than usual. Thus, I did not move a muscle when he stepped from behind his big desk and drew up a chair close to mine.

Among other things, he told me that he was proud of me and the effort I had expended on my lessons. After grading my tests he judged that I would rank about fifth in his class of thirty-five students. He then put his arm around my shoulders and said that if I worked hard at what I wanted, he knew that I would "make my mark in the world." He then stood up, blew his nose on a great white handkerchief that he always carried in a breast pocket, shook my hand and told me that he was proud to be my teacher.

I did not know how to respond to him, but I thanked him. I knew all along that he was going out of his way to help me. What I did not realize was how much I would learn about myself as he piled the work on. I learned that I could handle extra work and the responsibility of hanging in with it once I had started. I also felt the satisfaction, once again, one gets from knowing a job is well done. Mr. Thomas' influence on me in that one school term, I feel, was a great benchmark that carried me through many tough years that followed. Today whenever I see a good-looking Homburg hat, I smile and silently thank my teacher for what he taught me.

Grandfather's Library

My grandfather, who was largely a self-taught individual, was definitely pro education. He understood the value and the power of books for educational and/or recreational purposes. His library held a number of Zane Grey books, as well as many popular novels of the day. *National Geographic* came every month. *Time*, *Life*, *Newsweek* and business magazines, plus two newspapers came weekly. There was no lack of keeping up with current events.

I remember sneaking John Steinbeck's *Tortilla Flat* into bed at night so that I could read it under the covers with the flashlight.

One day when I was about fourteen or fifteen, I selected a book from the shelf, started reading and never put it down until I was finished. To this day I would have to say that book impressed me as much as any book ever has. It was *The Magnificent Obsession* by Lloyd C. Douglas.

Draney Inlet

While I was away from the camp at school, Grandfather had moved the logging camp into Draney Inlet. The entrance to Draney Inlet is through a very narrow and deep passage of water (Skookum Chuck) that lies near the mouth of Rivers Inlet. It can be entered only at certain times of the day, close to slack water. This is true because the narrow entrance backs up twenty miles of inlet. When the tide is either half way to full flood tide or half way to full ebb tide the narrows is impassable due to the four-foot waterfall caused by water either trying to flow in or flow out of the Inlet.

The twenty-mile run from the logging camp to the Skookum Chuck took about two and one-half hours and another half hour to Wadhams Cannery; thus, approximately a three-hour trip. Formerly it had taken only forty-five minutes to get provisions and mail from Dawson's Landing when the camp was located in the Hole-in-the-Wall. Also, there was the added nuisance factor of having to work with the tide in order to pass through the Skookum Chuck Narrows at the optimum time.

One afternoon Grandfather, Pete Gazzola, Roy Gadsden and I were headed for Wadhams Cannery. Draney Inlet was flooding at the time and that meant if we wished to pass out of the narrows any time before slack water, we would have to buck against the current. Grandfather kept looking at his watch and seemed to be in an awful hurry. We had been waiting inside the Skookum Chuck Narrows about one-half hour. As I recall, we had another hour or more to wait for slack water. Of course no one ever waited absolutely till slack water, regardless of which way one was headed. However, bucking the narrows was a far more serious proposition than running with it. Roy, the boat skipper, started up the eighty-horsepower Vivian diesel and we headed over to have a look at the narrows. The rapids still looked very turbulent and formidable and he was reluctant about committing the boat to the churning water, so he allowed the current to carry us back and away from the rapids once again. About fifteen minutes later Grandfather decided that we should go and have another look. This time it did appear as if the current had subsided significantly; nevertheless, it still looked pretty scary to me. When Roy hesitated, Grandfather said, "Go ahead Roy, we'll make her this time," so into the narrows we headed.

Once we were committed into the current, we could all see what we had bargained for. Many of the whirlpools were bigger in diameter than the length of our boat. A log twelve inches in diameter stood on end in a whirlpool and went around in it like a wooden spoon in a mixmaster. Our boat made headway until we were about halfway through. Roy had kicked the stool he normally sat on out of his way and was standing up literally wrestling with the steering wheel. The huge "barn door" rudder that the camp tender had fitted for towing purposes was receiving tremendous pressure from the accelerated water and holding the boat on course in all that current was an arm-breaking task for the skipper. We were unaware that the pressure and strain upon the entire cable steering system from the steering wheel back to the rudder post was about all the system could take. With the diesel wide open we had come to a full stop. That is to say, the trees and rocks on the beach were no longer going past; we were stationary. All of a sudden there was a loud report from somewhere beneath our feet and instantly the steering wheel spun uselessly. The skipper had no control. In a flash Peter Gazzola, who seemed to know what had happened, dropped down the companion way to the engine room and, locating the problem, had it jury-rigged (temporarily fixed) in seconds. The skipper had steerage again, but the current had us and we were headed for the rocks.

I was standing on deck as the boat swept over to the shore going sideways and backward and I could have jumped onto the shore without getting my feet wet, we were that close. Amazingly, the back eddy current along the shore "kicked" us away from the rocks. Luckily for us, the shoreline through the narrows is very steep and thus several fathoms deep against the rocks. Now that the skipper had steering control again, he took us back and away from the narrows to assess any damage.

The loud report that we had all heard from below was caused by a large steering control pulley block breaking away from its bulkhead mount. Pete Gazzola sensed this. Grabbing a large steel marlin spike, he jammed the point through the pulley block mount and into the bulkhead, then using his own brute force and the long spike as a lever, he held the steering chain taut so that steerage was possible to get us out of trouble.

I don't recall anyone saying much after the excitement had passed. The skipper and Pete were down below securing the steering block back onto the bulkhead with bigger screws. Grandfather looked at me though, with a wink, and said somewhat sheepishly, "Boy, that was something, wasn't it young feller?" Speechless, I nodded in the affirmative, thinking to myself that it was close to being an underwear-changing experience.

Nature Calls

In September, 1942, about 3:30 in the afternoon, I was again at Wadhams Cannery, this time with my stepfather and mother.

Mother and I were alone aboard the boat. The skipper was ashore on an errand. As often happens, nature's call comes at the least opportune moment. I asked permission to visit the public outhouse. My mother consented but warned me we would be leaving shortly in order to catch the tide at Draney Narrows.

Light of heart, I jumped to the floating dock, pleased to be moving and quickly made my way past the "rafted up" gillnetters, and up the ramp to the main wharf of creosoted piling and planks.

Even though it was near fall, the sun shone warm, if not hot. The smell of creosote mixed with the odor of rotting fish guts and seaweed boiled up from the mud flats beneath the wharf. The stench coiled up like a musty rope in the back of my throat. I forced myself not to breathe at such times, for I felt that putrid smells surely must be poison. After a brief period of controlled breathing and spotted vision, I would gradually get used to the stench and begin to breathe normally.

At the corner of the main cannery building I saw a pretty young Indian girl. She was about my age, lying flat on the wharf with her hand dangling in a waste water flume that emptied fish guts, including heads, from the Iron Chink to the odoriferous mud flats below. Alongside the young maiden was a galvanized pail, already half full of large fish heads. Just then more fish entrails sloshed down the flume trench and splashed against her waiting hand, including a large fish head, which she immediately snatched up and deposited in her pail with the rest of her booty. In doing so she gave me a knowing smile that only a twelve-year-old boy would understand. I was mesmerized by her activity. I watched her as long as I dared, without saying a word, sensing her appreciation of my interest. The outhouse was not far. I had been there before, or near there, but never inside. Now I hurried as nature was urging me on and I wished that I had found the Indian girl and her activities less fascinating.

I swung into the open doorway of the public toilet, a shack situated on the extreme edge of the wharf. It was one large room that might hold ten men, five standing waiting, and five squatting. Privacy was out the window. Along the outside wall were five holes in the floor, large enough to fall through. Above one of the holes an Indian fellow squatted with his pants around his ankles, smoking a cigarette, while a couple of his friends jabbered unconcerned in their Native tongue. I was profoundly embarrassed by my intrusion into this scene and wheeling around, was almost out the door, when the squatting figure called me back, "Hey, boy."

Returning with increased composure, I was intimidated by the size of the holes. It was a long fall to the slimy ooze below. As always, there was that ubiquitous, gagging fish stench rising up through the hole, wafting the hair on my forehead. The fearful challenge in squatting was to not lose my balance and fall backward through the hole. With controlled breathing and locked thighs, I somehow, managed to complete my business without catastrophe. Returning outside to fresher air, I hastened back to the cannery wharf hoping once again to see the Indian girl. She was gone. A few minutes later I discovered that the camp tender was also gone. Looking out to sea, I saw it a mile or so away and heading for Draney Inlet.

My heart sank. They had left me behind. I knew no one here and I feared they would not be back for at least a week. Two men were working on their nets close by. I approached them and asked if they knew of any fishing vessels going into Draney Inlet anytime soon. I knew that few fishermen ventured there and never twenty miles to the head where the logging camp was. I asked anyway, probably just to calm myself while I decided what to do. The two men looked up at the disappearing boat I was pointing at and said, "no," and went back to their work.

I had heard my grandfather talk of the cannery manager, a Mr. McLennan, as a friend, so I figured to go see him, wherever he was. No sense in standing around feeling sorry for myself. I might as well get started on a plan. As I walked away from the two men, I heard one of them shout. They pointed to the camp tender, as it had turned around. I ran full tilt down to the boat landing and arrived just as the boat was nosing into the dock. They saw me coming and were ready to back away as I jumped aboard the bow. My stepfather was very upset and swore at me. If we missed the slack-water period, he said, it would be my fault and it would be at least five hours before we could try it again.

My mother forgot that I had gone ashore, thinking I was on board below, when they left without me. Even though I heard her tell my stepfather that she had given me permission to leave the boat, he seemed unnecessarily upset by the foul-up and continued to belabor me about it. I became quite upset and cried. I noted that my mother never consoled me by admitting that it was as much her fault as anyone's. I said no more about it and I concealed my disappointment.

We made the Skookum Chuck on time and since we were running with it, we shot through with no trouble and in two and one-half more hours were back at the logging camp.

Float House at Ocean Falls

The fall of 1942–43 I no longer needed to board out with other families, as our family float house had been towed from Draney Inlet into Ocean Falls, a distance of about ninety-five miles. We were allowed to tie our float to one of the marine docks below the Chinese bunkhouses where it was out of the way of any harbor traffic.

Access to our floating home from the road above was first via a boardwalk and then a marine ramp. The ramp, being fastened at the shore end, had wheels that rolled in angle iron tracks on the floating dock end so as to allow for the change of tide, averaging an eight-foot change four times in twenty-four hours.

Everything we needed by way of food or fuel had to be carried from the road and boardwalk down the ramp to our house, a distance of about seventy-five yards. For most items this was not much of a problem, but a cord of wood was another matter entirely. The fuel truck would dump the rectangular blocks of fir and hemlock in a pile alongside the road. After school each day my two sisters and I would load each other up. Gradually, after several days, we carried the entire pile down to our float house, stacking the wood next to the shack that we used as a bedroom. The main house was the kitchen and living room and also our mother's bedroom.

We had hot and cold running water, but no full-size bathtub. Our tub was a round galvanized wash tub. When it was my turn to bathe, about once a week, I took the tub out to our sleeping quarters and placed it near the wood heater. As I bathed, I enjoyed the extra luxury of radiant heat. On a particularly cold evening I had placed the tub extra close to the heater. Drying off was an art, especially on a cold evening. I had developed a technique where I would stand up in the tub on one leg with the other foot resting for balance on the side of the tub and dry everything except the area below water level on the standing foot. This night the procedure was working well until I bent over to dry the toes on my balancing foot. One cheek of my rear squeezed solidly against the side of the heater and with a yowling screech, I was propelled out of the tub onto both feet running on the spot in an effort to deconcentrate the pain. A short time later when I examined my posterior in a mirror, I could see that I had branded myself with a fifty-cent-sized round bubble. I was perhaps fortunate that I had not received the logo of Western Stove Works Ltd. Luckily for me, it did not take long for the blister to heal and disappear, for another more serious problem had suddenly presented itself and was not nearly so easy to deal with.

Over a period of time my sisters and I had noticed the odd mouse and occasionally a rat. Nothing much was thought of this at first. Our float house was moored in a wharf area where one would expect to see a rat or two once in a while. Soon after this, however, we began to see many rats on a daily basis and some inside our sleeping quarters. We contacted townsite authorities who sent us the "rat man."

The Ocean Falls townsite employed a man full time to catch rats. He used a sawed off .22 with shot pellets, poison and huge traps. These were Norway rats and had bodies twelve inches long, not including the tails. The traps had to be loaded and cocked in the same manner as a smaller mouse trap, except these traps were more than a foot long and could easily break an arm. They were exceedingly dangerous. We had house pets, so poison was out and pot-shotting with a .22 did not seem advisable either. That left us with traps and the "rat man" loaned us about ten.

Every night when the lights went out, as if by cue the rats began their nightly prowl. Almost always they would start gnawing on something, usually the outer walls of the shack that was our bedrooms. They had holes chewed everywhere, almost large enough to put a tennis ball through. If we found the holes and plugged them, they would remove the plug in short order, or begin and finish a new hole in one or two nights. It was nothing to be awakened several times a night from rats bounding across our beds.

One night I was awakened and at first I was not sure why. As I laid quietly in the dark, I could feel my hair being softly chewed. I struck out frantically. The rest of the night I spent buried under my blankets, breathing through a small hole. Next morning I noticed bits of loose hair all over my pillow and realized that the rats were stealing my hair for their nests. I also found a big round rat hole in the outer wall right next to my bed, not a foot away. We had had some luck with the rat traps but not enough to do much good. However, I placed a trap right next to my bed near the newly chewed hole. The rat could not come through the hole with the trap positioned as I had it without dealing first with a big hunk of rat bait in the trap. After dark that night I lay in readiness with my flashlight. Pretty soon I heard scurrying by the hole and flashed on my light. Sure enough a big Norway rat had his nose through the hole, sizing up the situation. My light did not seem to bother him either. Off went the light; I lay back and waited. Slam, went the trap. On went my light and I had a huge rat right off. Without getting out of bed, I dumped him in a box and reset the trap. Minutes later another big one. I dumped him out and reset again. This went on for about an hour. If I remember right, I had more than a half dozen rats that night. The next night was about the same. For some reason the hole in the wall by the head of my bed was part of their nocturnal highway. I soon realized that I could not keep this up night after night and decided to change tactics.

The next night I set the trap as usual and waited. With the familiar slam of the trap, I flashed on my light and sure enough a huge rat had sniffed his last food. He was like all the rest, so large that his head and shoulders were caught in the wire trap, yet his body extended out through the hole in the outside wall with his tail dangling another ten inches or so. His body completely filled the hole and prevented any other rats from entering. I left things as they were, turned off my light and with the quiet soon fell asleep. The next night was the same. Now, I left the rat I caught each night in the trap till bedtime the following night, as he made a great hole plug during the day. Soon, though, I noticed another hole had been started alongside the old one plugged with the dead rat. I knew that inevitably more needed to be done.

When my stepfather, who was away most of the time at his job with the logging company, paid us a visit, I told him about the rats. It was his opinion that something we were not aware of must be attracting the rats. The next day the two of us climbed up into the attic of our bedrooms and discovered some old crates that apparently had been there a long time. They appeared to be full of odds and ends and mostly junk. One of the boxes about the size of an apple box had some boards lying across it. It was too dark to see clearly with flashlights. We rigged up a long extension cord with a 100-watt light bulb and had my sister Audrey stand on a chair holding the light up between the joists so that we could see better, and have both hands free to work. We had to balance on the ceiling joists and hang onto the rafters to keep from falling through the thin paneling. At this point my stepfather removed a board from the apple box and large rats started jumping out. It was an eruption of rats. Both of us had clubs and were whacking and flailing at rats as they passed us, it seemed by the dozens. Audrey saw all those rats bounding along the ceiling joists, most headed her way and some may have used her head and shoulders to get to the floor. Screaming loudly, she dropped the light and it exploded. Now we were in total darkness, still thrashing and swatting as rats continued to run over us. Finally, we used flashlights to get the apple box down to the floor. There we discovered that someone had stored a quantity of sugar and flour in the box and forgotten it. No wonder we were the center of attraction for the rats. We then examined everything stored in the attic to make sure there were no more surprises.

In less than a week I trapped most of the rats that were left hanging around and after that they all but disappeared. To keep out the north wind, I covered the round rat holes with tops off quart vegetable cans. The remainder of the winter was relatively pleasant, except for the snow.

That winter there was a very heavy snow fall. Ordinarily this would not pose much of a problem, except where a float house is concerned. Snow is frozen water and water weighs about eight pounds per gallon. In one week we had about three feet of snow covering the houses and the float. This much snow translates into tons of weight that was gradually sinking our float. That winter I spent hours almost every day for weeks pushing the snow into the surrounding water. The snow that slid off the roofs into the courtyard between the houses had to be lugged a fair distance to be dumped over the side into the chuck. Eventually, due to the cold weather, the snow I had dumped into the water began to freeze and form small icebergs trapped next to our float. It now became more difficult to slide the snow off. Gradually the snow stopped falling and as the weather warmed, the problem that seemed so ominous melted away.

Spring was, as they say, "just around the corner." Late one night we were all awakened by a very bright light. It appeared that the row of bunkhouses on pilings behind our float were on fire. Our mother was very nervous and excited and had all of us get out of our night clothes and get dressed. Indeed, if the bunkhouses were on fire, then we were in a bad spot and probably our place would burn too, as there would be little that the local volunteer fire department could do to prevent it. We were probably the first to see the reflections from the fire, but we could not actually see the fire itself as it was obscured by the bunkhouses. My mother sent me off running to alert her friend's husband who was one of the local constables of police. I ran like the wind, informed him of the fire and raced back to the scene. Actually, when I left to alert the constable, I could see that the fire was not close to the bunkhouses at all and we likely were not in the danger that we thought. When I returned not more than fifteen minutes later, a great crowd of people, many of them in their nightshirts under overcoats, had gathered near the top of our float house ramp to view the fire. Among the crowd I recognized five people with their arms full of their worldly possessions. They were my mother, three sisters and brother. Cherie's arms were burdened with a great amount of paraphernalia. Audrey held the family bird cage. I did not say anything at the time, but they all looked pretty silly. I pretended not to know them.

Luckily for Audrey, Cherie, and the rest of the family, I don't think anyone took notice of them. The firemen eventually arrived and could do little or nothing about putting the fire out, except keep it from spreading to the bunkhouses and the surrounding trees. The structure that burned was built by the Japanese community before World War II as a place for worship and study. It was a large building and well constructed, two good reasons why it made a brilliant fire.

Loaves and Fishes

I was always looking for new fields to conquer and so joined the Boy Scouts hoping to meet other boys with energy and imagination that would lead to exciting adventures. Instead, I mainly recall harrowing experiences on overnight campouts.

Our camping equipment was pretty meager. We had no sleeping bags or tents or even packsacks. Anything we took with us on a campout was stuffed into a burlap bag or flour sack and tossed over the shoulder for carrying comfort. The most vivid memory I have of overnight camping was how I always suffered from the cold. I had one old blanket for warmth and no ground sheet to put under me. As Boy Scouts, we were supposed to be capable of making "feather beds" from layering hemlock or fir bows together, but I never achieved any such thing. At best a bough bed was barely tolerable. Most were like trying to sleep on a layer of sharp stakes.

In front of a roaring campfire, even in the fall, it did not take much outer clothing to be warm enough. However, with the fire reduced to dim coals, it was another story. Curled up with boots removed under one ragged blanket on my bough bed, the ubiquitous cold and damp made sleep impossible. My consciousness was not aware of anything but the nagging cold, unless it was the crunching and gnawing of those nocturnal creatures that prefer the dark for their irksome activities. Needless to say, a sleepless mind tortured by a cold, shivering body focused like a laser beam on these noises surrounding our camp. Was some wild creature preparing for an attack, or what? Up I would get, massaging the numb spots on my backside and legs, shudder into my boots and stoke up the fire until it was producing real heat. There I would sit, knees up, with my blanket wrapped all around me and over my head. Soon others joined me in warming themselves and we would sit and talk until the sun came up.

One especially memorable Saturday morning at dawn, a dozen of us set out on a day hike that would take us out over rocky hillside trails and return us home at dinner time. This group of boys was a mixed bag consisting mostly of our Sunday School band and a few Boy Scouts. We were led by the local United Church minister who I suspect had never had the experience of shepherding such an irreverent gang.

The most remarkable and unhappy episode of this hike was lunch. The minister gathered his motley flock around him and announced to all of us that we were about to participate in a fundamental teaching of the Christian faith. Then he asked us all if we wanted to be Christians? I don't recall any great outpouring of enthusiasm from this group, only the muted sound of a few grunts and some snickering, as we poked at each other.

"All right then," he said, "lay your lunches out on the ground where all can see, for we are going to share what we have, just like Jesus did with the loaves and fishes at the Sea of Galilee."

At first this sounded okay until I began to see what the other boys were pulling out of their crushed paper bags, curled up peanut butter and jam, and worse. Instantly, I saw the handwriting on the wall. One thing I always made sure of when I went hiking or camping was that I had plenty of good food: sandwiches with meat, mustard and pickles. I was well acquainted with my appetite. Now I was in panic as it became obvious that most of the others had come ill prepared to deal with theirs. Worst of all, since this all took me by surprise, I had no chance to hide my O'Henry bar.

The minister instructed us to remove all wrappings from our sandwiches and display them fully. I will never forget how, upon examining my pile of food, he took my O'Henry bar and cut it up into many small pieces, grinning beatifically as if a beam from heaven had him in the spotlight personifying his rapture and devotion. Explaining once again, as if it would have had any real meaning to that mob, that they must share equally, he gave the order to eat.

In the elbowing rush that followed, others grabbed most of my food and I had to settle for some unfortunate-looking bread filled with a gooey mayonnaise paste and for a peanut butter and lettuce sandwich that appeared to have come out of someone's hip pocket. For dessert I did manage to get a small piece of my O'Henry bar. I was so thoroughly disgusted with this whole affair that I'm afraid that the lesson engraved on my brain that day was not the one the Reverend intended.

Windy

During the war years, it was difficult to get good men or any men to work in the camps. I know that my grandfather had his share of headaches trying to build and keep a good crew. The nucleus of Grandfather's crew, the old reliables that had been there for years, were the ones that were keeping things going. Most of the newer men had good reasons of one kind or another that kept them out of military service, such as medical or war industry deferments. Others were legally conscientious objectors.

I recall one such individual who told me that he had a medical deferment, although I never knew what it was. I cannot remember Len's last name, if I ever knew it, but everyone called him "Windy" because he talked so much.

Windy liked to fish for trout and there were two good trout lakes nearby. The only way to fish these lakes was by leaky rowboat that someone years earlier had left behind. It was only a short time before Windy ran out of fishing partners. He just plain talked too much. His complainers claimed that he scared all the big fish away.

At first, not having any reliable information on Windy, I agreed to go trout fishing with him and was pleased to be asked. The rumors, however, about Windy turned out to be quite truthful. Can you believe that a man could whip a fly rod around, manage the line, swat a swarm of mosquitoes, keep up constant chatter and catch a few fish, without dropping his rod or a vowel? Much of my time was spent in fear of being hooked by his flailing line while trying to answer his many questions. Alas, there were no cat tails around, or I might have tried stuffing my ears.

I thought lunch time would never arrive. One of the things I enjoyed most was opening my lunch box. My grandmother always packed in lots of beef and onion sandwiches, at least one piece of raisin pie and some cake too, plus a thermos of tea.

Usually, I would throw in a few candy bars, in case I got really hungry. Everything was wrapped in wax paper in those days, easy to get at. Today, with plastic wrap, the sandwich can go stale before you discover how to open it.

Windy had a big lunch too. I felt secure in that I would have a doldrums period of quiet while Windy gobbled his lunch. Windy did gobble his lunch but never stopped talking. Somehow he had mastered the art of masticating his food as it rolled from side to side in his mouth while he talked. To the observer it was a nauseating experience to see this mushy ball of food darting around in his mouth propelled by his tongue with dialogue spitting from the empty side like machine gun bullets. The trick, I realized, was to not look at Windy while I ate, allowing me satisfactory enjoyment of my raisin pie.

After eating, Windy, sucked his teeth while still talking. He lit up a cigarette and proceeded to grill me on what I knew about women. "You are now at an age where you should know how to handle yourself," he says. My answers to some of his questions brought looks of dismay to his face. Well he asked, "Of course you do know what is the first thing to do after you have had intercourse?" And then, there was the first silence in about three hours, as he waited for my answer. Finally I said I sort of knew but was not sure what kind of intercourse he was referring to. Leaning closer, he said, "Washing, of course; you must wash, right away, and get yourself clean, to prevent getting a disease. This is very important," he emphasized, looking at me from under his eyebrows and gesturing importantly with his finger as he elaborated further. I was quite unfamiliar with much of his discourse but, hoping not to appear a total nitwit, I replied, "Yeah, that sure makes a lot of sense. What else do you think I should know?" I figured that he thought me fairly sophisticated because now he offered me a cigarette. "Go ahead," he says, "I'll never tell."

Precisely a month later, at a birthday celebration for my Uncle Dick, Windy, with a few drinks of whiskey in him, was spilling his guts about me smoking on our fishing trip. Worst of all, he regaled everyone about how he had taught me about the birds and the bees. He could tell I needed it, he said, because I was so naive. Men like Windy were one level of passing influence on me. There were others too of a different cut that tended to balance my thinking and some were a permanent influence.

One such person was the Reverend Peter Kelly. Mr. Kelly was well known all up and down the West Coast of B.C. for his work with the United Church of Canada. He skippered the church's motor vessels, the *Thomas Crosby III* and *IV*, for years when I was growing up on the coast. The Reverend Kelly was a full-blooded Haida Indian, as was his wife, Gertrude Russ Kelly.

Big Game Hunters

The *Thomas Crosby IV* arrived at the logging camp once or twice a year to renew old friendships and perhaps even to extend the church's work where possible. Occasionally, the mission boat would carry a dentist affiliated with the church who would see to emergency dental problems wherever they went.

My grandfather and Mr. Kelly were old friends. Both liked to hunt. Mr. Kelly had established a reputation of being a knowledgeable grizzly bear hunter. Some years before he was involved in a bizarre hunting incident that was still talked about over hot toddies.

The story began with the Reverend Kelly and several of his friends and associates being put ashore early one morning at the mouth of an estuary where grizzly bears were known to be thick. Some of the men with Mr. Kelly on this day were along as observers, as was my grandfather, whose logging camp was where Mr. Kelly and his group were lodging. Most of the men were armed with high-powered rifles; however, only one or two were interested in hunting grizzlies. Mr. Kelly himself had not planned on this occasion to shoot a bear but wanted to get his friends close enough to a large grizzly to shoot some good pictures, as some were also photographers. Soon after going ashore a bear was spotted several hundred yards down on the mud flat, but too far away to tell if it was a black or grizzly bear. Reverend Kelly had previously cautioned his people not to shoot at anything that was not intended to be a kill and not in any case to shoot at anything out of range, just for target practice. This was serious business and he did not want anyone endangered. Nevertheless, disregarding the warning, someone did take a pot shot at the out-of-range bear, who up to this point looked pretty harmless, being so far away. Moreover, it probably had not even sensed them yet. Then another shot was fired and another. My grandfather claimed that he could see their bullets skipping on the pools of tidal water near the bear, but not within twenty feet of him. He was sure that the bear was not hit. Now, however, the bear's attention was aroused. Mr. Kelly, being quite annoyed at the men who started the shooting, got it stopped. They all were now bunched together and lined up on a high cutbank about fifteen feet above the mud flat, watching the bear as his senses searched for movement and the source of the intruder noise.

Inadvertently or not, the bear began loping in the direction of the men. When the bear came within the 100-yard range, some of the original shooters started to get nervous. Mr. Kelly told them to hold their fire. This was a grizzly, he cautioned, but was not a bear they wanted and he might just go away. The bear came much closer and could now see or smell the men. Unexpectedly, it charged the cutbank below where the men were standing. A shot was fired, hitting the bear. It fell rolling backward, stunned. Getting up, the bear charged the cutbank again and this time several shots were fired. The bear went down again, howling with pain. Seconds later it got up and resumed charging the cutbank, again and again. Now all rifles were blazing away, pouring lead into that bear. The men were so panicked by the grit and ferocity of the bear that they continued firing—even after the bear had fallen for the last time. After that show of courage by the bear, Grandfather said that none of Mr. Kelly's group was interested in pursuing grizzly bears anymore that day. They all got in the boat and went back to the camp. Mr. Kelly considered this episode to be a terrible blot on his integrity and reputation as a hunter of courageous animals. He said that he would never again consent to taking self-styled bear hunters into the field with him. It was not said whether anyone had captured this unfortunate episode on film.

Boiled Onions

It was custom, as previously mentioned, that all visitors to the logging camp were invited to eat at the cookhouse at the last sitting, when the cooks, flunkies and the family would all sit together and relax over dinner. It has been said by many that no class of working people eat better than loggers. At every meal there were always choices of meat, vegetables, bread, fruit, condiments, pastries or liquid beverages. Often there was raisin pie, lemon pie and peach pie for dessert, plus chocolate cake and matrimonial cake. I never had any problem with choices; I just sampled one of each. If I could not eat it all at dinner, I carried the other choices away in stacks with me to be consumed later. Often I would be back at "mug up" to get more. There is no question that I was very spoiled where food was concerned. With this in mind one morning, I found myself on board the *Thomas Crosby IV.* Reverend and Mrs. Kelly were used to seeing me around so it was no surprise to them having me appear in their midst.

Mrs. Kelly was quite outgoing and could generally be counted on to express her thoughts or opinions openly. I noticed that she was preparing to serve food in the ship's galley. A single pot on the galley stove was boiling furiously; the lid kept popping up and releasing steam.

As it happened, I was invited to stay for lunch. The Reverend and I sat at the table and from the single pot Mrs. Kelly served each of us, including herself, a single boiled onion and then she sat down. After the Reverend said the blessing, we three methodically sliced and ate our boiled onion as if we were pretending that it was pheasant under glass, filet mignon, cordon bleu or some other fancy dish. Nothing was said the whole time. Looking back, I believe that experience was one of my most intriguing challenges, to sit and pretend that I was enjoying myself. I have often wondered if the whole scene was meant to be a joke or an object lesson for me. On the other hand, I have also considered that, had I not been there, Mr. Kelly would have had to eat two boiled onions. Perhaps the real truth was that they were preparing their stomachs for a bountiful meal at the camp cookhouse later that evening. For my part, I showed up at the dinner table with renewed respect for the cooks and the variety of grub they had prepared for us.

Falling Camp

In Draney Inlet, Grandfather put Uncle Richard in charge of the "falling camp," which was several miles from the main camp. The plan was that once the main camp had logged off all of the felled timber in its present location, it would then move to the advanced location where newly felled trees were ready to be swung down the steep hillsides and into the chuck.

The falling camp personnel consisted of Uncle Richard and Aunt Phil, a handful of fallers, a female camp cook to prepare high-energy meals for the fallers, and a bullcook to maintain camp services. At the time, in 1943–44, at Doc's camp all falling of timber was still done with the crosscut saw.

The bullcook, a middle-aged man, had developed bad teeth and had to leave camp to see a dentist. Since they were temporarily short handed, I was asked to go to the falling camp and take over the bullcook's duties until he returned in about two weeks.

Because this was a small camp, all I had to do was split enough wood to fire all the wood stoves, including the cookhouse, sweep out the bunkhouses and make the beds, every day. Being thirteen, I was a little apprehensive about my responsibilities but found that I could complete what needed to be done by noon, daily.

By one o'clock most afternoons I was in a rowboat scouting the unfamiliar shoreline for interesting landmarks. Some days I accompanied Uncle Richard to the work site where the trees were being felled. On those days I hiked around in the area while Richard scaled the newly felled trees to record board footage and the faller's rate of progress. My uncle knew that I was used to being around falling or rigging crews during logging operations, so he paid little attention to me as he went about his duties. I had gotten to know Waldy and John, two fallers, and watched them as they felled a large spruce tree about four feet through at the butt. At the cry of "timber," the two fallers jumped from their springboards, never letting go of the falling saw, as they hit the ground jogging to a safe position. The tree was snapping and cracking in what sounded like a final lament, as it leaned more and more each second. Gaining momentum, the stricken forest giant succumbed to gravity and with awesome speed slashed its way to the forest floor, ripping and tearing huge limbs from itself and surrounding trees, in a final rattle of death. A large 150-foot tree impacts the ground with such crushing force that, if not skillfully placed by the fallers, the entire tree could be broken or split and thus ruined. Watching a 300-year-old tree die was chilling. Even though I belonged to a family of loggers, for me, repetition of this awesome sight never diminished the sense of wonder that I felt. I watched as Waldy and John jogged over to another tree they had marked as the next tree in succession to be felled. About an hour later I was circling back toward Waldy and John and could hear the swish, swish of the falling saw, but could not yet see them. Then they stopped sawing. All was silent. Now, I heard the smack of a hammer on steel and soon the swish, swish resumed. I knew then that another forest giant was near death. They had inserted wedges to insure the direction of descent as well as to free the saw in the last stages of cut. I moved closer to them, changing my angle, in order to verify the direction the tree would fall. Now, I could see them through the trees and a quick assessment suggested I insure my safety by swinging further to one side, which I did hastily. The sawing stopped and the wedging resumed. The sawing continued but almost immediately the familiar, ominous cracking and snapping and cry of "timber" underscored the end of another forest monarch. My eyes were on the tree tops, searching for telltale movement. There it was, and instantly I was on the alert, and started to run. I ran along a path provided by two previously felled spruce trees, glancing over my shoulder as I ran and in the last seconds jumped off the logs and dove to the shelter of a cavernous bushy hollow beneath them. I closed my eyes tight, curled into a ball with my arms over my head as the tree struck. The memory of it is still clear. It was only the last twenty or thirty feet (of a 100-foot-plus tree) of the tree top that reached my position. Nevertheless, as the top branches of the tree "cracked-the-whip," smashing over my hiding place, the air around me exploded with pitch, pollen and dust so thick that I could not see or breathe. My nostrils and throat burned with the taste and smell of turpentine. My eyelids were glued with pitch and it filled my hair and was down my neck. I scrambled, choking, out of my hole unhurt, but gasping for fresh air. Waldy and John came running to see how I had fared, their faces white and wide eyed from fear that I might have, as they said, "bought the farm." I waved at them and they waved back, shaking their heads at how lucky we all were.

That tree was the classic example of the tree that never quite fell where it was supposed to. It happens often in the woods and is why fallers and other woodsmen must have continual vigilance and never take anything for granted. As one of Murphy's Laws states, "if it can happen, it will." I brushed myself off as best I could and at a suggestion from both John and Waldy, we three decided not to tell my uncle of the incident. I was all for it because if the truth came out, I may have been quarantined to camp for a spell.

The falling camp cook was a middle-aged woman and married, but her husband was elsewhere at the time. She was small in stature, had graying hair and a broad, flat, tight-skinned, bony face, with a flat pudgy nose and rather large nostrils. She smoked heavily and when she exhaled most of the smoke exited through her proboscis. I often thought that she resembled a snorting bull. She kept very much to herself; however, she was an excellent cook, which was what the men cared about. She could have had two heads and three arms, but, so long as she kept them well fed, they were happy with her.

Her one interest aside from her job seemed to be gardening and she had several long planter boxes full of dirt where she could be found cultivating and fussing over her plants and flowers. One afternoon she had asked me to help her move some pails of dirt and after doing so she seemed to want to talk. I was standing beside one of her planter boxes when she turned and squatted down opposite me. In the isolated setting of the logging camp, I had no chance to acquire girlfriends but my interest in girls per se, was normal, given an opportunity. The cook was wearing a light cotton summer dress but as I noticed, was without underpants. At the age of thirteen, I was quite naive and had no idea of whether she was displaying herself for my benefit or not. She looked up at me a few times, smiled, and continued chatting. I was now becoming very uneasy, but somehow I could not move. My heart was pounding ferociously and taking my eyes off her crotch was exceedingly difficult. At this juncture, however, the bulge in my trousers had become very pronounced. My increasing embarrassment could be ignored no longer and I moved away in a bent over crouch, pretending to examine her posies as I left. On another occasion a similar incident occurred. I now feel that the cook was offering me an opportunity to learn something about the opposite sex. Regretfully, I let pass the opportunity for first-hand experience, where I surely needed it.

Teen Years

Indian Masks

The summer of 1945 found the Gildersleeve Logging Company camp at the head of Rivers Inlet. The Rivers Inlet Cannery or RIC was founded in 1882 by Shotbolt, Hart & Company of Victoria. It had long since been closed down, but still had a fisherman's store and net loft. During the summer a number of fishermen, mostly Indians, lived in old cannery shacks along the beach.

Our floating camp was anchored to the mud flat near some islands on the north side of the Wannock River estuary. When the tide was out the entire camp was resting on thick river mud. The Wannock River that drained Owikeno Lake was glacially fed and thus the lake and river were heavily laden with silt. During the spring and summer runoff, the entire upper end of Rivers Inlet is a silty, milky color, and seeing more than eighteen inches into the sea water is difficult.

The first summer we were there was again a summer of exploration. My sisters and I were off in rowboats to inspect our new surroundings. One of our first discoveries was on a small island that, due to swampy ground, was heavily overgrown with cottonwood willows. We went ashore to see if there was anything of particular interest on the island, e.g., evidence of human habitation. The very first things that we came across were huge round piles of fresh bear scat. This was somewhat puzzling, at first, because the island was so small, only about two or three acres. What would bears eat here, we wondered, that would produce such piles? We soon found the answer, old orchard fruit trees. There were apple, cherry and plum and maybe other fruit trees that we could not see. The brush was so thick in places that we had to crawl on our hands and knees to move around. Stinging nettles were everywhere, growing as thick as hair on a dog's back. Having never experienced nettles I whacked the back of my hand against a plant, and for the next few seconds I was on my knees holding my arm in agony. Almost as quickly, the excruciating pain was gone. It was a quick and simple lesson in plant identification. Stay clear of nettles.

Crawling around among the fruit trees, we discovered a row of cabins not far away. They seemed to be well-constructed cabins, but for some reason, none of them had any front stairs. We climbed through the front door of the nearest cabin, finding it clean and dry, but it had the look and feeling that no one had been there for a long, long time. Upstairs in the cabin we found pieces of furniture and an old trunk with clothing. The trunk had parts of an army uniform from the Great War and also newspapers from that era. We left everything as we found it and went to examine the other cabins. In one of them we discovered a large quantity of handcrafted Native ceremonial masks. They were of all sizes, and appeared from the odor to be made of yellow cedar. The smallest was the size of a human face, and some were eighteen inches or better across. All were beautifully hand carved and painted. Some were adorned with colored beadwork and feathers. From an early age we were taught to leave things be that did not belong to us, and although the temptation was great, we took nothing and left everything as it was. To this day, knowing the value of that art work, I can only hope that the rightful Native owners have long since taken possession of it.

On another day I was back at the island alone, and was standing inside one of the cabins when something by the door caught my eye. It was a nail driven high up into the side of the door frame. On closer inspection I could see what had attracted me— a small gold ring. A lonely wedding band hung there. I stared at it for a long time without touching it. I was wondering who the owner had been and what difficult circumstances might have brought the ring to this nail. After some time I carefully grasped the ring between thumb and forefinger and gently lifted it from the nail. Holding it thus close to my face, I could see that it was a wedding band for a small delicate finger. A very, very slight pressure caused the ring to bend. I returned it to its round shape, realizing that it was, probably, twenty-four karat gold. I knew intuitively that I could not keep the ring, nor did I want to. It belonged to someone once. Now, perhaps, it belonged to posterity. Life can be cruel. Someone's life of love and hopes may be tied up in that ring. It may still be there where I left it, hanging on that nail, in 1946.

Later on that summer we found where the Native Indians had nested coffins in large trees as burial sites. Most of the coffins and contents, however, had long since fallen from the trees. We also observed where personal effects were left atop grave mounds, e.g., a treadle Singer sewing machine, perhaps thinking, as I have read, that they would be useful in another life.

Spring Salmon

In Rivers Inlet, shortly after World War II, the sportfishing industry for spring salmon had not yet begun, and power boating as we know it now was almost nonexistent. Of course the spring salmon have been there for centuries, prior to going up into Owikeno Lake each year to spawn. Like anyone then who wanted to fish for spring salmon, we kids took to a rowboat. I was fifteen; Cherie was fourteen. We trolled a hand line with a #7 Gibs spoon and three pounds of weight. One morning Cherie and I were out trolling with the above equipment. I was rowing and Cherie was sitting in the stern seat holding the line. Actually, I had snubbed the line with a break away loop, I thought, to a ring on the boat transom. Cherie had reached out with her hand and was holding the strain of the line in order to detect a nibble or a strike. We had been out about one-half hour when Cherie reported mildly that she thought she felt something. All of a sudden a fish struck. Instead of the line popping loose from the snub ring as it was supposed to do, it tightened into a knot as the fish sounded. A few seconds later, the line pointing almost straight down came taut again with such force that the transom of our rowboat was pulled under. Instantly it popped up again, but not before shipping many gallons of water. Frantically I loosened the knot where it was tied to the transom ring, while Cherie, who had now gone to the bow of the boat, was whipping in the yards of line that had gone slack. Before long, the line went tight again as the fish was now out in front of us about ten feet down and going like blazes. The fish was so strong that Cherie was hanging out over the bow of the boat holding onto the fish line with both hands, while I hung onto Cherie. That fish towed us around the bay in great circles at about four miles per hour for several minutes without letting up. Finally the line went slack once more. I hurriedly yarded in limp line exposing the lead weight and twenty feet of leader. Suddenly the fish appeared. A huge spring salmon. It swam up to the rowboat, took one frightened gawk at us and sounded again. The three-pound lead weight caromed off the oarlock as it flew out of the boat, while Cherie and I ducked for cover. Again the line went slack and again I rapidly hauled it in, up to the lead weight. I saw now that the leader line had been slashed on striking the oarlock and only a strand or two was holding the fish. This state of affairs upset us greatly, as we were certain that we had never seen a fish as big as this one.

We had no hand net, no gaff nor even a club to stun the fish in order to help us get it in the boat. It sounded once again and we let it have all the line it wanted. Eventually, the fish played itself out. Luckily for us, the rowboat we were using was round bottomed and tipped on its side easily. Drawing the fish along-side, we slid the huge salmon in, along with many more gallons of water. We had a coffee can for bailing and promptly began to toss the water out. The fish, very much alive, started slapping the bottom of the boat with tremendous force, throwing fish slime into the air. We could do little about it.

Fifteen minutes later we landed at the commercial fisher-man's wharf, our clothing, hair and eyebrows coated with slime. Nevertheless, we were extremely pleased with ourselves when one of the fishermen hauled our fish onto his scale and weighed it at fifty-four pounds. We learned later that even larger spring salmon had been caught there. Our mother, years before, had caught a white spring much farther north, weighing seventy-five pounds. It had to be beached, as she could not get it into her row-boat.

Big Ben

Fishing took up quite a bit of time that summer. However, I also began playing cards with some of the younger loggers in camp and occasionally, two or three of us, between card games, would go trolling. We did not catch any more fifty-four pounders, but even the thirty- and forty-pounders seemed to fight as hard as the larger fish.

One evening, after stuffing myself with a huge dinner at the cookhouse, that included my favorite raisin pie, I went over to the bunkhouse where my card playing buddies were. Previously we had agreed that this evening we would play blackjack. As none of us had any money, we decided to gamble with .22 cartridges. Soon after the game got underway, one of our group brought out a fresh plug of Big Ben chewing tobacco and offered a chew to each of us. I declined as I did not smoke or chew. As I recall, Big Ben was basically tobacco leaves pressed with molasses. The aroma from the chewing plug smelled quite good. One of the fellows claimed that he did not swallow the juice and so he would not get sick. I stupidly believed him and decided to have a chew. It did taste pretty good at that. Like the others I had a can to spit in, and we continued to play cards. I was very careful not to swallow any juice and was spitting at least twice as much as the others, yet I began to feel a little light headed. Pretty soon I realized that something serious was wrong. I excused myself from the game and headed for the outhouse. My head was buzzing and I realized that I was going to be sick. With my head and shoulders hanging over the privy bench, everything was spinning as great heaves of food, bile and mucous erupted from my throat and nose, time after time. The outhouse had four sitting stations, but anyone who came close and heard my pathetic moaning and retching turned away to seek out a more tranquil place for contemplation. Word got around quickly that some poor devil was puking his guts out in the four holer.

I never went back to the game that night. I stumbled to my bunk on Grandma's porch to die. At least, I hoped I would die. When I opened my eyes the following morning, I felt rotten, but was glad to be alive. I have never touched a chew of tobacco since, and remembering as I write this fifty years later, my stomach is starting to churn. It was a rough but effective way for me to learn an important lesson.

Galbraithe

Early in the summer of 1946 I had the opportunity to work with a man who could have stepped right out of the pages of a frontier novel. He was one fascinating individual. His name was Clarence Galbraithe, a World War I British Army veteran, having served in the front line infantry in France as a boy of seventeen. I learned that he had been so seriously wounded, he should have died on the battlefield, but somehow did not. This may have been the reason why he was the toughest, two-fisted, iron-willed, humorous, devil-may-care personality that I had come across. I had not known him long when I realized that he was someone to be reckoned with.

Galbraithe was a road-building contractor and had come up to camp to build roads for the logging trucks. In his business, he was also an expert powder man. Grandfather had asked me to work with Mr. Galbraithe as his helper. Of course there was no pay involved; however, Grandfather allowed that I probably would learn a thing or two. Even though Galbraithe was forty-five or forty-six, he seemed oblivious to the fact that I was only a lad of fifteen. He treated me like an adult. That I liked.

One day while the two of us were sitting out in the woods by ourselves, eating our lunches, he reminisced that he had been a young soldier in the Great War of 1914–18. He was a big fellow, six-foot-six at sixteen, and had lied about his age. At the age of seventeen he was in the middle of a British Army infantry charge, was machine gunned and left for dead. He pointed to the large hollow spot on his left cheek where a bullet had gone in and lodged in the hard pallet, next to his brain.

Taking a swig of coffee, he offered casually that it was too close to the brain to remove, so they just left it in there. He added, "I have been what you might call living on borrowed time ever since." Then he stood up and with one motion, jerked his shirt out of his trousers and up to his neck. "Have a look," he said. I could not believe it. I got up, walked over to where he stood and counted one, two, three, four holes stitched across his stomach and chest. "From the same burst of fire," he said calmly. I could have put about one-half inch of my index finger into the healed cavity each bullet had created. After I had had a good look, he tucked his shirt back in his trousers, sat down, leaned back and winked at me. "Nothing's finished, lad, until it's finished," he said. "My time was not up." Then he paused, looking somewhat wistful, and said, "I have had some great times in my day since then," and added, "when your time is up, that is it, kaput, finished." He looked at me and grinned. He also knew from my dazzled expression that he had my complete and rapt attention.

In the days that followed, wherever Mr. Galbraithe went, I went. Whenever he spoke, I listened. When he was silent, I watched every muscle twitch and frown on his face, to better know his thoughts concerning his next move. Sometimes, I thought I knew what he wanted before he did. Often, things did not go right. Mr. Galbraithe could, without stutter, begin swearing, and spout a very long string of expletive language that I thought impossible to imagine, let alone speak. When he was through swearing, he would wink at me and laugh uproariously or develop a huge grin. I liked the laugh better because the grin usually meant that he was still mulling something over.

Most of our time was spent clearing a path through the woods in advance of his crew of road builders. All the timber in the path of the proposed road had been felled and removed. We were clearing the road bed of all stumps, some four feet in diameter, ahead of the tractors and other heavy equipment. My main task was simply to dig holes under the stumps where Galbraithe would set dynamite charges, often more than one charge per stump. He would inspect my progress on all stumps, as he was very particular how and where the charges were laid. It did not take me long to understand what he wanted. A little extra effort on a large, heavy-rooted stump could mean success on the first shot. A sloppy job might mean double or triple the work if it needed doing over again. After I had the holes dug, I would consult with Galbraithe. From the powder cache he would count out dynamite sticks—20 percent or 40 percent dynamite usually—and put them in a box that, along with a coil of fuse, I would carry out to the first stump. I never was allowed to carry the caps nor handle them. Galbraithe carried them in the breast pocket of his work shirt. As we strode along I could hear them rise and fall, sounding like loose rifle cartridges, echoing his long stride. When he caught me looking at the pocket in question, he would wink knowingly.

Galbraithe would squat or climb down beside the stump roots and I would hand him the number of powder sticks that he wanted. He would then cut off a suitable length of fuse, take a cap from the small box in his breast pocket and slip the open end onto the fuse. At this moment he would make eye contact with me and say "never bite the end of a cap," and then proceed to do so, using his eye teeth to crimp the cap to the fuse. I was aware, as he knew, that a small pair of pliers is normally used for such crimping. Then using a sharp twig, he punched a hole in the end of one of the dynamite sticks and inserted the cap and fuse. Into the hole beneath the stump went this charge, along with as many more sticks as he felt were needed. I then helped him pack dirt, mud and rocks over the charge before moving on to the next stump.

On this particular day we wanted to blow ten stumps, setting the charges up so that we could light all the fuses at once. Depending on fuse length, the shots would blow at about fifteen-second intervals. On we went, Galbraithe grinning and biting caps onto fuses, repeating "never crimp a cap with your teeth," while I handed him the dynamite. Finally we completed all ten stumps. At his request I gathered all of the ten fuse ends. Since the first fuses we cut were much longer than the last fuses, the ends drawn together were separated by only a few feet. We intended to walk away from the lit fuses in the direction of the last stump to blow (actually, the first charge we laid). He lit all fuses at once. Immediately my legs itched to start running. I knew how much dynamite was packed under those stumps and my thoughts were suggesting a much faster gait. Galbraithe was in no hurry. He acted like he was out for a Sunday stroll. I felt his act of nonchalance was mostly for my benefit. It irked me somewhat that I did not feel as macho. I feigned a confident attitude so as not to embarrass myself, as we ambled along.

It seemed far too long before Galbraithe motioned me off to the side of the path where a large stump afforded me protection from the inevitable blasts. Galbraithe took the other side of the proposed road where there was another large stump. I expected the first blast at any moment and pressed myself to my stump like a tree frog. I glanced over at Galbraithe. He was sitting relaxed, back to his stump with one leg and boot crossed over the other. The blast did not come as immediately as I expected. I relaxed and emulated Galbraithe, crossed legs and all. Presently he looked over at me, winked and held up two fingers, quickly put them down and held up one finger as the first blast erupted. Rocks, dirt and chunks of stump went flying in all directions. Suddenly, Galbraithe held up two fingers and the second charge exploded with a shocking crack. More debris was whizzing through the air and so it proceeded. As the shots got closer I drew my legs up and all but dissolved myself behind my stump. Over half the shots had blown now, with Galbraithe counting them with a show of his fingers. The air was acrid with the foul-smelling mixture of dynamite fumes and scorched earth. The smoke and gases produced from the blasts were hanging close to the ground; yet I could see Galbraithe clearly and on the shots went, coming closer. As he held up another set of fingers, I clenched my teeth and then, wham. Along about the ninth shot, I peered across at Galbraithe and he had his "makings" out preparing to roll himself a cigarette. Kapow, there went number nine. He was still tamping tobacco into the rice paper when number ten went right on cue. It was the closest stump and also the granddaddy blast. The explosion was ear shattering.

As I watched, Galbraithe hardly twitched, and immediately a shower of rocks and dirt began descending around us. He was licking the rice paper to complete his cigarette when a huge, pointed slab a foot thick and ten feet long descended from the sky like a wooden thunderbolt spearing itself upright in the dirt, not two feet from Galbraithe's outstretched legs. The cigarette paper went flying and his legs jerked apart as if to bolt up. He shot a glance at me to see if I had observed his instant of fear. I pretended not to have noticed the slab strike and he seemed convinced. Later, I did ask him if the slab spear had scared him. His reply was, "Well it did surprise me a little, but there was no reason in being scared, laddie. When your time is up, it's up." I nodded my head knowingly. I also understood now that Mr. Galbraithe, like all the rest of us mortals, was in no hurry to hasten that final moment of truth.

Five minutes after all ten shots had blown, we went back through the sweet-smelling, blue, choking haze to inspect our handiwork. Ear protection was unheard of in those days and my ears were buzzing so that I could not hear all that well. It looked to me like all of the stumps had come out fairly clean. I was eager to inspect their roots to see how well our charges had worked.

Standing near the first stump to blow, looking down into the hole, I felt a strange sensation. At first I thought my ears had caused me to lose my sense of balance. I looked up and saw Galbraithe waving his arms at me and shouting something, but I could not make it out. Then I realized I was slowly rising up in the air like I had antigravity. Galbraithe was still waving and pointing. I glanced around quickly and saw the problem. A large tree, some twenty feet from me had had its roots disturbed from the dynamite shots and was slowly falling away from me. I was standing on the fringes of its roots that were hidden with thick moss, and was being catapulted upward. I jumped to the ground, a distance of about three feet and dashed toward Galbraithe, as the tree went over, crashing to the ground. Had I remained on the edge of the roots I would have been slung off into the brush like a pellet from a sling shot. We both had a laugh at the odd incident and I decided that my time was not up that day either.

Chasing Sparks

Later on in the summer of 1946 it got very hot. It had not rained for weeks and the woods were tinder dry. Andy Torkelson, the woods boss, asked me if I wanted a job chasing sparks. The next day I was introduced to a five-gallon backpack water can and pump. This apparatus was used to extinguish small fires ignited

186

by sparks from the steam donkey smokestack. To my surprise, my first day on the job I doused a dozen or more small fires. All day long I heard the call, "Hey, kid over here, there's a bonfire getting started," and away I charged, with the five-gallon can bouncing along on my back. Being conscientious and close to a water supply, I filled my can every chance I got and always had a full five gallons that I lugged around.

One day as I sat thinking about this, I wondered, since water was so close, why was I carrying five gallons. A full water can weighed forty pounds. The smart thing, I concluded, was to carry about half and make my work a lot easier. Each fire, I rationalized, usually required only a few squirts. After dumping half of the water, I noticed when running to the next fire that the water in the can sloshed from side to side in rhythm with my stride. Actually, it was sort of amusing and I played with it a little, to see how much off balance it would take me.

A few days later, there was not much action. I was out scouting the area and squirting water on some of the running blocks in case they were heating up. I was heading back to the steam donkey, close to noon, when I spotted a huge spruce log more than 100 feet long all limbed, but not yet bucked into smaller logs. It appeared a great place to walk above the slash and brush, so up I went. I stood up a little off balance and ran a few quick steps to right myself. However, as I continued to run slowly, the water behind me sloshed to match my gait, like a pendulum. I never did get perfectly balanced. Running faster in an attempt to straighten out only made matters worse. The sloshing was my undoing. I tried desperately to leap to a soft landing in the direction of the pendulum force, but there was too much brush in the way. Instead I augered in head first, landing on my back in a brushy hole, with head and shoulders hanging down and my legs up over a log. The weight of the water can under my back had tightened the shoulder straps so that I was virtually pinned. I was trapped so that I could not use my legs or my arms. I was stuck. I lay there quite a while resting and thinking about what to do.

Presently I heard a voice calling, "Yimmy." That was Andy's name for me. I did not answer for I was more humiliated than hurt. "Yimmy," he called again, louder. I could hear his caulk shoes crunching toward me down the long spruce log that I had been on. Then he saw me. At first surprised, he stood and stared. Slowly a huge grin started to spread across his face, when he could see that I was not hurt. He took off his beat up "bone dry" hat and slapping it across his knee, let out a couple of war whoops, thinking, I guess, that I looked pretty funny. Still laughing, he hauled me up, dusted me off, and lectured me on the spot regarding such potential situations. Better late than never, I thought. Actually, he needn't have bothered with his lecture. I was a lot more careful after that incident. Also, I kept my water can full.

The Old Norwegian

Soon enough the rains came and my spark chasing job ended. I was told to go with the road-building crew, pounding spikes. This sounded a little ominous to me but I figured to give it a shot. They put me under the wing of an old Norwegian who was sixty-four, six-foot-two and skinny as an ax handle. He usually had snoose spit dribbling down from his lower lip and off his chin of three or four days' whisker growth.

Lucky for me, Larson was very experienced at his job and showed a lot of patience and sympathy with my obvious ineptitude. We had to drive nine-inch spikes through four-by-twelve fir planks into four-by-twelve fir ties for a truck road Grandfather was having built (Gailbraithe's road). Larson would start his spike by holding it in one hand and tapping it in lightly with the nine-pound hammer. Then he would draw back with a full, over-the-shoulder swing, wham, once, wham, twice and it was down, 100 percent in. I would follow his lead and start my spike the same way, then I would draw back and wham, bend the spike right over 100 percent flat. Or I would send it caroming off like a piece of shrapnel spinning into the brush. My other alternative was to miss the spike altogether with the hammer head and tear a great chunk out of the handle. The old Norwegian would not say a word of condemnation. "You will get it," he would say, "it will take a little time." About then, I was wondering if Grandfather could afford the hundreds of spikes that I ruined. Gradually, I did get better, but I never got nearly as good as old Larson.

Larson confided to me that he had been born in Norway to a woman in a railroad camp. He never knew his mother. He grew up in the camp like other kids in a similar situation. The camp was state owned and run. He was provided for until he was old enough to work, then he went to work on the railroad. I did not mention it to him, but it sounded almost like slavery to me. Larson immigrated to Canada as a young man and had worked in the camps as a logger ever since. He never married and said that he had no relatives that he knew of. He had worked for my grandfather off and on for some years, building roads and such.

As I mentioned, I chewed up a fair number of hammer handles. The old Norwegian soon informed me that we were short of hammers and that I needed to "hang" one that evening (that is, fit a forged steel hammer head to a wood handle). This pinched me a little, since after working under stress all day, I figured I deserved the night off. Larson gave me a few pointers on how to get started but said I must do the job myself or I would not learn. Thus, I headed for the familiar blacksmith's shop after dinner while Larson and my other buddies stretched out on their bunks.

I got the job done and after soaking the hammer head in a bucket of water over night, in order to swell the wood handle and further tighten it into the head, I proudly took the hammer with me in the morning. Right off, on my first swing, I could tell that it was not right. Before long I had changed to another hammer. An hour or two later, Larson approached me with the "problem" hammer and, taking his back, handed me mine saying quietly so as not to embarrass me, "it needed fixing." Larson was right, of course. Somehow in my haste to get it done, I got the head of the hammer a tiny bit out of line with the axis of the handle and it felt like swinging a lopsided monkey wrench. The next evening was also spent in the blacksmith's shop and that was not the last. Larson made me use the hammers I hung until I finally got the hang of doing it right.

Grizzly Capers

There were a lot of grizzly bears roaming the bush at the head of Rivers Inlet, but it was seldom that anyone had any problem with them. We had a brisk half-hour hike to our jobs each morning and we often joked with each other about rounding a turn and stepping up to a grizzly bear.

One weekend, for some unknown reason, a few of the Indian lads had shot a large grizzly. They then had dragged the carcass behind a large stump that was practically in the middle of our trail. As a joke, the bear was left sitting upright with his huge head propped up with a stick. It could not be seen coming up the trail until seconds after rounding the stump. Learning about the bear, a few of the loggers hatched a plot to scare one of their number who was terrified of grizzly bears.

The plan was to sandwich the "guinea pig" between a half dozen men who were in on the plot. When the man ahead of the guinea pig rounded the stump he would pretend to panic and shout. It happened quite by accident that at this particular spot on the trail there was no place to run to. The side of the trail away from the bear was a thick impenetrable jungle of heavy swamp vines with half-inch-long spikelike thorns. The intended victim could not run ahead and a column of men was behind him, so he was trapped, or so they thought.

At the appointed place the act was begun. Baker, the man who to me was the spitting image of the character "Flat Top" in the Dick Tracy comics, tore off screaming through the brier patch, oblivious of pain, and never stopped till he hit the river about forty yards away. The first-aid man had a tough job dressing all of Baker's thorn punctures and gashes. He was cut up very badly from head to toes. The whole episode was hushed up quickly by the perpetrators and I don't think my grandfather ever heard about it. Baker, the poor fellow, was greatly humiliated, and left camp soon after the incident.

Starvation Layout

The only other cruelty on the job that summer that I can recall had to do with myself. I was used to being fed by my grandmother, and when she packed my lunch, she knew what she was doing. I ate like a growing fourteen-year-old eats, like a horse, even two horses, and she knew it. For some reason, this particular summer my mother was packing my lunches and I about starved to death. She would give me two tomato sandwiches with nothing else except, ugh, mayonnaise, an apple or an orange, maybe a cookie, but rarely pie. I kept telling her that I could not wrestle twenty-foot four-by-twelve planks around and pound nine-inch spikes all day on tomato sandwiches. Alas, it was to no avail. At night I hustled over to Gram's cookhouse and smuggled out goodies for my next day's lunch pail. Lucky for me that I did, too, or I might never have survived that summer to record these lines for posterity.

Old Curmudgeon

The following summer at fifteen, I had not filled out much but I was stronger and I found myself working around the steam donkey. Little old Johnny Monks was a small curmudgeon of a man whose face held a continuous scowl. He had been engineer on the old steam pot longer than I could remember. I must have been a baby when he first went to work for my grandfather. I never knew how he felt, now that I was big enough to be pitching cordwood into his donkey's voracious firebox. Part of my job was to cut cordwood rounds from a large "fire log" using a steam drag saw that was powered via a pressure hose from the donkey. Later, I split the rounds into cordwood with a wedge and sledge hammer.

One of the first things that old Curmudgeon Monks said to me in warning was "never open the firebox door when the damper is down." Then he turned his back to me, leaning on his levers and controls as if that was that, and all I needed to know. "Where is the damper?" I wanted to know. Old Curmudgeon screwed his head around and looked at me with a kind of humorless pity. He turned arrogantly, reached up and pulled a lever down and latched it."The damper is down," he announced. Then he unlatched it, raised it up and turned back to his business. Okay, I thought to myself, that's pretty simple. He acted, I thought, as if he had been issued his steam engineer's ticket at birth.

To keep steam up when Mr. Monks and the rigging crew were having a good day yarding logs to the cold deck pile meant lots of cordwood needed to go into the firebox. When he needed steam, he opened the damper, and the fire would roar like thunder while the burning wood seemed to melt before my eyes. At first I did not understand the art of stacking cordwood properly inside the firebox and no one showed me. I discovered that if I tossed the cord wood in willy-nilly, it would fall every which way and prevent me from stacking it properly. Thus, it would be consumed rapidly. This caused many angry scowls from Curmudgeon Monks because the steam he needed was not being produced. Gradually, I learned to lay the wood in, stacked tightly against the back wall of the firebox. Then, I would begin a second stack in front of the first. This was no mean feat for me as the firebox door was only about eighteen inches by fourteen inches or less, and with the door open the heat often was too intense to stand directly in front of it. I had to swing the chunk of wood, thirty inches long by eight inches by eight inches, back, while aiming for its place inside the firebox, then heave forward pendulum fashion and pitch it end-o, through the firebox door opening, nesting it on the stack within the raging inferno. If done properly, the firebox was packed tightly with wood and I could lean against the woodpile and look forward to a short rest. Once in a while I got a rare friendly wink from old Curmudgeon Monks that perked up my spirits.

Monks was right about not opening the firebox door with the damper down. I did it only once. I learned from that one experience that if you live through the first time you make that mistake, you never make it again. Opening the firebox door with the damper down causes a solid tongue of vermilion red flame the exact shape of the firebox opening to shoot out instantaneously about three feet or more and burn to toast anything in its path. As

I say, I did do this only once, and scared myself half to death. I was soon cooled off, however, with the icy stare I received from old Curmudgeon. Somehow, my reflexes were sharp enough that day that my body was already moving to get out of the way the instant I made the mistake. I hit the deck hard and the gargantuan tongue of flame speared harmlessly over my back. Bear in mind the fact that at any time I was pitching wood into the firebox inferno, old Curmudgeon could have absentmindedly closed the firebox damper and singed the head right off my shoulders. Thank goodness old Curmudgeons don't make mistakes like that.

Lunch times were usually pretty interesting for me. Besides diving into my cram-packed lunch bucket of food that was helping to sustain my scrawny frame, I joined in the good-natured banter the older men engaged in while they ate. Much of their humor was at my expense, being the youngest crew member at fifteen. A man remarked one day that they should be careful what they say in my presence since the chances were that if it was about women, I likely would not understand. Not only was there laughing and general agreement on that score, but Jack Monks, Johnny's brother, allowed that if I ever saw a naked woman lying on her back with her legs spread I would probably drop my hat on her crotch and run for it. Oh, boy, they really had a great guffaw over that comment. To tell the truth, at that time, I was still pretty naive and he may have been right.

Another young lad, a few years older than I, had come to the camp to work with the rigging crew as a choker setter (a man who attaches choker cables to the logs prior to their being pulled to the cold deck pile). His name was Sam. He was a husky boy fresh from an orphanage home, or so he said. Sam tended to present a cockiness that indicated more experience than he actually had. This was not unusual at his age, and of course the other men saw right through him. It was pretty obvious to all that he had never worked in the woods before. A cocky attitude when one is green is sure to cultivate sadistic tendencies in co-workers.

One hot and humid day as I had just completed banking the boiler firebox, Sam came puffing into the trackside. Half shouting at old Curmudgeon Monks, he wanted to know, demandingly, where the choker holes were. Old Curmudgeon, without looking at Sam, jerked his thumb toward the back of the donkey in my direction. He then half turned and looking at me with a knowing wink and a seldom-seen insidious grin, said, "Jim will help you." Back Sam came sweating and snorting as if he had run all the way, which I am sure he had, due to the fact that the rigging crew had told him that they needed them right away. I was very familiar with the scenario.

Choker holes are those spaces that a chokerman finds or even digs under a log, if necessary, in order to get the knob of the choker through to the other side, then up around the log and locked into the choker bell. Thus, the log is "choked." I asked Sam, "How many choker holes did he want?" I told myself that I would not be going along with this form of cruelty unless Sam deserved it. I decided he did. Sam replied, "They said to bring a bucket full." On the back end of the donkey sled under the water tank was a large box of railroad spikes used mainly for securing guy wires to stumps. They were big, black and heavy. A bucket full, meaning in this case a fire pail, was a lot of spikes. I tossed about half a bucket full into a fire pail and told him that if they needed more to come back, but I figured that would do them. The half full pail of spikes must have weighed sixty to seventy-five pounds. Off Sam went, confidently dragging that bucket of "choker holes."

It was a very hot day and it no doubt took him a half hour or better, using a lot of sweat and muscle to get those holes out to the crew. Upon his arrival with them, they would jump up and down with delight and guffaw at Sam's expense. Most of the men would recall their own discomfort, in the not so distant past, when they too were sent to the trackside for "choker holes" or some other unlikely piece of equipment. Generally the men felt no qualms about perpetuating such a questionable tradition.

Sam was a hard nut to crack. He took his lumps without too much complaint, which gained him some respect. However, he persisted in attempting dangerous activities that he was not ready for. Sam had watched the high rigger go up the spar tree in a passline to adjust the angle of the mainline block. The rigger knew that he was not going to be up the tree more than a few minutes and so did not bother with a boson's chair to sit in. Instead, he often sat in a loop of chain attached to the end of the passline. Sitting in a chain like that even for a few minutes can be excruciating on the hip bones if one is not set just right and, besides that, it cuts off circulation to the legs.

A few days later, just before lunch, Sam asked old Curmudgeon if he would haul him up the tree in the passline. Old Curmudgeon's answer was "No." Sam pestered and pestered until the chaser who was old Curmudgeon's brother, said, "Do it and teach him a lesson." So, later, at noon, into the passline chain went Sam and slowly up the tree he went, using his feet to kick out from the tree as necessary. Old Curmudgeon hauled him up carefully, not knowing if Sam would panic because from only fifty feet up in the spar tree it looks one hell of a long way down. Also, Sam did have to pass by intermediate guy wires that he could have gotten tangled in. Sure enough, about fifty feet up Sam hollered to come down and we all thought we knew why. The chain was probably pinching his ass. Old Curmudgeon set the brake on the passline drum, put the damper down, grabbed his lunch box and sat down to eat, along with the rest of us. Sam continued hollering for the next few minutes as we chatted and ate.

At last old Curmudgeon got up, released the brake on the passline drum and slowly lowered Sam to the ground. Two men were standing, ready to grab Sam as he touched the ground and for good reason. Sam could not stand up and he was sobbing like a baby from the pain. He laid at the foot of the spar tree for some time, trying to rub circulation back into his legs. Eventually he got up and staggered away. I know that the men felt sorry for Sam, including old Curmudgeon. However, they were also hoping, but not betting, that Sam would soon start to develop better judgment, for danger in the woods was everywhere.

Not long after this incident old Curmudgeon was hauling in a difficult turn of logs consisting of several long (about eighty foot) boomsticks. He pulled them right up to the bottom of the tree and had them standing on end, prior to lowering the rigging and letting them settle into more or less stable positions. Mike

Monks, old Curmudgeon's brother, was chasing. His job was to run out to the logs and release the chokers so that old Curmudgeon could send the rigging back out to the chokermen for another turn of logs. This job, like most in the woods, can be dangerous. Logs, especially on a cold deck pile, often will appear to be solidly fixed when they are not. Constant vigilance is necessary. This particular time, as the turn of boomsticks appeared to be settled, Mike went out to unhook them. As I watched him release the knobs from the bells and straighten up, one of the boomsticks started to roll toward him. Ordinarily this should not have been a problem, as Mike had plenty of time to jump clear. A little fast foot work and he would be back alongside the donkey trying to pull my leg about something or other. Mike was much more outgoing than his brother (Johnny) old Curmudgeon. Mike's boot heel caught on a knot or thick piece of bark, as he skipped backward away from the approaching log. He went down on his back. I watched helplessly with his brother, as the boomstick rolled over Mike's legs and onto his belly, where it came to rest. The boomstick had to be rechoked in order to lift it off Mike. I admired the calm of old Curmudgeon, as he had to do it very carefully. Mike was rolled onto the stretcher that is carried on the back of all donkey machines and quickly transported away. Within a few hours he was on his way to the Vancouver General Hospital. We all heard later that he had a broken pelvis, but would recover. I never saw Mike after that. Old Curmudgeon, however, continued at his controls of the donkey.

The following summer I heard from the new chaser on the steam pot that my old friend Windy had showed up in camp the previous fall to take over my job as fireman. Windy, as he was still called, apparently had somewhere in the intervening years gone "hippie." They told me that he dressed strangely, had clothing covered with cloth badges and patches and wore a cloth rag around his forehead like Tonto out of the *Lone Ranger*. As the story goes, in the middle of the afternoon one day, a procession of Natives, all dressed up in their bright ceremonial regalia, filed by the steam pot with a coffin on their shoulders. They were conducting a very important funeral ceremony. A short while later, old Curmudgeon noticed that steam pressure was down drastically and went to check the firebox. The fire was almost out and Windy, the fireman, was nowhere in sight. Later, they learned that the Indian funeral procession had somehow mesmerized him and he helplessly followed them, joining in their ceremony. Windy was encouraged to leave camp, and that was the last anyone knows of him.

The Steam Donkey

I have no way of knowing how old the steam donkey was in 1947. Technologically speaking, however, at that time, steam power was being replaced by diesel "yarders" up and down the B.C. coast.

Gildersleeve Logging continued to use the steam pot for yarding and cold-decking purposes at the Tallheo Point operation up through 1949. Today the old Gildersleeve steam donkey rests silently in the woods near the beach about ten miles south of Bella Coola. Antique collectors have long-since cannibalized the old machine of most of its peripheral hardware. The large steam whistle of solid brass was among the first items to be taken. The 500-gallon steel water tank disappeared soon after and all manners of control gauges have also vanished.

The spruce sled upon which the donkey frame rests is all but rotted away and likely would not tolerate even a short move to the beach. Strangely, the shed roof that protects the machinery from rain, snow, falling branches, cones and leaves is in excellent condition, as if it was only a few years old. The machinery itself, being covered long ago in a heavy layer of grease and oil, bears little or no rust and so might be serviceable still if the boilers could be rebuilt. There it rests on its rotten sled, slumbering quietly under a sparse canopy of coniferous growth. It is a silent sentinel in representation of old-growth forests, when steam power at one time was king.

Sam Reading

I discovered quite by accident one afternoon that Sam, for all of his brawny, tough appearance and macho attitude, could not read even simple copy with any confidence.

Once Sam was aware that I knew he could not read, he admitted his problem. I offered to help him if he was willing to work at it. Every day after work for weeks, we would sit in an empty bunkhouse with stacks of pulp magazines around us. As I remember, they were discarded Rangeland Romances. For the first week or two Sam sat, open book on his knees, following the print with his finger and sounding out words like a second grader. As a matter of fact, I believe that Sam had learned to read at a second- or third-grade level where his reading education must have ended. Somehow he had forgotten this early skill. At any rate, after only a few weeks, with some coaching and encouragement from me, Sam was reading aloud, his confidence building every day. Soon the meaning of many simple words became a problem for him. Hence, I showed him how to look up words in a dictionary. It wasn't long before Sam would do nothing else in his spare time but read. His new-found talent had opened a whole new world for him. Many times after supper I would suggest to him that we go do a little cod fishing. However, Sam, now, was far more interested in getting back to his stories. I have thought of Sam many times over the years and wondered if his learning to read may have subdued his excessive macho outlook.

The Cave

During that summer of 1947, whenever I had the opportunity of an evening, I would visit an old Indian lady. She was the grandmother of a young girl who was a friend. Other kids and one or two adults, sometimes, would join the group. The old lady would tell us stories of Indian lore until well after dark. A number of her tales related strange experiences concerning her sons and a mountain peak that stood close by the area. The mountain peak we all could see appeared to have a large cave near its top. The old lady claimed that no white man had ever gone to that cave and come back alive, or dead for that matter. Holding my left arm outstretched in front, thumb up using it like a gun sight, my thumbnail appeared to be about the same size as the cave mouth in question. As the crow flies, I judged the cave mountain peak to be around ten miles away. Simple trigonometry shows that the cave mouth must be 500 feet across.

My grandfather also told me a story of this cave he had heard from a good friend who spoke of yellow metal. Apparently, gold ore was found there by an old Indian and he gave it to my grandfather's friend. The friend asked the Indian where he had found it and he answered, "The cave on the mountain." Subsequently, Grandfather's friend made a trip up this mountain to the cave. When they got into the cave they had no light to see, so one of their number threw several rocks ahead of their position into the cave. They claimed that they never heard any of them hit bottom. The group returned and never went back. (Apparently at least one white man did make it back.)

After hearing stories like the above, I was champing at the bit to go see for myself. The only team that I could come up with was Keaton and my cousin John Roger Gildersleeve. We decided that on Labor Day weekend we would climb the mountain to the cave. Friday evening after dinner, Uncle Frank agreed to take the three of us in a camp boat over to the shoreline where we decided we should start. As I was leaving my grandmother's house, she handed me a large piece of cooked liver wrapped in wax paper and suggested I could eat it as a snack along the way. I quickly folded it in half and slipped it into my back pocket. Foolishly we took very little food with us, as we planned to be gone only two days and two nights. If need be, we figured we would shoot a grouse or two. Since it was still hot and humid in early September, we also decided to take only one blanket for the three of us. Thus, we had only one small packsack that we would carry in turn. It contained our food and blanket for the trip. We planned to hit the beach about 7:00 P.M. on a Friday evening, climb until dark, then camp for the night. At first light around 4:30 A.M. we would climb to the top of the mountain, locate the direction to the cave, hike to it, reconnoiter it and be back on the beach by Sunday night.

The route we had chosen to get to the top we thought to be the shortest route. It also was a near-vertical climb in brush so thick that we had to crawl under it. There was crawling room, but then our rifles would snag on branches and force us to back up. It seemed as if we had to give up a foot for every two feet we went ahead. Since I was the youngest man in the party by at least eight years, I was elected to be the first to carry the packsack. That was okay by me. Early on I was at my physical strongest. Later, when I was pooping out, one of the others hopefully would take it. Roger and Keaton were always ahead of me and by the sounds of their groans and heavy breathing, were not having any better time of it than I was.

That first evening we climbed steadily for about three hours when we found a small trickle of water spilling from some over-head rocks. The rock ledge at that point was wide enough to make camp on so we called a halt for the night. We had preorganized the necessary camping duties. I was to get a fire going. Keaton was to rustle up water and make tea and Roger was to cut hemlock boughs for our common bed. I soon had a small fire going and was thinking how great tea was going to taste after that weary climb. By now it was getting dark and away from the fire it was difficult to see anything. Keaton stumbled over to the fire holding the packsack to the light searching around in it. He then shot a frantic look at me and asked, "Where's the tea?" and before I could answer, "and the sugar and the coffee?" Jumping up to grab the packsack, it was my turn to fumble around in its bottom, but sure as heck none of it was there. The tea, coffee and sugar were gone. We both stood speechless, as Roger stepped into the light of the fire, dragging a huge pile of hemlock boughs. He promised that on the bed he was making for us, we were going to sleep "better than kings on goose down." We told him there was no tea, or coffee, or sugar—somehow it was lost. Roger looked stunned, threw down his pile of boughs and sat on them.

"Well I'll be hornswoggled," he said, "don't that beat all; no tea, eh, lost, how could it be lost?" They both looked at me since I was carrying the packsack.

"If you ask me," I said, "we forgot to put it in, it was never packed."

A brisk discussion followed on who forgot to pack the tea, but then it was quietly dropped. We all knew that getting upset wasn't going to help. After a while Roger went over to the small stream of water and filled his cup. He took a great gulp, roaring out loud, "Son-of-a-gun, that water's good, you guys better try some." The water was cool and wet, which was the main thing, and we drank plenty. Roger now acted somewhat more indifferent about our "goose down bed," and was tossing the boughs into a loose pile of brush. The three of us laid down on it, our feet toward the fire under the one wool blanket with our boots for pillows. After a few minutes Roger yawned and asked, "Well, what do you say, guys, pretty damned comfortable, don't you think?" Roger got no definite reply from us, just a couple of recognizable grunts. Actually, the bough bed was bearable only for the first five minutes. The twigs jabbing my thighs and back or cutting off the circulation to my arm made me realize that this could be the granddaddy of worst sleepless nights spent in my entire fifteen years.

After a spell of trying to wiggle a comfortable hollow in our wilderness mattress, which I now visualized as the bed from hell, I spoke to Roger and Keaton with a half hearted, "You guys awake?" I got only groans for answers and was sure that their heavy breathing was faked. Suddenly there was a roar, accompanied by brilliant light. All three of us sprang upright in time to see Keaton's nylon jacket flare into oblivion. "I thought you guys were asleep," I said mockingly.

"Yeah, well I was," groaned Roger.

"Yeah, so was I," echoed Keaton.

Bull, I thought, and contemplated moving my bed to a flat rock with mossy covering I had noticed nearby. Since there was only one blanket, I decided to stay put.

The fire was about gone now and it was black as pitch. Soon I heard something big and heavy sounding moving around in our camp. After a while I realized that it had to be packrats. The amount of noise they made was surprising, like they were all wearing caulk shoes. First light came about 4:00 A.M. We got up and for the first few minutes attempted to unbend ourselves and beat the bloodflow back into our extremities. Since we had no tea or anything else to brew, we dispensed with a fire even though it was quite chilly. I never could tell who had my third of the blanket we were supposed to share, but it wasn't me.

We chewed some canned meat, washed it down with cold water and decided to move out. Up we headed. After a couple of hours climbing almost straight up over sharp rocks and thorny underbrush, my legs began to give out. The other two got quite a distance ahead of me. I was still carrying the packsack, plus my grandfather's large postcard camera and my rifle. I sat down to rest for a few minutes and shortly Keaton came back looking for me. He also rested while we chatted.

We resumed climbing and had gone a short distance when I realized I had left my grandfather's treasured camera laying on a rock. We both went back to search for it but could not locate where I had left it. Finally we had to give it up. This was a terrible blow to me. How would I be able to tell Grandfather? He had had that old Kodak postcard camera for years and had taken many wonderful photos with it—especially panorama pictures like the kind I was supposed to bring back from the top of this mountain. I was sick. The whole trip was ruined for me. I would rather have continued looking for the camera until we found it, than gone to the top of the mountain. Alas, I had to stay with the other two, so up we headed again.

A short while later we still had not found Roger and so we fired three shots. There was no answer. We kept on going and about half an hour later we broke out at timberline and found Roger sunning himself on a large boulder.

"Why didn't you answer our shots?" we asked.

"What shots? I didn't hear anything," he said.

The truth was that the underbrush was so thick and impenetrable near timberline that rifle shots from a distance of a few hundred yards below timberline were muffled and could not be heard. The view from that timberline position was breathtaking. However, as we took a good look around, we rapidly realized that we had made a very costly mistake. We had, in fact, climbed the wrong mountain.

From the channel at sea level we could not determine that the entrance to the cave we sought was high on the side of a distant valley beyond the mountain we had climbed. We could now see the cave clearly. It was slightly above our eye level at around 6,000 feet. To get to it, we would have to circle the mountain top we were on, descend about 2,000 feet, cross a narrow valley and climb up 3,000 feet or more to reach the mouth of the cave.

All three of us were now in such poor physical condition from our strenuous climb, not to mention a serious lack of food and drink and a night without sleep, that I figured we used good judgment in deciding not to proceed with our plan to reach the cave. The climb up to this point was much more difficult than we had expected. We did have some food left, which amounted to some moldy old army field rations. Opening the containers we found tinned butter and jam, plus cheese, crackers, chocolate and cigarettes. On close inspection, the butter was rancid, the cheese had metamorphosed into a scaly brown brick about the hardness of shale, the crackers were crumbled to dust in their cellophane wrappers, and the jam had gone to sugar. The solid bar of chocolate had turned white inside its wrapper, but we found it to be the only edible item in the entire pack. It too had gone brick hard and our teeth could not penetrate it. We had to smash it inside cloth like a piece of glass and then proceed to suck the chips. We foraged for whatever berries we could find but found them exceedingly scarce. Likewise there were no grouse of any kind. We shot a small bird with a rifle and found only its tiny legs remaining. Since we were not to meet Frank at the appointed sea level rendezvous till the following evening, we had the remainder of that day and night to spend on the mountain prior to starting down.

The weather was perfect for early September and there were no flies, so we decided to take our clothes off and hike around the top of the mountain in the nude. We found a small mountain pool about four feet deep of melted glacier water that was the color of azure blue. It looked extremely inviting until Roger stuck his toe in and found the temperature to be close to freezing. The rest of the afternoon we chose a huge flat rock that gave us a good view of the cave and sunbathed like three white sausages on a skillet. Later that evening we found ourselves a patch of thick heather and huddled together under our blanket, watching our small fire die out and feeling the cold creep in. That night was unspeakably miserable for us, due to the chill at 5,000 feet. We were up well before daylight, cold and wet from the mountain dew, stumbling around, flailing our arms at our bodies trying to beat the numbness out of our legs and rears. We decided not to head down the mountain until it was good and light, since the going was dangerous even in daylight. By now, we had been without significant food for over twenty-four hours. We were weaker than we realized from hunger and dehydration as well.

In patting my hip pocket before we started down, I discovered the folded piece of cooked liver my grandmother had given me as I left the camp two days before. The wax paper wrapping was gone, disintegrated. The liver was caked with mud and twigs, but we three eyed it like it was manna from heaven. I laid the liver on a smooth rock and carefully sliced it into small quarter-inch cubes. We then cut ourselves toothpick skewers and proceeded to spear a cube and eat, in rotation. Thus, we had our breakfast and lunch on the third day. Truthfully, the small amount of liver that each of us ate did little to assuage our appetites, but the ritual of eating something seemed to strengthen our resolve to make it to dinner that evening.

I have learned from hard experience that when heading back down a mountain that is unfamiliar, it is best to stick close to the route used in climbing up. The reason for this rule of thumb is that it will help to prevent some really nasty surprises. Because we were very fatigued, our judgment began to fail us. Roger found a route that seemed very easy going; he followed it and we followed him. We were aware that it was not the route we had used coming up, but the going was easy and we hoped it would work out.

We had descended about 1,000 feet when Roger, who was still leading, pushed through a dense hedge of scrub hemlock and literally stepped out into midair. He let out a yell and like a cat somehow twisted his torso around in time to grab the branches of a scrub hemlock as they were flashing by.

Roger had disappeared from our view, but we could hear him yelling. The terrain down to the scrub hemlock hedge where Roger had stepped through was quite steep, so Keaton and I made our way carefully down to the spot. Roger was now calling to us to be careful and to find good handholds because somehow we would have to pull him back. Keaton crawled on all fours down to the hedge and then, on his stomach, pushed his head and shoulders through it to where he could see Roger. I, too, was lying down, head toward the cliff and hanging onto Keaton's pantlegs. Roger was dangling by his arms over a 2,000-foot drop. We had looked at this particular bluff from the beach many, many times, but in our weakened states of mind, were not aware that the route we were taking coming down would lead us right to it.

Keaton managed to grab Roger by one of his arms and slowly Roger, with Keaton's help, pulled himself back up through the brush. The three of us sat around for a few minutes resting and joking about the close call; however, we all understood that we had made a serious mistake and it almost cost Roger his life. In addition, we had to laboriously climb back up, almost to our starting place that morning, in order to find the route we had used coming up the mountain.

Progress going down after that was very slow. We were not going to make any more costly mistakes. My legs would barely hold me up. If I stumbled, I fell and rolled and slid and crawled, not wanting to get back on my feet. The others were just as tired and we spent a lot of time resting. Around suppertime we were on the beach and had to wait only a few minutes before Frank was there to pick us up with the boat. When he drew into the beach with the boat and saw us he began to laugh. The three of us could barely stand up, let alone walk. I guess we looked pretty worn out.

We vowed on the beach that evening that we would return and reach the cave some day. We never did. The muscles in my legs were so spent that the next day I stayed in bed. I had food brought to me by my sisters. Roger and Keaton could not go to work and Roger had lost eight pounds, due to dehydration. I realize now that our loss of physical strength was not so much due to a lack of food as it was a lack of water. Foolishly, we carried no water bottles with us.

Twenty-five years later Keaton and I returned, in his Cessna 206. We had some difficulty locating the peak with the cave in it. We then discovered that because of the crowded mountain topography and dangerous flying conditions, we could not get close enough to get a really good look. The cave presumably has yet to be conquered by a white man. It appeared to us that the large dark spot at the peak of the mountain may not be a real cave but in reality a dark shadow caused by an enormous thick slab of rock that had fallen out. A much smaller and deeper cave could exist at the bottom of this huge rockfall, but alas, we did not see one. A party on foot would be necessary to find out for sure.

Mr. Moe

It was now the fall of 1947. I was close to sixteen. My sisters, mother and I all moved back to Ocean Falls so that we kids could continue our schooling.

It has always been my sense that the teachers employed by Pacific Mills and later by Crown Zellerbach, to teach in their school at Ocean Falls, were in the main good at their trade. Many of them are standouts in my memory: Miss Long, our music teacher; Mr. Nelson my seventh-grade teacher; Mr. Cochran the school science teacher. Mr. Bob Scott taught English literature and was also very active in developing high school sports; Mr. Moe was my teacher in grades nine and twelve. Then, of course, there was George A. Turner, the school principal. With his near skeletal physique, sharp face and deep set, piercing eyes, he managed tight control over his educational fiefdom. He ran a tight ship and ran it well.

The leather strap was still employed and used on those of us who managed to abuse the student-teacher relationship guidelines that Mr. Turner laid down. On a number of occasions, for being obnoxious, high school boys including yours truly were invited to the teacher's staff room where, with pants down, we were strapped on the fanny.

Beginning in the ninth grade, Mr. Moe took a peculiar interest in some of us boys. His curiosity it seemed was along the lines of documenting the growth and development of our physical bodies. For example, on occasion a few of us would accompany him to the teacher's staff room where he would use a tailor's cloth tape measure to record our chest, biceps, neck, waist and thigh measurements. The thigh measurement required dropping our drawers.

In junior high in 1946 and 1947 we were a pretty naive lot to say the least. We did not give Moe's interest in our thigh and waist measurements a second thought. By the time we left high school in 1949 all of us sensed that Mr. Moe's sexual persuasion may have been different from our own. He could have liked kangaroos for all I cared, so long as he didn't try to interest me in them and he didn't.

I remember Moe as a decent person. He had a positive and supportive personality, with a well-developed sense of humor that he shared with his students in a manner that enabled us to begin thinking of ourselves as adults. In retrospect, I believe that he was an excellent teacher.

To Tell the Truth

During one Ocean Falls winter and spring period, while I was attempting to master the ninth grade, I occasionally was employed by the Ocean Falls townsite authority. The real authority at that time manifested itself from beginning to end in the embodiment of Mr. Dwight Lee, who routinely rounded up several of us junior high school boys to tackle various odd jobs around the townsite that required someone's attention.

Mostly the jobs we were called upon to do could have been classified under the heading of aesthetic improvement. Typically, we hauled away ugly messes that others had left behind, such as building construction debris, remodeling residue or the gutted remains of a house fire. Other times we helped ready recreational areas for town celebrations or sporting events. We even painted equipment and buildings that were not too important. And we shoveled snow—lots of it. The task we were called upon to do quite frequently, and disliked the most, was one of clearing brush along the wooden walkways and plank roads that penetrated up, over and around the hills to all areas of the townsite.

Clearing brush is never an easy task and in 1944–45 we still had to rely on axes and hand saws for such a project. The ubiquitous chain saw and various other more modern brush-slashing equipment in use today was still waiting to be invented.

The brush in question consisted predominantly of young alder, salmonberry bushes and several species of thorny brush, including the honorable devil's club that thrived beneath the alder canopy. The alder trees commonly were about three to four inches in diameter or smaller and the salmonberry bush stalks often were an inch or better at ground level and grew in bunches six or eight feet in length. Attacking brush of this nature with an ax, we learned, was pretty close to the proverbial exercise in futility.

First of all, swinging an ax in brushy close quarters was a dangerous proposition. More often than not, as one took aim at a particular bushy stalk, the ax head encountered brush that seemed to be constantly in the way. Otherwise, if the ax swing ran true to the mark, often it shot back as if having struck a rubber tire. We learned, however, that we could successfully slice through these rubbery berry bushes with a pronounced downward ax slash at the trunk of the clump. Unfortunately, this tactic also drove the ax head firmly into the rocks, with plenty of sparks flying. We were careful not to use this successful technique while our boss Mr. Lee was around. On the other hand, I'm afraid that as adolescents we were not as careful as we might have been with company equipment. Actually, we finally resorted to the hand saws for the majority of brush cutting.

One memorable brush clearing episode took place over a period of several weekends. The rainfall in Ocean Falls averages around one hundred and fifty inches annually. It wasn't unusual, therefore, to be working weekends in the pouring rain. Most of us fifteen and sixteen year olds had not discovered gloves or probably could not afford them. We were paid thirty to forty cents an hour, which actually was pretty fair pay in those days for our brand of casual labor. Without gloves our tender palms were no match for the devil's club and other briar patches that we frequently encountered.

We also had inadequate rain clothing and after only a few hours on the job would be soaked through and shivering cold as the rain came down in sheets. However, we kept up our morale by regaling each other with corny juvenile jokes as we scrambled around in the mud and rocks, cutting, hauling and stacking the humongous piles of cleared brush that widened the roadway by several feet.

We were called the "Bum Boys." I have no idea where the name originated, but it certainly fit us as we appeared a motley, bedraggled-looking crew of six to eight boys.

Mr. Lee had a cardinal rule regarding tools: never be neglectful and leave any of them behind when leaving a job site. He had appointed me straw boss over the other boys and that authority he said included responsibility for all of our tools. He also insinuated that if tools came up missing I might have to reimburse the company for them.

Normally, I took responsibility seriously and made sure that we had all of our tools with us when we quit for the day. Nevertheless, after a grueling weekend of brush jumping, I did neglect to monitor our tools. When Mr. Lee noticed one of our axes missing, he asked me about it. For some inexplicable reason, I lied to him. Even though I knew I had forgotten the ax, I told him that we had searched thoroughly before coming in. I worried all week about my lie, fearing that he might himself go back and easily find it. That lie produced a lose-lose situation for me. If he found the ax easily, surely he would know I lied to him and my trustworthiness as far as he was concerned would be shot to hell. If anyone found the ax lying alongside the road and took it home that could mean that I might have to pay for it.

The following weekend we collected our tools minus "that ax" and got back to the job site. The first thing we did was scour the area for the missing ax, without success. It looked for certain now that someone had found and taken it.

I was not looking forward to seeing Mr. Lee that morning, but presently along he came in his brand new green 1945 company Ford pickup. Leaning out of the cab he wondered with a frown if I had found the missing ax yet. Nervously I looked him square in the eye and admitted that I had actually forgotten and left it behind the previous week and now someone must have found it and removed it because we searched thoroughly and it was gone. For a moment he just stared at me.

To my utter amazement, his scowl turned to a grin and reaching down, his hand came up with our ax.

"You sure as hell did forget and leave it," he said, still grinning. "I found it right after you guys left, stuck as big as life in that stump over there." He pushed the ax at me warning, "Let this be a lesson to you to take better care of your tools from now on."

I was still stunned as he drove off and was wondering if possibly he had lifted the ax from the stump even before we had quit work that fateful day. I wouldn't have put it past him. Nevertheless, I figured I had just learned two lessons: try to be more vigilant with responsibility; never compound a mistake with a lie or it will haunt you.

Keep It in Your Pants Stupid

As teenage boys in the late forties, we all carried a condom in our wallets. What for? Well, prestige among ourselves, mostly. What other good reason could we possibly have? All of us knew from talk via the grapevine that condoms were not really safe. That is, none of them could absolutely be counted on. For one reason or another they could sustain damage prior to use. Carrying one in one's wallet for months or even years, of course, was probably the absolute worst abuse a condom could have.

There was the fact (or so we believed) that by law all condom manufacturers must put a pin hole in the end of 20 percent of all condoms that were sold over the counter. This was easy for us numskulls to accept, for how else could the government be guaranteed of a rising population to sustain economic growth? Also, how about the need to produce more male babies to build armies and fight wars? In addition, the manufacturers even warned the public with fine print on their packaging that each condom needed to be blown up to insure its reliability.

Sure, can't you just see a potential Don Juan breaking the aura of the moment by suggesting to his already skeptical, if not anxious, sweetheart that she relax and think good thoughts while he blew up a balloon. Besides, after unrolling one of those critters, has anyone ever figured out how to roll one back up in the dark with one's pants around one's ankles. Give me a break. So there you have it, a double whammy, the fear factor, as well as the humiliation factor. Of course, no matter what one does regarding sexual activity, remember, there is always the ever-present fear of going blind. Blindness was foretold as automatic punishment where sexual indiscretions were concerned.

In my day, being found guilty of knocking up some nice young lass usually resulted in what is now regarded as an ancient and barbaric custom, having to marry the girl—thus forfeiting one's "opportunity" to investigate the mysteries of life prior to "writing that best-selling novel" or two. And believe me, in my day, you would surely have had to get married, no fooling about it.

The greatest mystery of all had been tampered with and now the genie was out of the bottle. The poor lass likely was the one to be pitied for allowing some pimple-faced clod into her pants. Yes, those were the days of comeuppance. Fathers were maniacal about such things as retribution and nearly all of them, where their daughters were concerned, were in agreement.

Today, fathers as well as mothers are so liberated that no one agrees on anything. The controls of using responsible restraint through fear of comeuppance are gone. There seems to be almost nothing anymore that is considered wrong relative to youthful sexual activity.

The telltale well worn ring in our wallets was, as I have said, mostly for boasting. Still, delusions of grandeur never escaped any of us boys as we set our eyes on some pretty young lass.

One unforgettable evening after a high school dance, misfortune of sorts struck one of my buddies. The never used only-for-show condom suddenly, unexpectedly, saw battle in the shadows of the tennis court out behind the school house.

The entire episode, as related to me, was a very hasty affair. Up went the skirt and down came the panties (no treacherous pantyhose then). Down came the trousers and on went the condom for a stand-up knee trembler. Wham, bam and it was all over. Up came the panties and trousers to rejoin the others so as not to arouse suspicion.

A short time later my friend, feeling very smug and pleased with himself, entered a washroom for the purpose of discarding his spent condom and was flabbergasted to discover that it had vanished. His humor also had vanished and was replaced by waves of panic. Desperately he dug around in his shorts for the missing rubber and danced around on his toes shaking his pantlegs, but it was gone. Further inspection of his penis showed that the sturdy condom ring was still firmly clamped in the appropriate place. No, why me, he thought to himself as more waves of panic descended upon him. The only other obvious place to have lost it was unthinkable, but that is where it was later found. Later, when she discovered this ghastly truth, she found that she could not get it out, and in her own emotional panic the following day sought help from her mother.

Her mother, bless her heart, who obviously was a very understanding woman, only suggested to her daughter that for the next few weeks to keep her fingers crossed, otherwise no telling what manner of idiocy her father was capable of. The father normally ate nails for breakfast. He had always allowed that if his daughter became pregnant, the boy responsible would fry in hell, after of course he personally beat the pulp out of him. Then, naturally, after all of that, the boy would have to marry his daughter. Not favorable prospects for my good buddy. He was now extremely depressed by worry. He lived in torment and terror for the next several weeks, continuously wringing his hands over his bad luck. Never once, however, did I ever hear him suggest that his predicament was not of his own making.

His pitiful situation was a perfect example to the rest of us for practicing restraint. My friend managed to live through the next few weeks till the all-clear signal was given. We all breathed a sigh of relief. Believe me, sharing experiences such as this one did more to promote celibacy among ourselves than anything else we could have imagined. "There but for the grace of God go I."

Murphy's Law

At the age of seventeen a young man's fancy very often turns to young women, whose fancy often turns to young men. My peers and I consumed hours of energy fantasizing ways in which one could be secretly alone with a girlfriend free of the embarrassment of being challenged by her parents, especially the father.

Most of us boys were capable of conjuring up schemes of daring-do, but only a few actually had the courage to attempt a real time scenario in order to capture the forbidden fruit. The beauty in one such plan was its utter simplicity and my friend was anxious to prove how easy it would be to pull it off.

One sultry evening in midsummer after her parents had departed for an extended evening of cards with friends, this young lass greeted my buddy at her back door. According to plan, he was waiting for her parents to leave, as she had alerted him to their evening agenda.

My friend brought along a few of his Nat King Cole and Frankie Lane records and for quite a while, they listened to music and danced. Later on she was showing him through the house and naturally they wound up in her boudoir.

On the bed and engaged in some serious necking, it shocked them when her parents came home long before they were expected. They came into the living room talking loudly and called to their daughter to locate where she was. She answered loudly that she had gone to bed. Satisfied that all was well, the parents decided to retire also.

Up the stairs they came and entered their bedroom near the head of the long stairway. After a few moments the mother popped into her daughter's room to say goodnight. She sat on the bed, gave her daughter a hug and kiss, and left.

At the first instant of hearing voices downstairs, my friend nervously crawled under the bed and began praying that they could not hear his heart pounding or his raspy breathing.

After what seemed a long while, he could hear quiet breathing coming from the parents' room. At this signal he slithered from under the bed and crawled over to the open doorway, lying there for some time wondering what to do next. While he lay there on the floor, shoes in hand, the girl watched him but said and did nothing. It was like a bad dream, a nightmare, like none of this was real. Finally he made his move. He slowly, carefully, stood upright in stocking feet, took a deep breath and stepped out into the hallway, pausing there an instant before continuing past the entrance to the parents' room, where he would be in full view of anyone looking.

With each cautious step the floor squeaked unmercifully. Reaching the top of the long stairway leading down, he was again in full view of the parents' room. It was then that a loud male voice from that room challenged him, asking him who he was, and from other sounds my friend deduced that the voice was coming to find out.

Up to that point my buddy had congratulated himself on his degree of self control, but now it appeared that an eyeball to eyeball confrontation was imminent. "The jig was up," as they say and he decided to run for it. Down the stairs he flew, bounding over several treads at a leap. Suddenly, he was at the bottom of the stairs and, feeling the cool evening breeze brushing his face from the open door directly in his path, he headed for it without breaking stride.

What transpired in the next several seconds of this amazing incident are not perfectly clear to me, as they were not at all clear to my friend who experienced it. Piecing his bizarre story together from his confused memory the following day, while he massaged many cuts and bruises, I do believe that this is what happened.

In my friend's extreme haste to escape through the open doorway, he failed to realize that he was looking through a fine-mesh screen door. Impacting the screen door with a full stand up body blow, he carried it completely off its hinges and still in full stride, shot across the short verandah, wearing the screen door like a suit of armor, and struck the hip-high railing of the porch while still traveling full tilt. Though his hips and lower extremities were stopped cold by the porch railing, his upper body continued to propel itself over the railing and into the dark. In so doing, the rigid screen door frame pivoted neatly on the railing, catapulting my friend out into the inky blackness and down into the salmonberry bush-covered rocky ravine about twelve to fifteen feet below. Somehow, inadvertently, he managed to stay glued to the screen door as it spun through the air and the two struck the dense brush below in a manner where the door and brush cushioned the impact. He lay there stunned on his screen door bier. Looking up through the tangled mass of thorny brush he saw the father, with the porch light behind him, gazing down into the dark abyss, presumably wondering where he had gone. The father said nothing. My friend was also silent.

Eventually the father went back inside, but my friend was certain he heard an amused guffaw as the door was closing after him. A long time later he crawled and stumbled away, amazed and thankful that every bone in his body was not broken.

There is no important moral to this story except that most seventeen year olds have not yet "peed on enough snow" to be familiar with Murphy's most famous law that states, "If something can go wrong, it will."

Strange Proposition

One day in Ocean Falls when I was seventeen, and heading into the local hotel coffee shop, I was approached by a friend of my stepfather. He mentioned that he was on his way up to his room and invited me to join him in a bottle of beer. Since he was a good friend of family members, I saw no harm in his invitation and went along with him.

As soon as we were inside his room on the third floor, however, I began to have bad vibes and had to ask myself why I was there. He opened two bottles of beer and, handing me one, invited me to sit on the bed. Indeed, there was no other furniture to sit on. Soon, too soon, I thought, he wanted to know about how I was getting along with the high school girls. I recall being both surprised and embarrassed at his sudden personal line of questioning.

Without warning his hand went to my leg and with eye contact he said, "You know Jim, girls can be very dangerous, they can get you into a lot of trouble. There are other ways to get the same pleasure and satisfaction..." I was 100 percent sure of his motives at that point. The stiffening hair on the back of my neck was my red flag and it spelled trouble.

I broke off eye contact, slowly set my beer on the floor, stood erect and headed for the door. At most the door was ten feet away, yet it seemed like a journey without end. Time seemed to be frozen. I recall focusing on the stainless steel door knob and I thought to myself, "What if the door is locked?" Instantly, I felt a strange sensation of power, as if I had grown much larger. I had full confidence that I could rip the door down if need be. Suddenly, the metal knob was in my hand and it turned easily. The door opened and shut again with a sharp click. I strode to the elevator ready to engage anyone who would stop me. No one appeared. Soon I was outside sucking in fresh air seeking a quiet place to regain my composure, for suddenly I was shaking.

Whistlepunk—Chokerman

In the spring of 1948 the Gildersleeve Logging Co., Ltd. was moved out of Rivers Inlet, north, once again, to South Bentinck Arm and a place called Tallheo Point.

I was seventeen that summer when I arrived in camp. My shoulders had precious little muscle on them and wrestling rigging blocks around was not my idea of fun. Our sixty-five-pound tail block must have been designed by the Spanish Inquisition. It had no smooth, flat spots on it where they were needed in order to hoist it to one's shoulder in comfort. It had only sharp protrusions that ground into my bony frame. Whenever I had to move the block, it was like an adversarial encounter. I stared at it with hate and it stared back. The pulley inside of the cast-iron frame formed the steel lips of a hideous grin. I was barely strong enough in a half crouch to flip the block from the ground to my shoulder. This procedure, however, was only moderately successful. Much of the time I miscalculated on technique, and the block upon reaching my shoulder would tear flesh and bone as it continued on its way over my shoulder, falling back to the ground.

This particular day we were moving the rigging into an area of very large newly felled spruce trees. Large spruce limbs were piled so thick and high that we had to negotiate our way over them about ten feet off the ground. Granddad had instructed me to hang the tail block onto a certain tree. To comply, I had to walk a large, crooked spruce limb high over a tangled mass of broken branches. Halfway across I lost my balance and down into the punji spears went the block. I purposely gave it the heave ho. I was not going down there with it. Unfortunately, Granddad looked back as I was dumping the block, and by the scowl on his face he must have thought I was doing it for kicks. The fact that I might have been skewered like shish kabab meat if I had fallen into that hole with the block seemed of no moment to him. He gave me his "now why the hell did you do that frown," ungloved his right hand, removed his battered Stetson and scratched his head, as if to say, "They just don't make seventeen-year-olds the way they used to." The worst part of it was that he was deaf as a post without his hearing aid, which he rarely wore. Communicating probable cause of events to him after the fact never seemed to work well, either.

Prior to graduating to the job of chokerman, which gave me the dubious opportunity of lugging rigging blocks around the hillsides, I began on the rigging crew as a whistlepunk, the lowest position on the rigging crew's "spar pole." The men would kid me each morning when I headed out away from them to a lonely stump "perch" somewhere on the hillside. "Hey, kid," they would say, "that's not a job you've got, that's a position." I was aware that all of them had blown whistles at one time or another and they knew how deadly boring the job could be.

The duty of a whistlepunk had not changed much over the years. Basically, it amounted to relaying signals. The chokermen

217

hooked up the logs scattered in the brush to the rigging system. In doing so they often required adjustments made to the lines; such as, go ahead slow, come back slow, slack the haulback, etc. The hooker shouted signals to the whistlepunk, who in my day relayed a signal via electric wire to a horn on the donkey machine. Back in the 1940s, whistlewire was still being used. It was not uncommon for the whistlepunk to have to drag around hundreds of feet of wire in order to reach a position of vantage where he was close enough to hear and possibly see the chokermen at work. The whistlepunk had to be vigilant and stay clear of all moving lines, especially the haulback line that frequently ran along the ground when the rigging was at rest. When the rigging was under power, either pulling logs into the landing or hauling the rigging back out to the chokermen, the haulback usually whipped around dangerously and could throw large broken slabs or tree limbs into the air, to come down who knows where. My stepfather's young brother, Jim Gadsden, was killed by just such a tree limb when blowing whistles at our camp in Moses Inlet in 1937. He was seventeen.

The whistlepunk, due to the nature of the terrain, often had to assume a position where he could not see the chokermen and had to rely solely on his hearing. I recall such a time, and being seventeen, I was nervously straining to hear signals, when a raven sitting in a nearby tree decided to clear his throat. I took it to be a single "ho," from the hooker (meaning "go ahead" on the mainline). The instant I squeezed the "bug" I knew I had erred and just as fast I canceled the signal. I waited for all manner of verbal abuse to roar at me from beyond the hill, but none came. Luckily I had canceled fast enough that the engineer hadn't time to move the rigging and so no reprisals were taken.

False signals were not at all uncommon. The whistle wire itself got old, and when the insulation cracked, often a short would occur and cause an erroneous signal. This situation could be highly dangerous since a single toot of the horn at the appropriate time could mean "go ahead on her." Visualize that a chokerman could be laying half under a log at that moment. They don't call logging a dangerous occupation for nothing.

The whistlepunk's main tool in my day was a switch called a "bug." It was nothing more than a hand-sized pair of "deadman" contacts that closed a circuit when squeezed and opened on release of palm pressure. Two leads from the whistle wire were attached to the exposed wing nuts about one inch apart at the bottom of the spring loaded "bug." Mild shocks were an everyday affair from carelessly brushing one's hand across the two contacts. Another and rather more insidious problem occurred when it was raining hard and everything, including the whistlepunk, was sopping wet, inside and out, and especially the palms of one's hands. At times like this, squeezing the "bug" was much like playing Russian roulette; now you get jolted, now you don't. Take it from me, a good wet contact grounded with twelve volts stiffens one's hair like nothing else. I carried a large roll of friction tape in an attempt to defuse electric shocks but when everything got wet I never quite eliminated them.

Andy Torkelson, camp superintendent and woods boss, also known to me as "Macho Man," would spend a fair amount of time daily with the rigging crew, especially if they were green and needed instruction at "choking" logs, and how to move clear and away from possible danger. One sunny day the chokermen had completed their task of "choking" (hooking up) two large fir peelers. On Andy's instructions, they had moved clear, while he remained standing on top of one of the logs with his hand lazily grasping the butt rigging shackles. Can you imagine my surprise when he glanced up to where I stood well in the clear and hollered "ho." Of course I did nothing, whereupon he stiffened himself and, still looking at me, hollered "ho" once again. Still I did nothing and he began cursing and shouting at me, asking if I was deaf, as he dismounted from the log and moved toward the other men. I thought that he must have been grandstanding for the men, but to this day I don't really know what he was thinking. Eventually, I sent in the signal and away went the "turn" to the landing.

The next "turn" was ready to go. Andy did the same as before; he gave me the "go ahead" signal while he was loitering on the logs, gazing around as if he was waiting at the old Birks clock site at the corner of Georgia and Granville streets in Vancouver, B.C. I saw that he had a clear, unobstructed path off the end of the log to get clear and I popped his signal into the donkey before he could even think "Jack Robinson." The logs took off like gangbusters. So did Andy. His short banty legs were pumping like revved up pistons on the old steam pot. He never quite made the end of the log before it began to lift into the air and Andy was propelled head over heels into the puckerbrush. When he finally staggered to his feet (Andy was well past fifty at this time) brushing himself off, he was looking at me with a glare. Not then, not later, did he ever say a word to me about it. In retrospect, I realize that I did a foolish thing. Andy could have been seriously hurt. He knew that I could see him. I should have waited until he got clear even if it took all day and resulted in more tongue lashing for me.

Dead for an Hour

One particularly hot and humid morning in the summer of 1948, another chokerman named Al and myself were making our way up a steep log with lunch boxes in hand. We were headed for the machine where we would sit in the shade and eat. Suddenly, in front of me, Al pitched forward and fell headfirst into a deep brushy hole about twelve feet below. I yelled at the machine operator and climbing down, found Al unconscious. We carried him up onto the machine sled and laid him on a stretcher. The machine operator, an older fellow, ran off to get help. Soon the woods boss, Andy Torkelson, came by and, kneeling beside Al with his hand on Al's neck, looked me squarely in the eye and said, "This man is dead." Andy then got a blanket from the back of the machine and drew it over the body.

I was astonished by this sudden event and hardly knew what to think. Nevertheless, seventeen-year-old boys need to eat and so, when Andy left to get help, I sat down beside the blanketed victim and nervously opened my lunch bucket. I had sunk my teeth into a huge beef sandwich with raw onions and was just about to get control of the mass, when I heard strange moaning sounds. I looked around and seeing nothing unusual, continued chewing. Suddenly the blanket over the "dead man" was moving. Then I heard more moaning. If there had been anyone else present, they could have knocked my eyeballs off with a stick. Dead men don't groan and certainly don't move. I jumped over and threw back the blanket. This man was not acting dead and was foaming at the mouth like he had swallowed a can of Burma Shave. His knees were raised tight against his chest. I remember pushing his knees down and his torso and head popped up. I pushed his head down and like a rocking horse his knees popped up again. He was rigid as rigor mortis could have made him. I could not straighten him out. There was so much foamy saliva spilling from his mouth that I had no success in putting a stick across his jaws, thinking to prevent him from swallowing his tongue.

About this time the woods boss came back on the dead run, bringing the first-aid man. Both were perplexed to find the victim alive and in convulsions rather than dead. After they carried him away, I was confused and shaky, but resumed eating my lunch. I needed strength and the way things were going there was no telling what the afternoon would bring. Later that evening I learned that Al had a history of epilepsy. According to workman's compensation rules, he should never have been employed in the woods. Amazingly, falling twelve feet and landing on his head did not injure him. Like a miracle, he recovered quickly, and left camp shortly thereafter. Apparently the exceptional heat of that particular day triggered his attack.

Skyline Crash

Not more than a week or two after the above incident, Andy Torkelson, Grandfather and I were standing together near the trackside cold deck spar tree. They were looking up at the skyline rigging that stretched back 1,800 feet to the rising sidehill several hundred feet above where we stood. The skyline was steel cable two inches or better in diameter and had a large carriage hung from it that was pulled in with the main line and out with the haulback. The butt rigging was hung from the carriage and included four long chokers that reached out to the sides of the

221

skyline road. The three of us stood there watching as the steam donkey engineer fought a "hang-up." That "turn" of logs had probably jackknifed behind some stumps. The old steam pot had tremendous power and it took skill on the part of the engineer not to tear up the rigging with the awesome force he had at his fingertips. Nevertheless, on this day, the strain on the skyline system was too much. The skyline tailhold stump at the back end, 1,800 feet away and up the sidehill, gave way. The entire skyline system and carriage crashed to the ground with a screaming snarl of whipping, slashing and coiling steel cable.

Andy Torkelson, who had rigged the system, knew instinctively what was happening, even before I realized anything was wrong. I heard a loud report like a cannon shot. A heavy blow to my shoulders put my knees to the ground and my face snorkeling into the mossy dirt. Suddenly, the air a few feet above our heads was filled with the slicing steel tentacles of a descending skyline cable gone mad, flailing about in giant circles and coiling itself at tremendous velocity and power into a monstrous spring. I suffocated on the sour odor of sweat from the heavy body on top of me and I could not move. Gradually, the pressure on my back relaxed. I raised my head slightly, snorting the dirt and moss from my nostrils and mouth. I saw that Grandfather also had his head plowed into the dirt and he had not moved a muscle. It was then that I realized I had a huge arm around my neck and so did Grandfather. Andy knew what was happening. Without regard for himself, he grabbed the two of us in hammerlocks pitching the three of us forward onto our faces with him on top holding us motionless.

Presently, Andy, sensing that everything had stopped moving, jumped up, giving us a slap to do the same. I got up slowly, and Grandfather staggered to his feet, a little shaken but managing a grin.

The bight, or looped end, of the two-inch skyline cable lay not thirty feet from us spun into a cork screw coil about twenty feet across. Granddad and Andy, realizing the seriousness of this breakdown, certainly were not happy about it. However, since there was not a single person hurt in the incident, everyone felt pretty good and there was a lot of handshaking, back slapping and general congratulating at being alive.

A few weeks later Andy asked me what I planned to do after high school. He wondered if I was interested in learning the rigging trade and becoming a high rigger (his understudy). He surprised me by asking. I was old enough and six feet tall, but of a slight frame. I suggested to him that I did not have the physique for such an occupation. He replied that size was not the key thing and, pointing to his forehead, he said the main aspect of being a good rigger "is up here." He asked me to think it over.

Students

In late September of 1948 I returned to Ocean Falls to resume my education and entered the twelfth and final year of high school.

My male classmates in the twelfth grade class that year were Leo Portelance, Allen Gilchrist, Ron Robinson, George Davies, Barry (whose last name I have forgotten), Roger Killin and Sid Fosdick. I don't know what they did over the summer months while I was off logging. Some may have worked in the pulp and paper mill. The female students were Maureen Brown, Beryl Vanatter, Katherine Mackay, Rosa Spence, Doreen Wheaton, Donna McLeod, and Doreen Miller.

Allen Gilchrist, Leo Portelance and Jim Portelance were British Empire Games class swimmers, as were other kids from Ocean Falls, and they may have spent their summers either training for swim meets or traveling away from Ocean Falls to compete in them.

Leo Portelance tragically drowned a year or so after high school graduation in a bizarre boating accident at Powell River. Allen Gilchrist later swam in the Olympics for Canada, as did Lenora Fisher, another swimmer from Ocean Falls.

Bucker

In the spring of 1949 I wrote my final high school exams and received my university entrance diploma. Soon I was back at Gildersleeve Logging which was still operating at Tallheo Point.

I had never answered Andy Torkelson's question regarding whether or not I was interested in becoming his understudy at learning the rigging trade. I have no doubt that my silence on the matter was all the answer that he needed. Although flattered by Andy's invitation, I felt that I was not equipped either physically or with the proper mental attitude to be a good logger.

That summer logs were being dumped into the salt chuck at a pretty fast clip, producing a serious need to sort and stow logs into flat rafts in preparation for towing to Ocean Falls.

There were many large spruce trees at Tallheo Point. Normally these logs were cut into forty-foot lengths prior to their trip to the beach. However, many were still ninety feet and longer upon reaching salt water.

The scale calculated on a sound log at that time (in thousands of board feet) was its overall length times the diameter of its smallest end. The difference in ends of those spruce "sticks" was as much as two feet. Grandfather introduced me to a six-foot crosscut saw and instructed me to buck them into shorter logs precisely where he would mark them. I gazed upon what looked to me like acres of huge spruce logs all floating and tightly stowed so that there was little danger of losing equipment overboard.

Power saw technology had not advanced in 1949 to where they were in general use. One hundred percent of falling and bucking at Gildersleeve Logging was still done with hand equipment. The company, however, did employ a full-time saw filer, so there was no shortage of sharp saws.

On average, the cuts were made through about four feet of spruce log, a few larger and some smaller. My first few days working with the crosscut saw seemed interminable. Bending over to operate the saw for hours on end was something I had to get used to. Initially I spent a lot of time straightening up to unkink my back muscles and clear the sweat out of my eyes. Once in a while one of the booming crew would drift over to see how I was doing and provide me with some moral support.

Since I was working close to the camp and the cookhouse, I walked in for lunch and consumed enough food for at least two men. Back to work after a half-hour lunch break, I would resume sawing up those giant logs.

One day after watching me handle the saw for a while, Granddad came over to me and asked me to step aside. He said, "You know Jim, like most everything else, there is a right way and a wrong way to using a saw like this. Here, let me show you what I mean." With those words he proceeded to point out, by demonstrating with the saw, how a lot of energy is lost "fighting" the saw. He demonstrated how not to attempt to force the saw through the cut in an effort to speed up the process. "If the saw teeth are correctly sharpened and set, they will do most of the work for you," he said. "Don't try to yank the saw through the cut; just take it slow and smooth and let the saw fall of its own weight. You, the operator, are mainly clearing the sawdust from the cut by manipulating the saw back and forth." He continued, "Once a fellow gets the hang of it, sawing can become a real pleasure, even artful, like it's not real work any more."

When Granddad left, with a smile on his face, I went back to work. Thinking about his short lecture on the use of the saw, it all sounded pretty simple and obvious, but after all, wasn't that exactly what I had been doing all along? Was he pulling my leg about getting so good with the saw that it became a pleasure and wasn't real work any longer? My aching back suggested otherwise. Nevertheless, as I worked, I began to visualize the saw's cutting teeth scoring the wood at the bottom of the cut on both sides of the kerf, and the rakers slicing or shaving off that pass of the cutters and rolling it up to kick it out as long fibrous fingers of sawdust with each reciprocating motion of the saw. I began to see clearly that any attempt at forcing the saw to cut faster would likely result in the teeth gouging, causing jamming and indeed creating more work.

After a few more weeks had passed, I felt myself becoming much more confident and sophisticated in the use of the saw. I began to notice that I was now completing cuts without a single jam and the work definitely was easier. How much of this change could be attributed to the fact that I was also becoming stronger, I have no idea. Now, however, I was constantly examining the sawdust and became quite critical of its appearance. Long specimens (sawdust) generally meant that the saw was working well. Once in a while a particular saw seemed to drag and stick, unlike other saws that I had recently been using. I got so that I questioned whether the teeth were "set" properly and in my opinion, if a certain saw worked too hard, I carried it back to the filing shack and discussed it with the filer. Usually, he told me that I was full of bologna and that the saw was just fine, except that he always gave me another one that to my way of thinking worked much better. I never did achieve that "hallowed" level of proficiency, however, where sawing ceased to be work.

Most good days I would make four or five cuts in those huge logs, thereby increasing the amount of board-foot scale appreciably. I felt that I was earning my wages and then some. I was being paid six dollars a day or seventy-five cents an hour, and very happy to get it. (A hired man doing the same job would likely have been paid at least two times more. But as I was part of the family....) I was lucky that I did not have to pay room and board, since I ate enough to keep two or three men going, and yet I hardly gained a pound.

One very hot afternoon I had just completed a cut and had put the saw aside to decide on the next cut. Grandfather indicated where cuts were to be made by a caulk shoe score mark in the thin spruce bark. The marks were quite easy to see, so there was no problem with that. The next mark was scored fully under a swifter (log) that was placed across the spruce logs and chained at both ends to prevent the raft from spreading. There was no way that I could get my six-foot crosscut saw into position to cut where it was indicated. I had not encountered this particular situation before, so I "scared up" a peavey and attempted to roll or skid the swifter aside enough to get the saw in position. No dice. I then tried to scoot the spruce log in question back enough to expose the cutting area. That too did not work. To hell with it, I thought, what's a few inches more or less, and began my cut about one foot from the optimum spot indicated.

Long after I had finished that cut Grandfather showed up to check on my progress. At first he seemed pleased with my efforts until he spied the cut I had made off his mark, and he let a loud bellow out of him. He pointed out to me rather excitedly that I had just cost him two whole feet of log. (This probably cost him a few hundred dollars, at least.) I had forgotten that log scale then went by the two-foot rule. Cut a forty-foot log short by two inches and immediately you have a thirty-eight-foot log, not a thirty-nine foot, ten inch log as one might think. When the log is four feet in diameter this does make quite a significant difference to the scale. I should have checked with the boss before proceeding.

Toward the Future

Time moved swiftly that summer and fall approached all too rapidly for my comfort.

When my two oldest sisters and I became teenagers, there was a definite change of direction to our association regarding summer activities and summer fun. We spent far less time with one another as a social unit. Gone were the excursions down on the beaches and around the coves in the rowboat to explore and report on things of interest. The girls spent much more time with our mother and grandmother doing whatever women do. I, in turn, was involved with minor maintenance projects.

The downside of all the summers through our teenage years, I felt, was the lack of social contact with people nearer our age. I know that I personally could have benefited from an exchange of ideas with young people harboring views different from my own. I may have emerged later on not taking myself and my ideas quite so seriously.

Nevertheless, I can say for certain that I enjoyed doing much of my growing up in the logging camp. The experiences I had, the things I saw and the people I knew were in many ways a priceless opportunity for a young lad. The pattern of alternating back to Ocean Falls for schooling was a regimen that I grew to count on as the years went by. It was an organized life and I was comfortable with it, up to a point. Of course, I knew no other. I had not given much thought to the fact that one day it would have to end—and then what? It made me uncomfortable to dwell on it.

227

On the positive side I knew what I did not want. I felt that I was not cut out to be a logger, as a life's work. Also, I did not want to become an employee in the local pulp and paper mill. My mind was in a lot of turmoil and I began to regard my potential options as limited.

I knew very little about life away from Ocean Falls and the surrounding area. Only once with my mother and sister Audrey did I ever leave Ocean Falls and travel to the cities of Vancouver, B.C., and Portland, Oregon. We were gone only two weeks. It seems odd to me now, but I was seventeen before I ever saw a modern passenger automobile.

In spite of my quandary about the direction for my future, I did have an inkling that I ultimately wanted to work for myself, like Granddad, perhaps even to be an entrepreneur, although at the time I hardly knew the meaning of the word.

My older sister Audrey had already enrolled in nurses' training at the St. Paul's School of Nursing in Vancouver. Cherie, my next oldest sister, was to enroll there also a year or two later. Both graduated from there as registered nurses.

I had enough saved to support myself for one fall and spring term at the University of British Columbia, and so about the middle of September, 1949, I caught the Union Steamship boat going south to Vancouver.

A day or so later I disembarked. I was still on the pier, attempting to get a taxi, when one of the steamship stewards approached me with a wallet in his hand. He asked if it was mine. Indeed it was and it held every cent I had in the world—about $900. The hick from the sticks had arrived in the city.

A Poke in the Eye with a Sharp Stick

When I completed my first year at the University of British Columbia, I returned for the summer to work at Ocean Falls instead of Gildersleeve Logging. Crown Zellerbach Canada had offered me a job booming logs in the harbor at Ocean Falls. Besides the good wages, I figured the extra social life might do me some good too.

In the early fifties it was a forty-eight-hour work week. I loved it. Often we worked seven days a week when it was necessary to get the work done. I surely needed the money. All of us students needed the money to sustain us another winter in Vancouver while continuing our studies at UBC.

Occasionally we did get a day off. I had so much energy at nineteen and twenty that if I wasn't going to be working, I planned to be climbing a mountain. There were several mountains to choose from, but the easiest to get to was Mt. Caro Marion. It was this mountain's foothills upon which the town of Ocean Falls was built. All one had to do was walk out the back door and head straight up.

Ocean Falls, situated at the head of Cousins Inlet, was at sea level. Caro Marion, less than 5,000 feet, was steep, with many bluffs to negotiate, and heavily wooded to timberline. One need not have gone to the summit to experience breathtaking views of the town and surrounding countryside, although a climb to the summit was almost always my goal. If I started after an early breakfast, I could be on the summit before noon and be back down by three or four in the afternoon, depending on time spent on top.

The most interesting climbing on Caro Marion, I found, was in exploring different routes to the top. Most of my explorative climbs failed to find easier routes to the summit and at least one came close to ending in disaster.

Generally, I had great difficulty in finding anyone interested in accompanying me on these outings. However, a co-worker about ten years my senior, whose wife had gone on vacation, agreed to join me one Sunday. His name was Phil.

The day began with a cloudy overcast, but I had high hopes that it would clear as we set out on that day in mid-July. The challenge this day was to explore for a manageable route to the summit from the front face of Caro Marion, the side facing south down Cousins Inlet.

A large area of the front face of the mountain is an old slide that is clear of timber and heavy brush. We chose to begin there. I had previously climbed on this slide and so we kept to the side of it where the going was steep but the footing solid. In an hour or more we had arrived at a point where the old slide appeared to have originated slightly below timberline. The rock face confronting us went almost straight up several hundred feet. Not being experienced rock climbers with the proper equipment, we began searching for a gully or a rock chute that would allow us passage up and around this almost vertical obstacle.

Moving off to one side onto some small bluffs still below timberline, we ran into residual snow. Working our way up the face of a bluff, we came out onto a clear outcropping of flat rock covered in several inches of hard-packed snow and sloping upward at an angle of twenty degrees extending perhaps fifteen or twenty yards ahead where another small bluff began. The area to the right, after a few yards, sloped dangerously down the mountain side and wasn't at all inviting.

We tested the snow and found that we could kick steps in it and so proceeded, with me in the rear carrying the pack. We had not gone ten yards when the slope increased measurably, causing us to reevaluate our situation.

The cloud ceiling, instead of improving, had dropped considerably and now it was noticeably colder as well. Both of us were wearing only light shirts and had no other outer garments. The route ahead from this vantage point was discouraging and so we decided to backtrack. In moving my feet to get turned around, they kicked out from under me and I came down hard on my back, pointed head first down the slope. The small pack on my back acted like a toboggan and away I went. The snow pack was hard under the first inch or two and my attempts to put on the brakes by digging in fingers and elbows seemed to no avail. As Phil described it later, I "shot" down the slope, angling to the right, away from our line of ascent and "disappeared into space." He was right about that.

All of a sudden I was floating. I was well aware that I had left terra firma. As I recall, the only thought I had was how upset my mother was going to be when they found my body. Almost at the same instant I felt a knifelike blow to the back of my neck, just above my shoulders. I must have blacked out momentarily, but then realized that I was standing on my head in some kind of snow hole. Supported by my shoulders, I was looking up at my feet, with a bright circle of light beyond. My eye glasses had vanished but I needed them only for distance viewing, so that was no problem. I felt a frigid draft on my left cheek, causing me to turn my head. What I saw made my hair stand on end. In my upside-down deployment, my neck and shoulders were supported by a small ledge of hard-packed snow about the width of my body. Alongside me was a deep narrow cavern like a chimney of hard-packed snow and ice that extended a long way down, curving out slightly, following the shape of the mountain. Daylight shining on the snow from the outside came through to the inside and cast an eerie blue glow, allowing me to see that the hole was very deep. I had to be extra careful of my movements. If I had managed to slip into that crack head first, it would have been bye bye baby. I would have been entombed for the ages, like one of those frozen mastodons one reads about in *National Geographic*.

While I was contemplating all of this, I realized that my friend Phil was calling for me from above. I was careful in replying, so as not to move suddenly. Soon I saw his face about five feet above the hole I had made plunging into my precarious position. He could not see me and was confused by the sound of my voice. When he realized where I was, he climbed carefully down and peered into my hole.

"Jesus," he asked, "are you okay? We are on the edge of a sheer cliff," he said, "we won't be able to get down from here."

"Never mind," I said, "first I've got to get out of this hole." Phil had nothing with which to reach me. It was up to me to try and get turned around to where I could stand up. Carefully, using my elbows and back, I worked myself into a sitting position while balancing, jack-knifed, on that small ledge.

Standing up, my outstretched arms could almost reach the hole opening, but I had no way to climb out. There was nothing to stand on so that I could boost myself up. I was afraid to jump up from my ledge for fear of collapsing it and doing a disappearing act into the blue hole. Finally, after some discussion, Phil removed his belt and braced himself, while I used it to haul myself out of that ice house. We then climbed back up the route Phil had used descending to find me, before crossing over to our original track. Being somewhat nervous at this point and a bit tired, we moved slowly and carefully. Soon we again began our descent, but found that our troubles were far from over.

Fog was beginning to move in and around our position on the mountain. We were still near timberline among the bluffs and in snow when we were completely enveloped in thick, wet fog. It's difficult to appreciate unless one has experienced it, but the fog was so dense that, separated by only a couple of paces, we could barely see each other. We sat down and waited for perhaps five minutes and it got even colder. All of a sudden it was snowing and this was July. Our altitude could not have been more than 3,500 feet. The ledge we were resting on, I remembered, was perhaps thirty or forty feet above a small snowfield of considerable slope.

I suggested to Phil that I try climbing down a few feet to see if I could get a glimpse of the snow slope below. Anything, I thought, was going to be better than freezing to death on that ledge. Phil wasn't so sure and wanted to stay put even though his skin was turning blue. I recall how he put it to me.

He said, "Goddamit, Sirois, my wife is due back from Vancouver on Tuesday's boat and I fully intend to be there to meet her."

I suggested that he might be there all right, but "frozen stiff."

"I'll take my chances here," he said. "Where I can't see, I don't go."

Pretty damn good advice, I thought, especially on a mountain. Nevertheless, something told me that things were going to get worse, not better.

The essential problem climbing down in that fog was that one could not see much beyond a few feet. It would be really easy to get into a fix where one could not see how to get down further and yet could not get back up either. This sort of situation can happen even without fog. Anyway, I thought I should try, and told Phil I was starting down. After a few feet Phil could no longer see me. He stood directly over the place where I started down so that I would have some idea of my movement from there. I remembered coming up in almost exactly this same place, so I knew that the rock itself was not difficult. I could only grope with my foot to find solid footing before lowering myself to grope with the other foot. When I judged that I had come down fifteen or twenty feet, the going got tougher. I kept staring down, hoping between the swirls of fog to catch a glimpse of the snow-field. Stare as I might, the continuous billowing of the fog seemed hypnotic to the point where I began to imagine I saw snow. Now I could not seem to find places for my toes and my arms would not extend far enough to allow my toes to drop another inch or so to a firm support. Getting a little exasperated, I decided to stay put for a few minutes to regain my composure. For the time being at least I was stuck.

Phil called and asked me if I was okay.

"I am fine," I said, "just resting a bit."

I remembered that the snowfield below butted hard up against the rock face, with no loose rock scattered in the snow. The snow surface itself lay at a steep angle to the rock bluff, per-haps thirty-five degrees, before leveling out further down the slope. If I jumped to it, I thought, the initial steep angle of the snow would cushion my fall prior to sliding further down the slope, not unlike how a ski jumper uses a steep hill for a "soft" landing. That was how I figured it anyway. Even so, I wanted to get as close as possible to the snow before jumping. Fifteen feet, I thought, would be close enough. Of course, there was a small possibility that this was the wrong rock face and maybe there was no snow down there.

I began staring down again, and thought I saw something darker than the fog. Was I imagining it? No, there it was again. The fog was billowing into my face like smoke from a genie bot-tle. There I did see it. It was snow. I called to Phil and told him that I was going to jump the rest of the way and to come down to my position to follow me. No answer from Phil. I knew that he was thinking about it. I waited a moment longer to see if I could glimpse the snow once more. Yes, there it was for sure. I pushed

233

off, expecting a twenty-foot drop and prepared my mind and body for a stiff jolt. Almost instantly after jumping I could see the snow and the drop was less than expected, perhaps ten or twelve feet and the landing was a piece of cake. I guess the impact did produce a large grunt from me because Phil's voice was calling down to me.

"Are you okay? Is everything okay?"

I was so damn pleased with myself that I did not answer him right away. Phil called again and I could detect the fear in his voice.

Calmly, I replied, "I'm okay, Phil."

"How was it?" he wanted to know.

"It's not bad at all, Phil," I answered, "better than a poke in the eye with a sharp stick. Come on down."

Presently I could hear movement above and I moved further away from the rock face in case Phil dislodged a rock on top of me. Then I saw Phil's feet appear through the fog as if he were emerging from another dimension. I called to him and asked if he could see me.

"No," he said, "but keep talking."

"Well, Phil," I said, "it's about twelve feet to the snow; it's steep and soft and no rocks. Just push off, you will do fine."

It wasn't that easy. The fog was getting worse. I could not see Phil's feet anymore, but I did not tell him, and it was snowing again.

I suggested to Phil that we best get moving, the fog was getting thicker and we still had a way to go. Down he came with a great thud, landing almost perfectly in my own tracks, skidding at least ten feet. He let out a big whoop, made a snowball and threw it at me. He was happy to be in one piece. We both were.

"Nice going, Phil," I said, "now let's get the hell out of here, fast, while we can still see where we're going."

We lost no time from that point getting off the mountain. By the time we had reached the 2,000 foot level the fog had followed us all the way down and it had begun to rain and blow. Arriving at the bottom we looked back up to see where we had been but the entire top half of the mountain was totally shrouded in huge black clouds and fog. It's possible that we could have survived a night on the mountain clothed as lightly as we were, but not likely.

We walked home in the rain, in very good spirits, discussing the possibilities of another climb one day in the future.

Ocean Falls Night Life

During the summers (early 1950s) in Ocean Falls, the social life, as I remember it, centered around private house parties or private room parties at the Martin Inn Hotel. Two of my good friends, Ray and Ted, who at that time worked the year around in Ocean Falls, were often involved in party activities no matter where they went.

I recall a Martin Inn reception I attended with Ray and Ted early one summer. The party had generated a full head of steam even before we arrived. I don't recall what the celebration was for, but when we pushed through the door, someone shoved a bottle of beer into our hands. The rooms were so crowded with people and the pushing and jostling so pronounced, that it was dangerous to drink from a beer bottle for fear of losing one's teeth.

We had been there about ten minutes and were becoming acclimatized to the din when some boisterous fool thought it funny to fuzz up his beer and squirt it into another's face, causing shrieks of laughter from some onlookers. Naturally, the squirtee responded with a generous suds blast of his own into the face of the squirtor, with about half of the foamy mass reaching innocent victims. This sudden suds shower caught people off guard and provoked even more shouting and shoving, which caused indignant cursing, ultimately promoting more beer facials. Predictably, someone got an elbow in the nose and the melee was on.

I stood in awe, until an empty bottle soared past my head and crashed against a far wall. Instantly, I was on my knees and found myself staring into the faces of my two friends. Without a word we headed for the door, and on the way met other intelligent folk, crawling in the same direction. Scrambling out the door, we found to our amazement that people there were still trying to get in. It was a great pleasure to exit and make room for them.

Shortly after the above episode I escorted an attractive lady friend to a local community dance. All that evening I did everything I could to make a good impression on her, so it was with pride that I informed her that we were invited to a private party later, if she was interested.

"Sure, why not," was her reply.

However, I had reservations, as I didn't know the people that well. Some of my friends would be there, I was told, and there would be drinks and further dancing.

We showed up at the apartment to find that we were the first to arrive. The host introduced us to his attractive wife, and shortly we were all dancing to some lovely music. We were offered drinks, which we accepted, and innocently asked our hosts where the others were. We continued dancing under subdued light but shortly the lights were turned completely off. Then our hosts suggested that we switch partners, which we did, and continued dancing in total darkness. I realized by now that no other guests would be coming and that this so-called party was some sort of a setup.

When the lights came on again, the host's wife brought out a picture album full of snaps that she laughingly said were some of her husband's recent pictures. Photography apparently was his hobby. As soon as I saw the first photo, I realized that my boy scout act all evening was out the window. It showed his wife in a sexy pose displaying some very attractive lingerie. Ninety percent of the photos were of her in various stages of undress. So much for my Mr. Nice Guy act. I felt sure that my date would think me in cahoots with our hosts, especially now that the husband was suggesting that both women disrobe while he got out his camera equipment.

What could I say? I was caught between a rock and that hard place. In a feeble attempt to regain my composure, I said simply, "No offense intended, but we should be leaving." We got out of there in a hurry. Once away from the apartment we both got into a laughing jag, which was the most fun I had had all evening. My date did, after all, display some sense of humor. She confided in me that she had trouble undressing in front of her mother, let alone some geezer she didn't know. I apologized for the evening's outcome and escorted her home.

Three weeks later a few of us were in Ted's room at the Martin Inn engaged in quiet conversation and drinking some beer. Without warning, the door crashed open. In burst some fellow in a wild panic, his face flushed and eyes flashing with rage.

"Where is she? I know she's here!" he shouted.

We all gaped in disbelief as the intruder lunged to the closet, threw back the door, thrust his arms through the clothing and finding nothing, dropped to his knees cursing, shooting looks under both beds before leaping up and dashing out the open door. All of us were flabbergasted, except for Ted, who acted calmly as if this strange event had happened before. Slowly, he got up with a knowing smile, but not a word of explanation, and closed the door softly.

"Christ, Ted, what the Sam Hill was that all about?" Ray asked.

Ted remained silent, but the smirk remained.

"Must be dicking some poor sap's old lady, eh Ted?" someone else ventured.

Ted only continued his silent smirking as he swigged some of his beer, not looking at anyone in particular.

"Hell, Ted," I said, "you must be living on the edge."

"No, no, nothing like that," Ted finally said quietly.

"Well, Ted," I pursued, "would you believe I know who that guy is, doesn't he work over in the paper mill?"

Ted's grin widened further, but he said no more.

"Dammit, Ted," I continued, trying unsuccessfully to be humorous, "banging his old lady while he is away working graveyard is dirty pool. I was under the impression that we were all gentlemen here. I guess maybe all that counts is your big ego."

Ray, who was Ted's longtime best friend, spoke again, smiling, "Listen to me, you Australian bastard, one of these days I'm going to come up here for a beer and quiet conversation and I'm going to find a pair of Australian balls hanging on your door knob. You ain't going to like that one bit."

"Ah, come on you guys," Ted said, "you have the scenario all wrong, it's not like that at all. The truth is that guy, whoever he was, had the wrong room, right Ray?"

Ray laughed. "I don't know a damned thing, Ted," he said. "And by the way, why the hell don't you keep your goddamned door locked. I come up here and expect privacy among friends. I don't like the idea of some big ape busting in like that."

"For godsake," Ted said, "this is no opium den, who are we trying to keep out?"

"Weirdos," Ray said, "anyway, I've had enough of this bullshit, I'm getting out of here before any more crazy bastards bust in. Anyone want to play some pool?"

"Good idea," I said, as we all got up to leave, including Ted, who said, "Well, screw you guys, I guess I'm coming too." Then he added grinning, "I might need some protection," as he shot me a telltale wink.

I never confided further to my friends that the brash intruder I recognized in Ted's room that evening was the host who wanted to photograph my date and his wife together in the nude. His wife might have been playing around with Ted and possibly others. All I could think of at the time was that that kinky bugger was getting his just desserts. Or how do they say it, "Time wounds all heels." Knowing that knowledge is power, I settled down to await future developments.

A few weeks later, on other fronts, five of us were congregated in Ted's room once again, all hoisting a bottle of suds. As I recall, the five included were Ted, Ray, Smokey, Pat and myself. The subjects of conversation never changed—they ranged from work, to booze, to women, to international affairs, to our own affairs, not necessarily in that order.

We were all relatively young men then, full of ourselves and we individually stood ready to defend our honor (or false pride) from any insult, imagined or otherwise.

Ray and I were born in Ocean Falls. Ted hailed from Sydney, Australia, and was a grand fellow. The other two, Smokey and

Pat, I knew only casually, even though we all worked as part of the booming crew in the harbor. Smokey seemed a decent sort, fairly outgoing, but he had a reputation to anger quickly. Pat I hardly knew at all, except that he was recently from Ireland, did not talk a lot and tended to have a negative outlook. One could say that Pat was the misfit in our group that evening. Both Smokey and Pat were physically well put together, but Smokey had powerful shoulders, and arms as large as my thighs.

The five of us were sitting facing each other, beers in hand, on two low steel cots that took up most of the room. Ray was on my left, Smokey to my right. Ted and Pat faced us from the other cot. Bent forward in conversation, our foreheads would almost touch.

I don't recall what was being discussed, but something was said by Pat that upset Smokey enough that he retaliated with a remark of his own, directed at Pat. In a flash Pat had smashed the neck off his beer bottle on the steel bed frame between his legs and thrust the jagged manifold of razorlike glass past my nose into Smokey's face. An instant later, and without a sound, Smokey's fingers were closing around Pat's throat in a death grip.

Our first reaction was to get out of the way. Then we realized that Smokey's face was gutted, laid open to the bone. The slash began at the extreme outside corner of Smokey's eye, moved back toward his ear and down his cheek, to curve forward and exit in the corner of his mouth between his lips. A huge flap of flesh swung out and flapped around like a chunk of beef liver splashing blood over all of us.

Smokey went out of control. His eyes bulged as he clamped his huge hands about his attacker's neck, hunching his powerful shoulders for even more leverage, while grunting and rolling in a mixture of spittle and blood. Pat's kicking and clawing at Smokey's arms was to no avail.

Suddenly it was clear to us that Smokey would kill Pat. Simultaneously, the three of us jumped on the pair and by some miracle Smokey was talked into releasing his grip on Pat's throat.

The two of them were taken quickly to the hospital for repairs. Smokey healed up with the help of more than 100 stitches, but when I saw him a year or so later, he had a terrible disfiguring scar. Pat was fined $100 by the local magistrate, fired from his job and kicked out of town. No one I know ever heard of Pat again. It may be that he now communicates through sign language.

Going in for Two

One pleasure of being a young man in British Columbia in the early 1950s was reaching the age of twenty-one and being legally allowed to enter a licensed premises (beer parlor).

Now there, in my opinion, was an institution that was distinctive and had merit. It seemed a place where working men could go and feel comfortable with pals, no matter who they were, what they were or how many. Any form of clothing was permitted, no matter how dusty, greasy or wet. It was a place crowded with bent frame tables and chairs. The tables were laden with glasses of golden beer, the chairs populated with animated patrons eager to take their turn in buying a round for the table— some needing to prove their financial liquidity.

Beer slingers lofting full trays of beer overhead, often fully oiled with their product, glided serenely between tables where seemingly no passage existed. No empty glass was ignored for long.

The beer parlor did hold a certain fascination for me. As a man needs sex, he also needs the opportunity to associate and be sociable—to be able to "peel the onion" with friends. Surroundings can be of the least importance.

While home one summer from the university, I found that the beer parlor was also a place where grandfather and grandson could meet for a couple of hours before 6:00 P.M. and be near equals over six beers. The establishment closed from 6:00 P.M. to 7:00 P.M. This intelligent and humane rule allowed everyone a chance to get home for dinner.

Six glasses of draft beer on empty stomachs, as I recall, put quite a twinkle in our eyes. When Grandfather and I arrived at my mother's dinner table giggling and elbowing each other, she was thoroughly unamused—disgusted with the two of us, may have been closer to the truth. Potatoes and other vegetables landed on my dinner plate as if fired from a catapult. The clever remarks, bursts of laughter and winks from my grandfather only infuriated his daughter more. I tried to pretend, with only moderate success, that I was unaffected by the beer by keeping my mouth shut.

At the first chance, I ducked out of the house and left Granddad to take any further heat. He knew how to handle my mother. He just joked with her about her anger. I was a student at this time and felt damned lucky to be getting free room and board for the summer; thus, I tried not to make too many waves. If I had tried taunting her, I surely would have been looking for room and board elsewhere.

Later in the evenings, if I stopped in at the beer parlor, I might run into a friend and kill the rest of the evening socializing over a few more beers. Occasionally though, a party would develop at a private home or apartment and last all night long. More times than I like to remember, I arrived back at my mother's house in time to change clothes, grab my caulk shoes and head for work without breakfast.

More than once after an all nighter, I'd feel nauseous aboard the tug boat heading out to the booming grounds, where there was no escape for the next eight hours. One such morning I felt a serious barf coming on and leaned over the side of the tug to let her fly. A startling volume of brilliant tangerine yellow vomit disgorged with unusual force, narrowly missing several contemporaries. The yellow puke had everyone, including me, wondering what had happened to my insides. More than likely the problem was a lack of food in my belly. One of the more enjoyable aspects of a night out on the town was an early morning breakfast of bacon and eggs, hashbrowns, toast and coffee. That particular morning my stomach received no food at all and perhaps the violent reaction was an act of rebellion.

I was convinced that morning that my final hours were numbered. Sucking on cubes of sugar was all that kept me going.

241

Bending over on the end of a rolling boomstick to thread a chain up through the hole was an exercise conceived in hell for one with my skull-cracking headache.

Nibbling a sandwich or two at our half-hour lunch break perked me up; by three o'clock I actually felt that I would live. At four-thirty when we "clocked out," we all had to pass by the beer parlor and inevitably we went in for "two." Then it was four beers; and then six. Soon it was 6:00 P.M. and home for dinner. "See you at Ray's later," someone shouted. "Okay," I answered laughing, as I now felt like I could lick my weight in wildcats. Another evening was just beginning.

Recollections

Animals

When friends of mine learn that I was raised in a rural area on the northcentral B.C. coast (the "boonies"), the subject they most ask about is the wild animals. "Did you ever see a bear? Were you ever attacked by one?" Where I grew up, on the sparsely populated area between Smith's Inlet in the south and Butedale in the north, there were bears galore, black bears and grizzly bears; and there were also wolves, deer, moose, goat, cougar, bobcat and wolverines, to name only some of the larger animals.

Bear, deer, goats, wolves and cougar always seemed to be the most plentiful, as they are seen on a fairly regular basis. To my knowledge no one in my family has experienced an unprovoked attack by a wild animal.

A female bear with young cubs will act aggressively if you get too close to the cubs or, worse, get between the cubs and her. This to me would be considered as provoking the animal and care must be taken to avoid this. At times, the mother bear, if annoyed in this manner, will suddenly execute what is called a false charge, snarling with teeth showing, rushing a few yards at the provocateur with a great display of emotion, then just as suddenly, retreat with the cubs. Often cubs are never seen when an incident like this occurs, and people will think that they did nothing to arouse the bear.

I treat all wild animals with the utmost respect, especially bears. If our paths cross, as they do quite often, I remain motionless and pretend not to see the bear (eye contact is considered unwise). The bear appears, most of the time, to be performing the same act of nonchalance. I never move off in the same direction as the bear if he is close. If he is blocking my direction of travel, I give him a wide berth and go around. On occasion, when on a narrow and dense path, I have about faced and retraced my foot-

243

steps for a hundred yards or more because the bear sat down and waited for me to leave, which I did once I got the message. There is not a thing in the world wrong with letting a bear know that he is king of the forest, because for all practical purposes, he is.

In my experience, bears make a lot of noise as they move through the woods and underbrush. They just seem not to care; after all who or what can bother them? Usually one hears a bear and spots him a fair distance off, but not all the time.

Once, on the Dean River in the early fifties, full of youthful vigor, I was running full tilt along a twisting narrow foot path in a pine forest. It was challenging to see how fast I could run and negotiate all of the turns without running off the trail into the trees. With the wind whistling in my ears and concentrating on placing my feet, I shot around a tight curve and slammed into a black bear sitting broadside on the trail. He had been gobbling huckleberries when I struck, sending him "ass over tits." I smacked him dead center and bounced backward, landing on my rear. At first I was stunned, not sure what I hit. The bear was up before me and, by his look, he was also confused. I quickly gave him maneuvering room and scrambled on down the trail. He went right back to his huckleberries.

On another occasion, not long after, also at Dean River, while out walking I met a tourist hiker at a fork in the trail. After comparing notes he moved off down one fork and was gone, while I started down the other path. Moments later I heard a terrible scream that grabbed my attention. In the next instant I was aware of much thrashing and breaking of branches. Something like a wild tornado was headed out of the brush directly at me from the direction of the other hiker. I was rooted to the spot in surprise, and in a flash judged the frightened bear would run over me in about three seconds flat. I carried my pistol, barrel down, in the oversized hip pocket of my ski pants. In one second I reached back and grabbed the pistol by the butt thinking to swing it out, but the barrel was caught in the cloth of my pocket. In the next second, I jerked at it to no avail. In a fearful frenzy of superhuman strength I ripped the gun out as the terrified bear suddenly swerved to avoid me by twenty feet, going by like an express train. It was gone before I thought to cock the gun for firing. Actually, I would never use a pistol on the likes of a bear. My only intent was to create noise so that he would see me and not run me down.

I was still standing there shaking, gun in hand, when the hiker dashed up to me out of breath shouting excitedly that he had just seen a huge bear. It was then that we noticed the rear of my ski pants hanging down like the trap door on an old pair of winter longjohns. In my moment of terror I had ripped the ass right out of my pants. It was a breezy walk the rest of the way to camp.

After dinner one evening, a year later, Uncle Dick and I were fishing for salmon in the Dean River. About dark we left the river carrying a fifteen-pound coho salmon. Dick elected to carry the salmon, giving me the fishing poles. I followed him in the dark, using my nose and the smell of fresh fish. It took us a while to locate the trail but once we did the going was easier. After a spell he said, "Here Jim, you carry this fish awhile. Give me the poles," but he remained in the lead. I had walked only a short distance carrying the fish when I heard movement behind me and to the side. I stopped suddenly listening intently, and sure enough, I heard the soft crunch, crunch of padded feet before they also stopped and went silent. I tried this a time or two making sure that I was not imagining things and called out to Dick who was now a long way ahead, that something was following us. Dick, laughingly, called back in a loud voice, "Of course there is. Why do you think I gave you the fish?" and he guffawed again, louder. Then he added, "It's probably just a wolf, nothing to get excited about."

But I noticed he never offered to take the salmon back. Luckily for me I never saw any shining eyeballs or I would have jettisoned the fish and raced Dick back to camp.

In contrast to bears that one sees regularly, wolves, in my experience, are seldom seen. I see their sign everywhere, and hear them howling in the fall, but rarely see them. They are quiet moving about in the woods; unlike bears, they do not attract one's attention with ground noise. On the few occasions I see a wolf, it is usually a long way off. Or suddenly I will focus on one standing still thirty or forty yards away, staring at me and then it vanishes, but this is rare. They always know you are there and see you first.

Although bears are potentially more dangerous, I am more nervous regarding wolves because of their manner of being silent and crafty acting. In actuality, no one that I know personally has had any serious problems with wolves, such as being attacked by them.

Once when I was about eight, Grandfather and I were boating in a skiff on the still water up Johnston Creek in Rivers Inlet. He asked me to stay in the boat while he went ashore to heed nature's call. When he was out of sight, I first sensed and then heard movement in the tall swamp grass surrounding our skiff. The only weapon I had in the boat was Granddad's double-bitted falling ax, and it was razor sharp. I sat ramrod stiff clutching that ax until Granddad returned about ten minutes later. He had a big grin on his face when he saw me clutching the ax and asked me if I had seen the wolf. He had seen it and I had not, but surely the wolf saw me.

Often wolves smell bad from rolling in rotten material. Being downwind from a wolf can betray their presence due to their smell alone. Once when my mother, aunts and my sisters were starting out from camp on an afternoon hike, they encountered a terrible smell on the trail that to them was unmistakably a wolf. They lost no time in returning home. It is likely that the wolf was watching them from a distance, or following them out of curiosity, but probably would have done nothing more.

Grandfather, as mentioned, was hard of hearing; he was alone cruising timber one afternoon. Walking up a long sloping spruce windfall he thought he heard someone call out to him. Looking behind him he saw a huge timber wolf standing on the other end of the log. The two stood for a few seconds staring at each other when Grandfather picked up a broken limb in the form of a club and charged the wolf, waving the club and hollering at the top of his voice. The wolf's nerve broke. He jumped down from the log and headed for tall timber. Grandfather headed down the sidehill for the beach where we had prearranged that I would pick him up in the rowboat. About ten minutes later he emerged from the underbrush still carrying his crude club. Getting into the rowboat, he asked me if I had been hollering for him. I shook my head; then he told me this story.

Our experience was that wolves generally do not confront people in this manner, unless they are extremely hungry. Perhaps this one was. I could tell that Grandfather, an experienced woodsman, was very agitated by the incident. I wonder how the wolf felt? It seems that this was a situation where the wild animal was attacked by a human.

Mini-the-Moocher

We once had a cat in camp that strayed into the bush one day and returned many days later pregnant. The prevailing wisdom at the time was that some wild creature of the cat family, possibly a mink or a martin had impregnated our pet.

The litter produced in due course were, as expected, very strange-looking critters. As domestic cats, they were smaller and thinner of body, with small heads and sharply pointed ears, placed very close together. Eventually, our mother took the pick of the litter and had the rest stuffed into a weighted sack and consigned to Davey Jones. She named the survivor Mini, short for Mini-the-Moocher.

Mini was a mottled orange and black color and when full grown appeared to be about half the size of a normal house cat. She definitely had a wild animal look about her; nevertheless, she was an exceptional house pet.

At this particular time in 1947, Uncle Keaton, home from the wars, was passing through Ocean Falls on his way to Alaska and was staying with us for a few days.

One evening Keaton, Mini-the-Moocher and I were left alone in the house while my sisters and mother went out for the evening. After a short period of boredom, Keaton produced a bottle of gin and proceeded to make the two of us a gin fizz.

In short order things began to liven up and then we noticed Mini the cat stretched out comfortably under the kitchen stove. Thinking she might be thirsty down there amid all that heat, I got out a saucer of milk and offered it to her. She responded immediately. Mini was very thirsty. She seemed all but dried out.

I poured Mini more milk and the second time I added a few drops of gin. Mini lapped it down. I poured more milk and more gin. Again Mini consumed it all. Then we noticed that Mini staggered when moving away from the dish. We thought she was hilarious and so offered her more, which she lapped up immediately and looked for more. We were somewhat astonished at her capacity. By now, Mini could not negotiate at all. Her legs sort of slithered out from under her and she seemed to have no forward momentum, or backward either for that matter. I grabbed Mini around her middle and lifted her to her toes, but on letting go, her legs again assumed a form of the cat splits. For all practical purposes, she was a limp rag doll cat. Mini seemed to be in no pain whatsoever and still responded favorably to a belly scratch. She appeared to be in total comfort. In fact, she still drank from the saucer from her belly position with her head over the edge of the saucer. Her tongue continued to work well, while the rest of her body was paralyzed. Mini definitely was pie-eyed, falling down drunk. With help from my shoeless foot, I scooted her back under the stove to soak up more heat and to sleep off her inebriation.

The following morning I left for school not giving any thought to the previous evening's activities and returned, as usual, for lunch. Coming onto the back porch a burlap sack, lying there, caught my eye. It was unusual, especially since a cat's tail was protruding from it. I chuckled, thinking to myself that Mini had playfully crawled into the sack to hide, as cats will do.

I leaned down and gave the tail a yank expecting immediate retaliation from Mini. Instead, to my horror, the tail was as stiff as an ax handle. I yanked the cat out and held her up by the tail as if I was holding a giant lollipop. I had never seen anything like this and immediately wondered if the cat was as brittle as she was stiff; however, I refrained from tapping her against one of the porch columns. With consternation I stuffed Mini back into the sack and composing myself, entered the house.

Once inside, I sensed the tension that follows some horrific incident. Soon I was hearing in gory detail, from Mother, the worst of it. Mini the cat had apparently had a seizure and gone mad. While Mother and Keaton were enjoying a leisurely breakfast, they heard strange rasping sounds emanating from beneath the stove. Without further warning, the cat, foaming at the mouth, shot out from under the stove and tore around the kitchen, claws at the full, making all manner of gagging and choking noises before darting into the living room. According to testimony, Mini then flashed across the living room rug in a berserk frenzy, screeching, yowling and squirting cat poop all the way. She streaked straight up the window drapes, across the top and down the opposite side, followed by steady and unrelenting blasts of cat gas and manure. Upon reaching the floor she let out a last cry of agony, had a final spasm and fell over dead; elapsed time from start to finish, about twenty seconds.

It had happened, was over and done with before anyone could attempt to throw the cat out. The mess was abominable, to say the very least. Mother was a fastidious housekeeper and was mortified. "Poor Mini," she said, "what a terrible thing to happen to her. She must have gotten into rat poison."

Keaton and I were stunned by this event and hardly knew what to do except keep our mouths shut and go along with the rat poison theory. The two of us had been willing accomplices in other escapades, but nothing as serious as this. Of course, we would never be 100 percent sure, but in our minds we were, inadvertently, the murderers of Mini-the-Moocher.

Dogs I Have Known

When I was a kid of five or six living with my two sisters at Grandma Gildersleeve's house in Ocean Falls, a dog magically appeared among us. He was a Spitz cross and seemed full grown, but probably was about a year old. Someone named him Curly on account of the way he carried his tail in a curl high and proud over his back.

I was told that Curly was my dog, but that didn't last long. Grandma must have decided that she had enough mouths to feed without Curly added, and underfoot as well. Whatever the reason, suddenly Curly was banished to the logging camp. In no time

249

Curly was bonded to my grandfather and followed him everywhere for the next fourteen years.

It's a known fact that loggers are well fed, and no doubt Curly got his share. I don't believe his nose ever touched actual dog food.

As time went on, Curly developed a flatulence problem to where his farts were incomparable. A ghastly putrid rotten fish smell caused involuntary closure of one's throat, resulting in an explosion of movement toward open spaces and away from Curly. I'm almost positive that it was a dog-produced derivative of mustard gas. With one innocent fart Curly could clear a room faster than the cry of "fire."

In Curly's golden years he spent much of his time snoozing behind Grandfather's chair. From this favorite position he absorbed daily drubbings as he attempted to sneak wind. The first screech from anyone triggered Curly's arthritic scramble for the open door, hoping to avoid Grandfather's flailing newspaper and the rush of bodies headed for fresh air.

The frequent newspaper beatings, however, were not the worst insult Curly's body had to absorb. In shadowing Grandfather, Curly had managed, somehow, to get his beautiful tail caught in the spokes of an engine flywheel and as a result had it torn off at the root. Curly's claim to fame was gone. Although he did recover from this ghastly physical insult, he never regained his old pizzazz. His stabilizer in the dog world likely was that curly tail, providing him with a special identity among his peers. He gradually became cranky and withdrawn and was reluctantly helped to his final reward by those who remembered his many years of faithful friendship.

Spunk arrived at Grandma's house not long after Curly had been sent out to the logging camp. He came as a tiny pup inside the leather jacket of Uncle Keaton. Spunk was a golden Labrador cross with big round eyes, a large square-jawed head and sturdy, bowed legs.

It was fall and chilly at night. Keaton made a bed for Spunk in a box behind the wood-burning kitchen stove. After the fire died, the little fellow screeched and yowled something awful the whole night long. It was probably the first time that he had been away from the rest of the litter and his mother. Grandma was not impressed with Spunk either, and, like Curly, he was soon banished to the camp.

As contemporaries, Curly was perhaps a year or two older than Spunk. While Curly's character tended to be high strung, standoffish and aloof, Spunk, possibly due to his Labrador ancestry, was more gregarious and seemed to like everyone. He was very playful, and unlike Curly, wanted to follow us kids everywhere, and did, to our delight.

Spunk was as interested as we were in roaming the mud flats, squinting under rocks and old logs to see what might run out. He accompanied me on many a rowboat sojourn to explore the beaches and rocky coves near camp. He was with me on that never-to-be-forgotten day when a mud shark rose to the surface alongside the rowboat and scared the dickens out of both of us.

Spunk was the first to see that devilish-looking fin rise and stand motionless in the water only a few feet from our boat. I rowed away in a panic of my own thinking Spunk in his excitement might jump overboard to attack the aquatic beast.

Spunk had no peer as a swimmer. Naturally, there were times when we didn't want him with us, especially when we had important secret stuff to do, where dogs would be a nuisance. When we took off without Spunk, that was no big problem for him. He came anyway. He just dove in and swam behind. I could only row faster than he could swim for short distances. Spunk always arrived at our destination only shortly after we did. He would be so pleased with himself when he caught up with us that he would dash right over and shake in our midst, then, still wet, jump all over us, in glee.

One day we had gone to Wadhams Cannery in the camp tender, a distance of about two miles, and left Spunk behind in camp. Unknown to us, he jumped in and proceeded to follow. It was a calm day with the chuck smooth as glass, and I suppose it's possible our wake served as his lodestar. We had been at the cannery it seemed for hours, when out of nowhere dashed Spunk, still wet and leaping all over us. Somehow, he had swum the whole distance and then ran around the Cannery until he had nosed us out. He rode back with us in the boat, leaning forward off the bow bulwark looking cocksure, as if he was navigating us home.

Up until that time, as kids, we often felt that Spunk might drown as he plowed along back of our rowboat, pushing a bow wave that indicated prodigious effort to keep up. Worried, we would stop rowing and let him cruise alongside, eyeballs up, looking to come aboard. We had learned to grab him by the scruff of the neck, with his paws hooked over the side of the boat to heave him in. Our attempts to hide behind each other as he exploded into his undulating dog shake was in vain as every frigid water drop found some part of our recoiling bodies. Then he would jump all over us before proudly taking his place on the bow, his ears lifting triumphantly in the breeze like two signal flags.

Grandmother never seemed too keen on dogs and surprised all of us by deciding to get a "real bear dog," presumably for her protection while on numerous forays into the bush after wild berries. No doubt she felt that Curly or Spunk couldn't cut the mustard where bears or wolves were concerned.

Gram got an Airedale. When he arrived in camp, he was still a pup but stood about twenty-four inches high at the shoulders. His head, his most prominent feature, was square, about the size of an apple box and solid bone. Gram named him Scout. The rest of Scout's frame was also heavy boned and covered with a short, rusty brown, kinky hair interspersed with darker patches. Its texture was that of a Brillo pad. Scout displayed no fat anywhere and although he ate enough for two normal-sized dogs, he gained weight only because he grew much larger.

Big as he was, Scout was friendly and playful. He never understood his strength and frequently would bowl us over just nudging us as we romped around with him. He easily carried my eight-year-old sister, Cherie, bareback. One dangerous maneuver we learned to avoid with Scout was nuzzling our heads too close to his when wrestling with him. A sudden toss of his bony cranium and a glancing blow to our cheek, forehead or jaw felt about the same as being bludgeoned with a bowling ball. It hurt plenty.

Scout seemed to prefer Cherie; it seemed to have something to do with her odor. If Cherie was hiding apart from Audrey and me, he would home in on Cherie's scent. We played a game where one of us held him back, while the others would run and hide. He easily tore a woodpile apart to get at us if he smelled us in there.

One day to test Scout, I talked Cherie into trading clothes with me. On cue we dashed into Scout's view and ducked around the corner of the house to hide from him. On he thundered at full gallop. I exposed myself to him, again, so that he could see Cherie's clothing and ran for all I was worth. In a bound or two he had me knocked to the ground and, not getting the expected smells, he sprang away to find Cherie's hiding place.

I don't know how effective Scout was in protecting Gram from bears, but I never heard of any complaints. Gram and my sisters, by now three, Audrey, Cherie and Marilyn, seemed quite comfortable taking off to search for pie berries so long as Scout was accompanying them.

Curly, Spunk and Scout were contemporaries and there were others. Peanuts was my mother's dog, a wire-haired terrier. She was a house pet but very feisty. Her claim to fame developed as a mouse chaser. Many times she had us helpless with laughter as she rocketed after mice darting across the linoleum floor of our kitchen and dining room.

When Peanuts spied a mouse, she went bananas. Out came her toenails for better traction, but unfortunately the linoleum underfoot did her in. Her legs were a blur as they raced pell-mell, toenails out, in one spot, while she slowly gained momentum. Once she had speed then she could not stop as she crashed into a wall or corner where the mouse had sought refuge. Out the mouse would dash right past Peanuts' nose as she was pirouetting around and clawing grooves like sixty on that cursed linoleum. To my knowledge she never caught those mice but they certainly could have died of cardiac arrest after several terrifying dashes around the room with that cursed dog clawing and caroming after them.

Then there was Rusty who followed Peanuts as a family pet; he was a golden cocker spaniel, and was a favorite of my stepfather's. As Rusty got older he grew somewhat cantankerous and possessive and growled menacingly at friends who called at the house.

One day a young fellow came calling on my oldest sister Audrey. Rusty was being his overprotective self and acted as if he might bite. Roy assured the lad that Rusty was only bluffing. The lad advanced with confidence and promptly was nipped on his ankle bone.

The next evening I saw Roy with a large gunny sack and boom chain getting into a rowboat with Rusty. Shortly thereafter, Roy returned without the dog, having completed a very distasteful task, especially since Rusty had trusted his master right to the bitter end.

Lastly there was the legendary Pat. He was a black Labrador and came to the Gildersleeve camp about 1947–48 from Ocean Falls. Pat was like most Labrador retrievers; he was very playful and, more than anything else, he loved to return sticks thrown for him.

At this time the Gildersleeve camp was at Tallheo Point south of Bella Coola. Truck logging roads were being planned and lots of blasting was going on, clearing stumps and other obstacles in preparation for road beds.

Pat took to following the powder man around and discovered a new play thing: spitting fuses. When the powder man lit a string of fuses and headed for cover, Pat would often be seen lunging and barking at the fuses until he was called away. At first when called, Pat was inclined to obey the powder man. After a few narrow escapes, however, Pat began to lose his hearing.

My grandfather, who also was deaf, possibly felt some sympathy for the dog and came up with a silent dog whistle. The whistle seemed to work and for a time Pat responded and all was well. It wasn't long, however, when Pat ceased to respond to any audio commands, including the silent whistle, and the day came when he had to be tied up prior to doing any blasting.

This particular day Pat had been left behind in camp, tied up. After setting a charge of several sticks of 20 percent dynamite and lighting the fuse, the powder man was heading for cover when Pat, having broken loose, appeared on the scene looking for his friend. It didn't take Pat long to discover the smoke and sparks of the burning fuse that he loved and, pouncing on the spot, he soon had dug up the charge and proudly went looking for his buddy. Horror struck, the powder man, helpless to avoid disaster, had headed down the road as fast as his caulk-booted feet would carry him with, Pat bounding along some distance behind, his sparkling booty clamped happily in his jaws.

Fortunately for everyone, Pat dallied with the dynamite sticks, tossing them about and snapping occasionally at the rapidly diminishing fuse. The powder man had gone into hiding when Pat appeared in the road near the camp, puzzled as to where his friend had gone. In the few seconds that followed, Pat caught sight of another friend, Andy Torkelson, who was standing about fifty yards away examining the new log dump built on fresh piling out into Tallheo Point Bay. With renewed enthusiasm Pat headed in Andy's direction with the smoking package. It is only speculation regarding what Pat may have been thinking (if dogs think) at the moment of the "big bang." One thing is for sure, Pat died a happy dog, grinning from ear to ear. Pat became an instant legend. Andy breathed a big sigh of relief, muttering a barely audible, "Yeasus." He had seen Pat approaching with his sparkling bomb and was crouched, ready to leap from the dump into the bay.

Reminiscing

One evening in 1955, at our Dean River logging camp cookhouse, Uncles Frank and Dick, Granddad, a few loggers and myself were swapping stories of unusual or humorous experiences. Granddad had just told us a tale that had occurred many years previously (early 1920s) and not long after he had arrived in B.C. from Oregon. It seems that a man had bet everyone in camp that he could toss a number of dynamite sticks from a rowboat and row away fast enough to escape the blast. The entire camp had chipped money into a pot to induce him to try it, and had all lined up along the floats to watch the result.

This was long before the days of duct tape, which he could have used to secure the dynamite and fuse together. What he did have was a ball of cotton store string that he wound around and around the parcel and tied it off. When he was ready, he lit the fuse, tossed the bundle over the stern of the boat and started to row like hell, with everyone on the floats cheering him on. All eyes were fixed on the spot where the explosive bundle had entered the water, while unknown to everyone, including the rower, a length of the string wrapping the dynamite had somehow caught on the back of the boat. The dynamite was being towed beneath the surface, about ten feet down and ten feet behind the rowboat.

About this time in the story, Granddad was laughing so hard, with tears in his eyes, remembering the incident, that he could hardly continue. "Well sir," he said, "when the blast came it was not where everyone expected it to be. It blew the ass end right out of the rowboat, and the boat and man disappeared in the foaming convulsion. By George," he said, "that fellow was pretty shook up when they fished him out of the water, but wasn't hurt much, put a few gray hairs in his head was all. But, by golly, everyone was so impressed with the show that they all let him keep the money." We all laughed hard at the story, knowing the crazy things that men in camp often do to combat boredom.

Goat Skins

I asked Granddad to tell us about hunting back in the 1920s when he and Grandmother and others were still living in shacks on the beach at Nootum Bay. My mother, Elsie Gildersleeve, was only nine or ten years old in 1920. Granddad allowed that hunting back then was a "very frequent activity, and not so much a sport as it was a necessity." He went on to tell us: "We had to hunt for meat, we had little choice. You must realize that we had no refrigeration and no way to keep fresh meat from spoiling. We hunted black bear, grizzly bear, deer and goats for their meat and their hides.

"Goat meat was a favorite in the cookhouse and since goats were plentiful in the mountains back of camp, we hunted them on a regular basis.

"By golly, there was this time when Almon and Lloyd Owens and my brother Jack and I were all hunting together. It was late in the year, October I think, and unseasonably warm, almost like an Indian summer. We had left camp at daybreak and fully intended to be back by nightfall. It was so warm that none of us took along heavy jackets.

"We hunted all day long, keeping close together, and by late afternoon we all had shot a goat. Unfortunately for us, the weather high on the mountain had turned cold and the fog rolled in. Well sir, it then began to rain, which very soon turned to snow. Visibility quickly dropped to only a few yards, and we could not see a damned thing. It's funny how the fog distorts things and makes directions so confusing. We were on the side of a mountain, but with the fog all around and covering us, it appeared that we could just walk off in any direction. Fortunately for us, we knew that mountain well and knew better than to move too fast. Slowly we worked our way down into the timber.

"By then we were pretty well soaked through, but in the interest of our own safety, we decided to go no further. We would hole up for the night. We all agreed that spending the night shivering was a mite better than stepping off a 100-foot cliff in the dark.

"Then someone had an idea. We all had goat skins rolled up on our packs and it was suggested that we drape the skins over our shoulders and backs and huddle together for even greater warmth. We found a quiet spot out of the wind, dropped our packs and crawled into our goat skins. Surprisingly, even though it was close to freezing and snowed off and on, we actually spent a fairly comfortable night.

"At first light, most of the fog had lifted and we made our way down the mountain and back to our camp on the beach. Those were some of the finest goat hides we ever got. Somewhere we have pictures, taken the morning we got back, shows us with the goat hides on our shoulders."

The Giant Goat

Uncle Dick then asked Granddad, "What about that giant goat that Uncle Jack claimed he saw that time?"

"Yeah, well, that was the time when your Uncle Almon, Jack and I were hunting down on King Island near Snow Mountain. The three of us were spread out at just about timberline when all of a sudden brother Jack starts to holler at us to come quick and look at what he sees. He is waving his arms, jumping up and down and hollering at the same time. Well sir, by the time Almon and I got over to where Jack was, there was nothing to see. Whatever it was, was gone. We asked Jack, what was it? He said, 'It was a giant goat, biggest goat I have ever seen, in fact it was as big as a horse, a big horse.' Of course, both of us, Almon and I, laughed at him and that made Jack awful mad. I said, 'Well, Jack, you know a goat can't be as big as a horse, leastwise, I never heard tell of one that big,' trying to humor him a little. But Jack was adamant and he was shaking he was so upset and mad at seeing whatever it was and us not believing him. 'For God's sakes, you fellows, you know me, I've hunted plenty with you and shot lots of goats with you. I know what a gosh-darned goat looks like, dammit, you guys know that. I tell you, this was a giant goat.'

"Okay, we told Jack, you saw something, but it ain't there now. Well sir, Jack was no good for the rest of that day, he just sulked and would not talk to us.

"I don't rightly know what he saw, but knowing my brother Jack, I know that he was right about one thing, he did see something that startled him, even scared him."

Uncle Dick asked, "Well, if he saw something, what in tarnation could it have been?"

"Well, mind you, I can only speculate, but sometimes when a person sees something that scares the dickens out of them, the mind can do strange things. It may play tricks with you. As I said, I'm only speculating, but supposing Jack actually saw a sasquatch? A sasquatch is not supposed to exist to Jack's mind, and so he does not see a sasquatch, but he has to tell us that he saw something awful big. Why not a goat, since that's what we were doing, goat hunting, so, Jack saw a huge goat. That's the best I can come up with."

Uncle Frank spoke up at this point to say, "I recall that Uncle Jack's experience was not the only strange thing that happened on a goat-hunting trip."

"Well, yeah, you're right, that Snow Mountain area back of Nootum Bay where we had our first camp after coming to B.C. was an interesting place to hunt. It's where I had a doggone crazy thing happen to me, again while I was alone goat hunting. Frank, you were only a baby, then, of two or three. Dick you were five or six, no more. Jim there, has likely not heard this story, so I'll tell you about it.

"We needed to hunt a lot in those days, as I have mentioned. Meat would not keep long, as we had no way to keep it cool. At least weekly we had to go shoot a goat or two to keep the cook-house supplied.

"On this particular day, I set off late, and by the time I had shot a goat, it was getting on to suppertime. I skinned it out, wrapped the meat I wanted in a canvas bag that we used for this and stuffed it inside of my packsack. I rolled up the hide and, securing it to the packsack, decided to go the short distance to the top and spend the night there. For sure I could not make it back to camp before dark.

"In fact," he told us, "I had a campsite that I had used a number of times from where I would watch the sun go down over the Pacific Ocean. It was a beautiful spot, and a wonderful experience to see the sun drop away like that, with the colors and all.

"I went right to a spot where I regularly cached my packsack for the night, especially if it contained fresh meat. My cache place was a deep, narrow crack in the otherwise unbroken flat surface of the surrounding rock. I had to lay on my stomach and push the packsack down into the crack, jamming it in place about an arm's length down. My meat had always been safe and never touched in this crack, because there was absolutely no way that any animal could reach down and pull it out. The crack was too deep and too narrow even for a small dog, let alone wolf or cougar."

At this point in Granddad's story I have to digress to remind everyone that this man was no novice hunter or greenhorn. This man was a logging pioneer in B.C. Pacific Coast history and a wilderness survivor and about as serious when telling this story as a sledge hammer blow on your thumb.

He continued, "My campsite was about fifty feet or so from the cache and against an enormous rock, as big as a house. There was no way I had found for getting on top of it. Nothing could climb it. It was just too bald and too steep. I had selected this spot partly because it was close to the cache, but also because of the safety it afforded me. My fire was four or five feet from the rock so that I could sit or lie between the rock and the fire. It wasn't long after I had eaten when it became very dark. I was dozing from the heat of the fire, when I sensed something very large pass over my head from off the top of the rock and land outside the glare of the campfire. Actually, I believe it was large and heavy because I felt the ground shake or vibrate when it landed, whatever it was. It spooked me bad. I grabbed my rifle and sat back of the fire, my eyes wide open the whole night, waiting for further developments. At first light I went immediately to retrieve my packsack from the cache and was astonished to find it lying on top of the rock with the canvas sack removed, opened and the meat gone. The goat hide remained.

"Now, to my way of thinking, only an animal with a long arm and opposing thumb could have grasped my packsack and hauled it to the surface of the crack, to say nothing of untying my knots to get at the meat. I know positively that no one from our camp was up on that mountain with me. It is out of the question to think that there was anyone else around who would steal my goat meat. There is no question, at all, in my mind of what done it. It was bigfoot, the sasquatch, same as the one Jack saw."

Out of respect for Granddad, I am sure, his story ended in silence. I tried to hide my amusement at his story unsuccessfully. He caught me smirking and allowed that "You young whippersnappers think you know it all, but I am here to tell you that I have experienced a thing or two, and so have others, that would make you want to change your underwear, by golly, young

260

feller." "I'll attest to that Doc, you damn bet," one of the older loggers agreed. They all then had a good laugh at my expense and the group broke up.

Bigfoot

I went from the cookhouse straight to bed that evening, as I had previously agreed with Granddad to do some mineral prospecting for him the next day. That meant scaling the steep rock bluffs behind camp. About midmorning of the following day I set off. Late in the afternoon I reached a narrow ledge where I could sit and view clearly the rock face that I wanted to examine, although there was no way that I could get over to it. It was a sheer rock wall about 2,000 feet above the valley floor and at least several hundred feet distant from where I was perched like a mountain goat. To enhance my inspection of the rock wall, I dug out a small brass eight-power telescope of Granddad's that I used for such purposes. I had my eye to the telescope and was confirming the truth about the intense red smear of color that could be seen from camp. It definitely was not of mineral origin, but instead was a lovely red-orange lichen. As I gazed at the fungoid growth and marveled at the richness and beauty of its organic coloring, I sensed, or heard, from a long way off, the sound of a bugle blowing. At first it confused me because my mind could not rationalize what I heard with where I was. Then I heard it again, loud and clear, and there was no mistaking it was coming from a ledge above and behind me.

I have no reason at all to deny that it just plain scared the heck out of me (as my Grandfather prophesied, in such cases, I might need a change of underwear). I was definitely spooked. Nervous as hell, I had to crawl backward along my narrow ledge where there was no room to turn around. I felt that something was challenging me and that I needed to be where I could maneuver. Once off the ledge, I sat and looked around for a few minutes, waiting to hear the noise again. There was only silence. By now all I wanted to do was get off that mountain, because it would be dark in an hour or less.

The quickest way down from those bluffs to the narrow valley below was a rather unorthodox descent down the fir trees that grow against the bluffs. There were many bluffs all about fifty feet high. The general procedure for sliding down a fir tree is to jump out from a position on the bluff landing eight to ten feet below the top of the tree, giving the tree a bear hug with your arms and sliding lickety-split down to the larger branches where you then climb to the bottom. Walk to the next bluff and repeat the tree-descending procedure again and again for a rapid descent of the mountain.

By the time I was down on the valley floor, it was dark. I groped my way slowly through the wooded terrain, feeling jittery that whatever had produced that bugling sound was close behind. Normally, being in the woods after dark causes me no fear. In my experience, the last thing that any animal will do is attack in the dark. Usually, they hear you first and then they are heard crashing their way rapidly off in the opposite direction. Being spooked, though, is a whole different kettle of fish. It deals more, I think, with the mysterious nature of the subconscious mind.

What does it mean to be spooked? It's like a sudden allergy. Nerves sprout blisters causing thought processes to fracture. Judgment becomes transparent as window glass while the icy shadow of fear forms a damp mildew over one's skin. Fortunately, this state of mind is recognizable and the most courageous thing to do when it strikes is to sit down and do nothing, until the feeling passes and often it does in a matter of minutes.

At breakfast the following morning I mentioned my previous afternoon's experience to a man who I thought would regard my story sympathetically. He nodded vigorously, smiled and, putting a hand on my shoulder said, "Well, Jim, you are back in one piece anyway. Oh, by the way," he added, "I am going trout fishing at that small lake below those bluffs you were climbing yesterday. Do you have any spare fly line that I might use?"

At supper that evening I noticed that, as he ate, my friend seemed engrossed in thought.

"How was the fishing," I asked, "catch anything?" Instead of answering me, he asked me in a rather subdued voice, unusual for him, "Tell me again about that noise you said you heard up on the bluffs." So I did, and again he grew quiet.

Then he spoke, "Funny," he said, "I was fly casting in that small lake, you know, the one I told you about, when out of nowhere comes this bewildering racket, not so much like bugle notes but more like a shriek, repeated, and loud as hell, like it was right behind me." He was silent for a moment. Then he said quietly, "I took off running like I was possessed. Later, after I regained my composure, I looked down at my fishing reel and saw that all of your line was gone. I panicked and forgot to reel it in. Sorry old man," as he again patted me on the shoulder.

Now this story is even more interesting because this man was no "Mr. Milque Toast." He stood about six-foot-four, a big, raw-boned Scotsman that weighed around 225 pounds. During World War II he had been a Regimental Sergeant Major in the Canadian Army. (I am told that those fellows ate nails for breakfast.) At this time he was employed by my grandfather as a cat-skinner and certainly was not the type to lose his nerve or spook easily.

What did Uncle Jack Gildersleeve see or thought he saw? What took Granddad's goat meat? What did both the cat-skinner and I hear on two different occasions? I don't have the slightest idea and probably never will have. But I know that there is something mysterious out there. It is food for thought.

One thing is for certain, there are no elk or caribou anywhere in that area of B.C. Moose just don't sound anything like what we heard; besides, it was not the proper season for moose calling. Who knows, maybe it was sasquatch after all.

Doc's Rock

It has been forty-three years since I first heard the story concerning "a rock as big as a house" and the sasquatch that made off with Grandfather's goat meat.

For me as a young man there was never any question regarding the veracity of grandfather's story. However, in repeating it to

263

others over the years, I have puzzled over what his "rock as big as a house" that "nothing could climb" must have looked like.

I have four treasured, old, yellowed photographs. They were taken on Snow Mountain behind Nootum Bay between 1917 and 1923 on one of Doc's goat-hunting trips and show recognizable terrain near the summit of Snow Mountain. Doc probably took these pictures, because he is not in them. They do, however, include his two regular hunting partners and brothers-in-law, Almon and Lloyd Owens. Two significant details in the pictures are a small mountain lake in the foreground and a mountain ridge with a prominent single sawtooth feature against the skyline. I have kept these four photographs handy of late, to study in leisure moments. Somehow I felt they might be key to future adventure.

My curiosity regarding Snow Mountain caught up with me during August of 1997. I finally had the opportunity to seek Doc's Rock—the "rock as big as a house" that "nothing could climb." Snow Mountain was never recorded, as such, on any chart of the area. They may have chosen that name because, although only slightly more than 4,000 feet tall, I was to discover that their most practical hunting area faced north and thus retained considerable snow into late summer.

My first challenge was to identify which of the several peaks back of Nootum Bay was Snow Mountain. I had remembered from childhood being told that it took one hour of tramping to reach the base of the mountain from their Nootum Bay encampment. According to a topographical map of the area, that narrowed the options to three mountains.

We left Kimsquit on the Dean River at 6:10 one morning in Danny Hodson's R-44 Rainbow West helicopter and proceeded south down Dean Channel crossing over King Island into Burke Channel. In the distance I could make out the summits of several peaks girdling the Nootum Bay area. Naively, I had thought identifying Snow Mountain quickly would be easy. Now, up in the air and viewing the options, I had serious second thoughts. They all appeared large, steep and heavily timbered. None of the options seemed reachable by one hour's hiking from Nootum Bay tidewater. I was, of course, forgetting to factor in the mindset of Doc Gildersleeve's generation of woodsman. The truth of the matter was that Doc and his partners often did hike to Snow Mountain's base, climb to 3,000 feet, shoot their goat or goats and then return to tidewater by nightfall.

Suddenly, a feeling of chagrin possessed me. What the heck was I doing, attempting to find Doc's "mystery rock," itself just a blip of granite somewhere ahead of us on a mountain that I could not identify—when all I had for clues were four old photographs. The photographs were before me, as if I had expected them to indicate which of the options was Snow Mountain, not to mention direct us to a spot near Doc's favored goat-hunting area.

Finally, because I was silent, Danny asked me, "Which mountain?" I thought to make a joke of it by replying "eenie-meenie-minee-moe," but instead had to say "I don't know." He gave me a smile and somewhat sympathetic look, I think, sensing my confusion. "No problem," he said, "I'm familiar with this area, so let's fly around a bit and maybe you will recognize something." His words relaxed me somewhat and I began to study more closely the sawtooth ridge profile shown in the photographs.

Minutes later, to my everlasting astonishment, that sawtooth detail, I noticed, compared favorably to a mountain ridge on our left. Danny saw the similarity, also, and he headed for it. Closer still, we soon had no doubts that this was Snow Mountain. Bewilderment to certainty had occurred in a scant few minutes. What luck. It was almost too good to be true—and what a relief for my sagging self-confidence.

Our approach to Snow Mountain was above timberline, skimming a few hundred feet over treeless, weather-beaten rock that closely resembled the terrain in all of the photographs. Suddenly before us was a small mountain lake recognizable as the one in the photos. This I felt was inscrutable luck.

Danny lowered the helicopter slowly onto a small patch of lush green alpine grass alongside the diamond clear water of the lake. This spot was photographic "ground zero," from which all Doc's photos were taken. After all my misgivings about locating the right mountain, we not only did that but honed into their lakeside rendezvous with laserlike precision. How about that? Was this outcome preordained or what? I was ecstatic. Smiling like Alice's Cheshire cat, I disembarked from the chopper to set foot on Snow Mountain's "historical" patch of greenery.

With other business on his mind, Danny quickly offloaded my pack, and checking his watch, we agreed he would return to this spot for me in about seven hours. Then he was gone. It was 7:00 A.M.

After many previous hours studying the pictures of this spot on Snow Mountain, the surroundings I now saw were very familiar—so much so in fact that I had a twilight zone sensation of being in one of the photographs.

Hurrying over to a welcoming row of chest-high boulders, I draped myself over a well-rounded example in the form of an affectionate bear hug. The immediate chill I received through my light clothing confirmed that I was not hallucinating.

To control my excitement, I began to consider a brief plan for the day. What to do first? Reconnoitering the area seemed a good idea. Remember, I thought to myself, I'm here to look for Doc's Rock—"a rock as big as a house."

My view at our landing site beside the lake was restricted by the surrounding granite basin that sloped gradually away from the pool of water to a height in places of perhaps fifty feet. In just a few minutes I walked up the slope and stood on the rim of the lake basin where I encountered a marvelous vista. At about 3,500 feet altitude I had a 200-degree view of the north and west sides of Snow Mountain, encompassing hundreds of acres of treeless, wind-scoured, ice-cracked bare rock to include numberless bluffs, gullies and shear ravines. Snow still prevailed in most of the nooks and crannies but also lay deep in broad areas protected in shadow from long hours of summer sun. The lake area behind me nestled comfortably in the approximate center of this mostly barren goat haven, and was set hard against a summit ridge on the east side that rose hundreds of feet higher.

The narrow, boomerang-shaped lake is perhaps a quarter mile long by seventy-five yards wide in places. It is created by summer snow melt collecting in the rock depression formed at the base of the summit ridge. The water was crystal clear and very deep at its center. A shallow, sandy bottom at one end invites ankle wading if one enjoys glacial temperatures. The continuously filling lake has an outlet through a short granite trough and slips away in silence over the west edge almost unnoticed.

I devoted the next half hour to circling the lake area, acquainting myself with its landscape details, especially as they related to the photographs. During this time I easily located the places by the lake where each of the old photographs was taken. By lining up a few pertinent landmarks such as lake contours relative to certain large boulders, I found the specific rock that my Uncle Almon sat on while posing for one of the old pictures. This was a real kick for me, so I took a time exposure of myself with a smirky grin sitting on Almon's rock.

The sawtooth rock skyline feature in the background of the photographs began to interest me more and more. Did that sawtooth detail have an importance I wasn't aware of? Time would tell. Once or twice I considered it just might be the "rock as big as a house," but I dismissed the notion because from my vantage point by the lake, it loomed more like a major section of the mountain—and it was.

There were now about six hours left to explore and I wanted to cover as much ground as possible. I was out to enjoy myself first and finding Doc's Rock would be "frosting on the cake." My plan was to climb the ridge of several hundred feet behind the lake to the summit where I could survey all below. From the top I would traverse southwest across and down the ridge to the distant sawtooth formation and from there descend even further, returning to the lake level where I began.

Shouldering my twenty-pound pack, I skirted the north end of the lake and started up. My eyes eagerly surveyed the slopes and gullies for the easiest path. I followed smooth, upward-sloping rock outcroppings bordered in many places with a variety of blue and purple heather mixed with long-stemmed yellow buttercups. A goat path suckered me to a breathtaking shear drop where cliffs soared even higher above me before plunging hundreds of feet to an alpine graveyard of tumbled boulders. Looking down I

267

saw many among them that were as large as a house, yet all would be easy to climb. I dropped my pack to rest a spell and contemplate the enthralling sights and distances.

The view for miles was seductively clear. Everything in sight was in focus and solid looking, no matter that it might be ten miles away. The closest crag might be a mile distant; however, I felt that I could have tossed a rock to it. Relaxed, my thinking flowed as clear as an eagle's vision, provoking philosophical thoughts. I mused about the possibilities of mind over matter. Flirtatious whispers hinted that I journey across to the next hilltop where a lush green meadow beckoned. Why not just float on over, it shouldn't be that difficult. I wished!

All was silent except for the snow melt bubbling away into the gullies, chased by a playful breeze that carried the scent of wildflowers and hummed a soft tune among the rocks. Is this where heaven began?

Refreshed, I bounded upward to seek an even higher perch. Large stones of every description crowded the way. Some were half buried, some squatted solidly fixed, while a few large examples were teetering and appeared to have done so for eons. None were "as big as a house." A few wind-stunted trees gestured with gnarled limbs the way up a narrow goat path with the now energetic breeze pressing gleefully from behind. Goat trails led everywhere, seducing my interest to go this way or that way. I hesitated to choose a path and noticed cougar tracks followed the trails where goats had left tufts of their wool on scratchy thickets. Soon my pockets were full of oily wool.

Finally, at the summit, my view was unobstructed. From this high vantage point the now lower sawtooth formation began to better delineate itself. It was perhaps a mile away. I was now beginning to grasp its true size and shape. Could this be Doc's Rock? It looked enormous.

Sun shadows indicated noon and time to eat. I devoured two meat sandwiches, washing it down with water from my flasks. Resting my back against a flat stone, I gazed westward out over Burke Channel and across the lower end of King Island to Fisher Channel. The cruise ship *Rotterdam* had just emerged from Lama

Passage, heading south. The scene was like an immense mosaic panorama with azure and green pieces as fjord water, interrupted by dappled brown, green, gray and yellow pieces for interspersed bare rock and densely wooded side hills all locked together for "show and tell," with the bone white *Rotterdam* superimposed, as with a skyhook, over this scene. Since the cruise ship was the only moving element in this "mural," I fantasized a hidden puppeteer behind one of the mountains giving the *Rotterdam* motion.

I dallied too long. My legs were stiffening, and as I rose to leave I winced at the cramping in my thighs. This was a new experience for me. My thoughts raced to a time while in Oregon hiking with a group in the Columbia Gorge when I heard a call for help. Hurrying to the sound of the voice, I encountered an individual lying on the path locked into a fetal position unable to move a muscle. Upon the advice of others, I forced a quart of water down his throat. To my surprise and his, within minutes his muscles began to relax, beginning with his fingers and arms and then his legs. He literally unfolded like a flower responding to the first rays of dawn. Minutes later he rose to his feet and declared that he was okay. Later that day, however, he was admitted to the hospital. It turned out that his body potassium level was so low that his dehydrated state triggered major cramping of all his muscles.

The August afternoon air was very hot and dry, and thinking I might have the beginnings of a similar problem, I quickly guzzled another pint of water from one of my flasks. Now I was facing the decision of continuing on or returning the way I had come. I figured I might have covered about half the distance on my journey from the lake across the top of the mountain and back down to the lake. However, the route ahead was unknown to me and I might still reach an impasse that would force me to retrace my steps. About three hours remained to complete the journey back to the lake, whichever route I chose. I was unmistakably tired and thought that perhaps I had taken on too much on such a hot day. My greatest danger was exhaustion. I did have flares with me and reasoned that Danny would find me wherever I was, if I did not make it back to the lake by the specified time. It upset me tremendously to think that I had come this far and might not

269

be able to cover the planned distance. Therefore, I decided to go on with caution. I continued to drink more water and gradually the cramps ceased. The fatigue remained, however, so I just dealt with it as I moved on carefully at a reduced pace.

Nearing the sawtooth formation I could now look directly down upon it and from a quarter mile away it took my breath away. I just knew that I had found Doc's "rock as big as a house"; no, it was more like an apartment building.

Eventually I was standing alongside this gargantuan "rock" and to say that I was astonished at its immense proportions would be a serious understatement. I had to wonder if Doc had purposely minimized its size. No one, I felt, would have grasped the hugeness of this rock, even if they had believed his sasquatch story. It was at least four stories high and rested on a rectangular base approximately 150 feet by 75 feet. Just as Doc had described it, however, the sides were near perpendicular and smooth, with no cracks, crevasses, bumps, ledges or vegetation that would allow any known creature to scale its sides. Its peak was sloping in the manner of a mine shaft roof.

Wearily I removed my pack and began a survey around the base of the rock. From a rise of about eight feet I descended along the south side of the base into a small depression about ten feet by twenty feet. I was facing the rock and before me, about four feet from the rock base, were the unmistakable burn scars of a long unused fire pit. Hardly believing my eyes and feeling like an archaeologist who had just unearthed an ancient tomb, I crouched low to study the blackened ground where moss and roots had been consumed to create a shallow circular depression. Curiously I reached out and touched the charred remains of turf, reflecting as I did so on Doc's night of sasquatch terror eighty years earlier.

I am almost certain no one had stood and gazed upon that spot since Doc left in a hurry the morning after his mysterious sasquatch episode. I felt a disturbing connection, not exactly déjà vu. The fact was that my long-lived vicarious association with Doc's memorable old sasquatch story of this place had unexpectedly hardened into reality. Here I was gazing down at the "scene of the crime," so to speak. I felt like hollering "Yippee!" In fact I did.

I thought that if Doc could have spoken to me at that very moment, he might have asked in surprise—"How the devil did you find this place?"

I recalled Doc's story as I sat back against the rock facing the fire pit. The creature that he claimed leaped from the top of the rock over his head and the fire would have landed on solid rock about eight feet above where he was sitting (and where I was now sitting). Looking to my right I had an unobstructed view out toward the Pacific Ocean. Indeed he would have been able to sit in that position of safety and, as he said, watch the sun sink into the sea.

It seemed so improbable to me that I should ever have found the setting of Doc's sasquatch story—and yet here I was. The photographs were the keys to discovery after all. That jagged sawtooth rock on the shoulder of Snow Mountain is, for sure, Doc's Rock. I do agree that it sure as heck is "as big as a house" and no creature I know of could ever climb it.

Time was running out for me and I reluctantly had to leave. My knees were worn out, no longer would they hold my weight, and my balance was shot. I had to move slowly. It was very steep and so I slid and crawled down from rock to rock. I was so cautious and quiet that I surprised two goats basking in the afternoon sun. I watched them at close range for a few minutes. They were licking and cleaning each other's fur, as I have watched cats do. It's likely they had never seen a human before and therefore took their time before bounding out of sight.

Finally, I stood beside the lake where I had started out almost seven hours earlier. My energy was exhausted. I removed my pack and stretched my body full length onto a large slab of warm granite, where spread-eagled I allowed my consciousness an immediate holiday. In about twenty minutes, although it seemed much shorter, the thump, thump of the helicopter returning stirred my dreaming.

Looking down at Doc's Rock as we lifted away I had the distinct feeling there was more to discover and that I would be back.

Epilogue

Before 1900, when sawmills began to proliferate, the mills turned to small logging contractors to supply them with logs. The mills habitually paid their contractors with scrip (paper certificate used in place of money). The scrip was often discounted or considered worthless by the local merchants, because the mill owners had gone broke or reneged on honoring the scrip. Either way, the contractor was blamed, and thus the term "gypo" was applied to them.

In later years the term gypo lost most, if not all, of its early derogatory connotations. Any small logging contractor could be referred to as a gypo operation. It is very likely that some of the best logging contractors in B.C. history have been called gypo operations, even though they were well managed and financed.

Family-owned and -run gypo operations, such as the Gildersleeve floating camps that I grew up on, are likely close to extinction. If this is true, it may not be a good thing. The reason for their demise probably has more to do with government legislation, i.e., availability of Crown timber, tree farm licensing, etc., than anything else. Though the lifestyle in the camps was challenging, it was manageable.

Work at the camps was physically hard and dangerous. Isolation from extended family and friends was another hardship. All these hardships, however, were acceptable to the owners as they also got the opportunity to take charge of their lives, assume responsibility for their own welfare and ask little from anyone. For almost forty years, the Gildersleeves provided employment for hundreds of coastal families willing to assume the challenges of the gypo-logging lifestyle.

In the last fifty years, modern technology has created radio phones, fax machines, satellite TV, power saws, articulated off-road vehicles, mechanized mobile steel spar trees and self-loading log barges; as well, there are north coastal aircraft operations that transport personnel, mail, supplies in and out of isolated camps without much bother. None of this was possible in the first half of the century. Logging and loggers are not the same as they once were.

My grandparents, Doc and Amy Gildersleeve, never got to retire. Typical of pioneer stock, they both gave too much of themselves during their thirty-nine years of coastal logging. They died prematurely of heart problems; Amy died in 1955 at sixty-five years and Doc died a year later at sixty-four. Doc Creek, Amy Creek and Gildersleeve Lake are how we remember them at Nootum Bay in Lower Burke Channel. This is where they lived on the beach for their first five winters after coming to B.C. from Oregon. During that period they built the large floating rafts that later served their mobile logging operations into the 1950s. Gildersleeve Bay inside Fish Egg Inlet is also named after them.

Of Doc and Amy's five children who grew to adulthood, only one survives at this writing—Aunt Pearl (Gildersleeve) Evans. Pearl and Uncle Leyton had three children: Leslie, Sandy and Brian. Elsie Gildersleeve (Sirois) Gadsden, my mother and the oldest sibling, had six children: Audrey, James, Cherie, Dolores, Marilyn and Terry. Uncle Richard and Aunt Phyl (Gadsden) Gildersleeve had one child: Penny Lynn. Richard in later years was employed by Crown Zellerbach at Ocean Falls. Uncle Frank and Aunt Joyce (Casperson) Gildersleeve had five children: Barry, Jill, Debbie, Karen and Megan. Frank was a logging contractor living in Bella Coola. Uncle Keaton and Aunt Maria (Brady) Gildersleeve had one child: George. Keaton left the camp at age eighteen during WW II. He flew Spitfires and Mosquito bombers and at war's end was twenty-three. He went to Alaska and was a bush pilot for the next forty years.

In 1956 I was working in Ocean Falls for funds to further my education. That fall I transferred to the University of Washington in Seattle and graduated from there in 1958 with a degree in industrial design. After graduate school at Pratt Institute in Brooklyn, New York, I was hired in 1960 by the Whirlpool Corporation of Benton Harbor Michigan. There I worked in their advanced industrial design section. I helped support product concept development on all major household appliances, initiated by many technical disciplines at the labs. Before leaving in 1965, I worked the last two years exclusively on the feasibility and design of the life support systems for the first-generation astronauts.

In 1955 I met my wife Gerry Mooney at Ocean Falls while working at summer employment there. We were married in Brooklyn, New York, in 1959 and moved to Benton Harbor, Michigan, shortly thereafter. Our fist two children, Eric Harrison and Casey Ellen were born there, while Christine Lee came in 1965 shortly after I moved our family to Portland, Oregon.

My intention in moving to Portland was to start a new design firm. Together with partner Perry Rosen, we founded Rosen-Sirois Industrial Design Inc. We specialized in product development, design and packaging of industrial equipment, instruments and various mechanical devices. In 1974 I bought out my partner and the firm became Sirois and Associates. Geographically, we served manufacturing clients from California to, and including, B.C.

The year 1975 was an especially difficult year for my family as Eric passed away from cancer at the age of fifteen. Casey now has two daughters, Jessie and Heather. Christine has a son, Brandon.

All my sisters, save one, live in California. Audrey and Cherie moved there shortly after graduating as registered nurses fro the St. Paul's School of Nursing in Vancouver. Audrey passed away in 1996 of cancer. Cherie is retired and lives with her husband John Bauer in Martinez, California; Dolores and husband Brad White live in Los Gatos, California; Mary Sirois lives in Orangevale, California; brother Mike Sirois and wife Connie live in Salt Lake City, Utah; Marilyn (Gadsden) Wilson lives in Lewiston, Idaho; brother Terrance Gadsden and wife Marilyn live in Port Alice, B.C.

My wife Gerry and I divorced in 1989. Thus, my circumstances allow me to spend most of the year at my Kimsquit property on the Dean River. After my rustic beginnings in the outback of British Columbia and subsequent minor contributions to the world's "market economy," here I am, full circle, back where I started. This puts me in mind of the proverbial salmon returning to its place of origin.

Chronology of British Columbia, West Coast and Gildersleeve History

(Bold type indicates historical Gildersleeve dates)

1513 Vasco Nunez de Balboa crossed the isthmus of Panama and claimed the Pacific Ocean, including all shores it might wash onto, for the Spanish Crown (Barman).

1534 The Algonquin Indian word Canatha means "a collection of houses" or "a village." Jacques Cartier in 1534 took this name to be the name of the country. Thus, we now have the name Canada (Lyons, 1969:l).

1579 Francis Drake sailed the west coast of North America as far north as San Francisco Bay (Manning, 1905:307).

1670 Hudson's Bay Company was created to exploit the fur trading potential of North America (specifically beaver, at that time) (Barman).

1728 Captain James Cook was born October 27, at Merton, Yorkshire.

1728–9 Vitus Bering, a Danish sea captain in Russian employ reconnoitered islands off the North American coast and discovered Bering Straits (Lyons).

1740–41 Vitus Bering, again for Russia, explored North American coast along the Aleutian Islands. He wrecked on Bering Island, where he died (Lyons).

1760 New France was lost to England; French General Montcalm lost the battle of the Plains of Abraham to English General Wolf (Barman).

1744 First Spanish expedition under Juan Jose Perez Hernandez sailed to the Queen Charlotte Islands; no land was claimed (Manning, 1905:308).

1745 British Admiralty offered £20,000 for discovery of a northwest passage (Lyons).

1755 Second Spanish expedition under Bruno de Hezeta and Juan Francisco de la Bodeza Y. Quadra. They claimed land as far north as fifty-eight (north latitude into the Alaskan panhandle) (Manning, 1905:308).

1757 Captain George Vancouver was born at King's Lynn, Norfolk.

1764 Sir Alexander Mackenzie was born at Stornoway, Scotland.

1778 Captain Cook explored the northwest coast of B.C. above forty-five (north latitude) searching for a northwest passage. First Englishman known to have visited Nootka Sound. In spring of 1778 he spent the month of April there and mapped it thoroughly. He named Cape Flattery (Cook referred to it as "King George's Sound") (Manning, 1905:306) (Barman).

1779 Third Spanish expedition reached 60 (north latitude; as far as Kodiak Island) (Barman).

1779 Captain Cook was killed (and some say eaten) by natives at the Sandwich Islands (Barman).

1785 Captain James Hanna sailed from Macao and anchored in King George Sound (Nootka Sound). First trading expedition to North America (Lyons).

1786 Captain Hanna's second voyage to Pacific Coast (Lyons).

1787 Captain Barkley, accompanied by his wife, cruised B.C. coastal waters and reached Nootka Sound.

1788 Captain Mears in May established a trading post at Nootka Sound (Friendly Cove). He had brought fifty Chinese artisans from China. With their help he had erected a two-story house and built a ship of fifty tons named the Northwest America. In October they all returned to China. The following spring (1789) Mears' associate captain Colnett returned to Friendly Cove with two ships, the Argonaut and the Princess Royal. "In addition to their crews they had several artificers of different professions and near seventy Chinese who intended to become settlers on the American coast." Unfortunately, the Spanish, who claimed Nootka Sound, had arrived a few weeks earlier in ships commanded by Captain

Martinez. The Spanish impounded the British ships, their supplies and crews. Thus began the "Nootka Sound Controversy." All personnel were taken to San Blas, Mexico. Whatever happened to the Chinese artisans is not clear (Manning).

1790 In the late eighteenth century it has been said that 80,000 or more Indians lived in B.C. Further, it is estimated that almost half of all Indians living in Canada at that time of first contact with Europeans lived in B.C.; coast nations then were: Coast Salish; Nootka; Kwakiutl; Bella Coola; Tsimshian and Haida (Jean Barman).

1793 Captain George Vancouver in June of that year explored Dean Channel; named Raphoe Point after Reverend James King, Dean of Raphoe, Ireland in 1791 (Ramsey) (Raphoe Point is approximately six miles south of Dean River mouth).

1793 Alexander Mackenzie reached the Pacific Ocean at the mouth of the Bella Coola River on July 10, 1793 (Kopas).

1792–4 Captain Vancouver proved by examination of coast that the Northwest Passage connecting Atlantic and Pacific Oceans through the North American continent did not exist (Lyons:727).

1798 Captain George Vancouver died at forty-one, May 10, at Petersham, Surrey (Lyons).

1804 Lewis and Clark expedition to Pacific organized. November 7 expedition reached estuary of Columbia (Lyons).

1805–8 Simon Fraser reached the Pacific Ocean at Vancouver, B.C. via the Fraser River (Barman).

1806 Nicholas Appert system of preserving food (boiling in hot water) was developed (McKervill). He was awarded a prize of 12,000 francs in 1909.

1810 David Thompson came down the Columbia River to Fort Astoria (Barman).

1811 Beginning of agriculture in B.C., at Fort St. James.

1820 Sir Alexander Mackenzie died, at fifty-seven.

1821 Fort Alexandria established July 2. Amalgamation of Hudson's Bay Company and Northwest Company (Lyons).

1825 Hudson's Bay Company established Fort Vancouver on Columbia River.

1825 Treaty between Great Britain and Russia defined boundary of territory afterwards called Alaska.

1825 Sea otters on the Pacific Northwest coast in serious decline.

1829 Salmon curing began at Fort Langley. Fish became B.C.'s second industry (fur the first).

1831 Fort Simpson (north of Prince Rupert) established by Hudson's Bay Company on Chatham Sound; this was the market for all of the northern Indian tribes of the mainland and Queen Charlottes, plus Alaska. Approximately (14,000) Indians traded there (Rain Coast).

1833 Fort McLoughlin—Hudson's Bay post, at Bella Bella, established; torn down in 1843 (Rain Coast).

1835 Coal discovered on Vancouver Island.

1840 Fort Durham: Hudson's Bay Company purchased a Russian post on the Stikine River, presumably closed it, and then established Fort Durham on the Taku River (Rain Coast).

1843 Hudson's Bay Company first arrived on Vancouver Island; construction of Fort Victoria began; this was approximately 170 years after the creation of the Hudson's Bay Company in 1670 (Akrigg).

1846 Treaty of Washington signed by Britain and the United States put the international boundary west of the Rockies at the 49th parallel of latitude (Akrigg).

1849 California Gold Rush. Later gold rushes: Australia, 1851; Pacific Northwest, 1858; Transvaal, 1886; Klondike, 1898 (Barman).

1851 Gold discovered at Queen Charlottes.

1852 Victoria, B.C., named: first it was Fort Albert, then Fort Victoria, then in 1853, Victoria, and in 1868 became capital of B.C. (Barman).

1853 Bella Bella—New Hudson's Bay trading post built (Rain Coast).

1857 Death of Sir John McLoughlin, father of Oregon.

1857 William Duncan established a Christian mission at Fort Simpson (Rain Coast).

1858 Governor James Douglas fixed price of land at two dollars fifty cents per acre.

1858 Matthew Baillie Begbie sworn as judge; rule of fur trade ended, rule of law began.

1858 The mainland colony of British Columbia under Governor Douglas was inaugurated, August 2, 1858, with the provisional capital at Fort Langley. It was raining (Barman).

1858 Approximately 200 white inhabitants in mainland B.C.— soon to be 30,000 coming to gold rush on the Fraser River (Downie).

1859 Hudson's Bay Company's lease to Vancouver Island terminated May 30, 1859. Britain then took control over sovereignty of all of the Pacific Northwest north of the 49th parallel (Barman).

1860 Major William Downie and others explored B.C. coastal inlets including Dean Channel and Kimsquit area for a short route to the interior gold fields (Downie) (Akrigg).

1860 Waddington's men attempted a wagon road at Bute Inlet to the interior; ended in failure (Downie) (Akrigg).

1860s Smallpox, measles, tuberculosis, and whooping cough decimated B.C. Indians; reduced Indian population by 70 percent (Rain Coast).

1862 Victoria incorporated (Barman).

1862–5 Caribou Road completed from Yale to Quesnel, 400 miles and eighteen feet wide.

1862 Simon Fraser died, April 19.

1862 Overlanders left Fort Gary for Fraser gold fields, June 2.

1862 William Barker made big gold strike on Williams Creek, August 21.

1862 Overlanders crossed Yellowhead Pass. Mrs. August Schubert was first European woman to cross Rocky Mountains in Canada, August 22.

1863 Barkerville, B.C., had 10,000 residents, mostly miners. The colonization of British Columbia began in earnest with the gold mining prospectors (Barman).

1864 First commercial canning of salmon at Washington Cal. on the Sacramento River (Lyons).

279

1865 Dean Creek (River) land speculation (sham) by Victoria promoters. Faked a road to be built to the B.C. interior from Kimsquit Flats (Downie).

1865 Dr. William Fraser Tolmie, Chief Hudson's Bay Factor in Victoria, when consulted, wrote a letter strongly urging Great Britain to accept a Russian offer to sell the panhandle. On the other hand, the Royal Navy's Commander-in-Chief for the Pacific, Rear Admiral the Hon. Joseph Denman recommended that Britain get rid of Vancouver Island and British Columbia. He noted that half of the 14,000 inhabitants were foreign, had to import food from Washington and Oregon and could not defend themselves. He wrote "I consider it would be greatly for the interest of England to divest herself of these possessions by any means consistent with honor and justice to the English settlers" (Akrigg:320). Two years later the U.S. saw a bargain in the panhandle, later known as the Alaskan Panhandle, and bought it.

1866 Six entrepreneurs filed a claim with the Lands and Works Dept. of British Columbia to 960 acres of land on the Dean Delta. Transfer never took place (Prince 1992:48).

1866 Two colonies, Vancouver Island and British Columbia, merge to become the United Colony of British Columbia; the capital was New Westminster (Barman).

1867 Bella Coola: Hudson's Bay Post established at Bella Coola (Kopas). (This was twenty-four years prior to Doc Gildersleeve's birth.)

1867 First Canadian Dominion Day. North America Act went into effect uniting four Canadian provinces into the Dominion of Canada. They were: Canada West (Ontario); Canada East (Quebec); New Brunswick and Nova Scotia (Akrigg).

1867 U.S. purchased Alaska from Russia, March 30, 1867, for 7.2 million dollars.

1868 Victoria made capital of B.C. (Akrigg).

1870 First commercial salmon canning in B.C. on the Fraser River (Lyons).

1871 British Columbia entered Canadian Confederation on July 20, 1871, and became a province of Canada (Barman).

1874 Dean River: Railroad exploration survey from Dean River to the Blackwater River Valley. Possible terminus at Dean River for the Trans Continental Railway—(Canadian Pacific Railway) (Barman).

1876 Private entrepreneurs, the Oppenheimer Brothers, applied for a tract of land at the head of Dean Channel "for fishing purposes." Transfer never made (Prince, 1992:51).

1876 Dean River and Kimsquit Bay: Further investigation of harbor possibilities for the Canadian Pacific Railway Terminus (Barman) (Prince, 1992:49).

1876 First red spring canning on Skeena: 1877, sockeye salmon on Fraser (Lyons).

1877 Kimsquit Indian village bombarded by H.M.S. Rocket (Prince 1992:53).

1880 Construction of CPR Railway through Fraser Canyon began in 1880 (Barman).

1881 Letters patent issued to Canadian Pacific Railway for building ocean-to-ocean railway; government to give 25 million dollars and 25 million acres of land.

1882 Bella Coola: Hudson Bay post closes (Kopas).

1882 Rivers Inlet: RIC (Rivers Inlet Cannery) built by Shotbolt, Hart & Company of Victoria (Lyons).

1882 Superintendent of Indians, Powell, recommended that Kimsquit Indians get compensation for the shelling of their village, and petitioned Ottawa for 1,200 dollars to purchase lumber and other building materials (Prince 1992:54).

1883 Bella Coola: Methodist Church established (Kopas).

1887 First Canadian Pacific passenger train from Montreal reached Vancouver, May 23.

First recorded rail shipment of salmon from B.C. coast eastward, June 28.

1888 Kimsquit River and Kimsquit-Dean River Indian Reserves were surveyed in 1888 and approved in 1913.

1888 Stanley Park in Vancouver was opened (Barman).

1889 Amy (Owens) Gildersleeve born Nov. 29, Oregon (Doc Gildersleeve's wife).

1889 Union Steamship Co. started service to upcoast canneries and logging camps (Rushton).

1890 Petroleum discovered along Athabasca River.

1891 Gildersleeve, George Harrison (Doc) born May 3, Washington State.

1891 British Columbia at this time had twenty-five operating canneries (Lyons).

1893 Robert Draney (older cousin of Tom Draney) formed the Namu Canning Company Ltd. (Lyons).

1894 Norwegian colonists arrived in Bella Coola led by Reverend Christian Saugstad, 150 strong (Kopas).

1897 Wadhams Cannery built in Rivers Inlet (Lyons).

1897 Big year for salmon. Fifty-four British Columbia canneries had output of 1,015,477 cases.

1898 Yukon established as a separate territory.

1900 Tom Draney (younger cousin to Robert Draney) and John Clayton started a cannery at Bella Coola called the Clayton Canning Co., later to be known as Bella Coola Cannery (Lyons).

1900 British Columbia population hit 180,000 souls (Barman).

1901 Kimsquit Cannery (on Kimsquit Bay) built by Robert Draney (Owned and managed by Namu Canning Company Ltd.) (Lyons).

1901 Smith Butchering Machine "The Iron Chink" came on the market.

1902 The British Columbia Packer's Association of New Jersey took over forty-two B.C. canneries with land, buildings, machinery, fixtures, fishing gear, ships, boats, scows and trademarks, also two cold storages (Reincorporated in B.C. in 1910).

1904 Dean River Valley: Mark Smaby cruised timber for the company that would become Pacific Mills Ltd. and still later Ocean Falls Division of Crown Zellerbach Canada Limited.

1905 Dean River: Robert Draney in 1905 deeded one-half acre behind Kimsquit Cannery to Methodist Church. This one-half acre was deeded back to Bella Coola Indian band by the United Church in 1985–86.

1906 Iron Chinks installed in five B.C. canneries.

1906 Canadian Fishing Company Ltd. formed in Vancouver to engage in halibut fishing.

1907 The Kildala Packing Co. Ltd. had agents Dawson and Buttimer build Manitou Cannery on the west side of Kimsquit Bay (Lyons).

1911 Dean River: Pacific and Hudson's Bay Company proposed a railroad between Dean River and Hudson's Bay (Kopas).

1912 Robert Draney, age sixty-two, sold Namu Canning Co. to four men who formed Draney Fisheries Ltd (Lyons).

1913 Indian Reserve of eighty acres at mouth of Skowquiltz River in Dean Channel was approved.

1913 Dean River: Railroad proposed to run from Dean River Flats to Quebec (Kopas).

1914 Kimsquit Cannery in full swing, manned by whites, Native Indians, Chinese and Japanese and run by Draney Fisheries Ltd (Lyons).

1914 Bella Bella: Dr. George Darby set up residence and medical practice (Kopas).

1914 Grand Trunk Pacific's first transcontinental train reached Prince Rupert, April 8.

1914 Great war began. Seas closed to salmon shipments. British Columbia bought two submarines.

1916 Gildersleeve-Owens logging operation established at Nootum Bay in Burke Channel, by Almon and Lloyd Owens and Doc Gildersleeve.

1917 Railroad logging on the Kimsquit River, a Pacific Mills operation.

1917 Women granted right to vote in B.C.

1917 Tallheo Cannery—B. F. Jacobsen of Bella Coola helped found.

1918 Namu and Kimsquit Canneries came under control of Northern Fisheries Ltd (Lyons).

1918 Canadian Pacific Steamship *Princess Sophia* foundered in Lynn Canal, 343 lives lost.

283

1924 Gildersleeve: Doc and Bill Gildersleeve moved their logging camp north to Gardner Canal. Owens Camp had already established there.

1924 First fishing motor boats in Rivers Inlet.

1925 Owens Brothers Logging took over management of Pacific Mills railroad show at Green Bay.

1925 Floating canneries were prohibited.

1927 Robert Draney died, age seventy-seven (founder of Namu and Kimsquit Canneries) (Lyons).

1927 Gildersleeve: Doc and Bill towed their camp back south to the head of South Bentinck Arm.

1927 Owens brothers finished logging at Green Bay (brothers-in-law to Doc Gildersleeve).

1928 British Columbia Packers Limited was formed through the consolidation of British Columbia Fishing and Packing Company Limited and Gosse Packers Company Limited.

1929 Lloyd Owens moved his family back to Oregon.

1929 Stock market crash in New York—beginning of the Great Depression.

1929 The Gildersleeve brothers, Doc and Bill, split their camps and went their separate ways.

1930 Bill Gildersleeve moved his camp to Nascal Bay in Dean Channel.

1930 Sirois, James, born December 31, 1930 at Ocean Falls, B.C.

1931 Bill Gildersleeve was logging in Burke Channel.

1932 Bill Gildersleeve moved his camp to Dean Channel to log at Elcho Harbour and Jenny Bay.

1933 Gildersleeve: Doc Gildersleeve was logging at Bear River (Mussel River).

1935 Bill Gildersleeve moved his camp to Evans Arm in Dean Channel.

1935 Lord Tweedsmuir appointed Governor General of Canada.

1936 Bill Gildersleeve moved his camp to 1000 Islands in Burke Channel.

1936 Gildersleeve: Doc towed his camp to Moses Inlet.

1936 Great Fisherman's Strike: No unemployment insurance or welfare, in those days (Lyons).

1937 Bill Gildersleeve made a long tow to the Nekite River, Smith Inlet.

1937 Appointment of Rowell-Sirois Commission on Dominion Provincial Relations (Canada).

1938 Gildersleeve: Doc Gildersleeve towed his camp to Johnston Bay near Wadham's Cannery in Rivers Inlet.

1939 Bill Gildersleeve moved to Naysash Inlet—off Smith Inlet.

1939 Second World War began September 3. September 10 Canada proclaimed a state of war with Germany.

1940 Bill Gildersleeve moved to Boswell Inlet—off Smith Inlet.

1941 Gildersleeve: Doc Gildersleeve's camp was towed to Draney Inlet (logged there most of WWII).

1941 B.C. salmon production highest on record—2,248,870 cases.

1942 German submarine sank a cargo vessel in St. Lawrence.

1942 Japanese submarine shelled Vancouver Island.

1943 Bill Gildersleeve moved to MacBride Bay—off Smith Inlet.

1944 Gildersleeve: Doc's camp was towed to the head of Rivers Inlet.

1945 Bill Gildersleeve moved to Burnt Island—off Smith Inlet. This was his last logging show before retiring.

1946 The combined thirty-one operating B.C. canneries canned salmon pack was 1,348,138 cases, composed of: 543,027 cases sockeye; 8,100 cases springs; 4,115.5 cases steelheads; 100,154.5 cases coho; 116,607.5 cases pinks; 576,133.5 cases chums (Lyons).

1947 Gildersleeve: Doc's camp was towed to Tallheo Point.

1950 Bella Coola Cannery stopped canning; continued as a fishing center.

1951 Gildersleeve: Doc's camp was towed to Fish Egg Inlet.

1954 Gildersleeve: Doc's camp was towed to Dean Channel; Carlson Inlet; Kimsquit at Dean River.

1955 Amy Gildersleeve died January 13 at Ocean Falls, age sixty-five (grandmother of James Sirois).

1956 Doc Gildersleeve, pioneer West Coast logger, died April 7, 1956, age sixty-four (grandfather of James Sirois). The last logging shows for Doc Gildersleeve were at Deep Bay

(Carlson Inlet), Iron Island and at Kimsquit on the Dean River. The Doc Gildersleeve camp including floats, houses and equipment were sold to Neal Duncan in 1956.

1958 Mike Sahonovitch had a logging show near Manitou Cannery in Dean Channel.

1958 Ripple Rock in Seymour Narrows removed by an underwater dynamite explosion.

1961 British Columbia government approved taking over of B.C. Electric Co. as a Crown Corporation.

1961 Canadian dollar officially pegged at ninety-two and one-half cents.

1962 Namu Cannery burned: the offices, cannery, cold storage, machine shops and other major plant buildings were obliterated (the cannery was rebuilt for 1963 season).

1969 Gildersleeve: Bill died age eighty-two (brother to Doc).

1982 Elsie (Gildersleeve, Sirois) Gadsden, died in March, age seventy-two.

1982 The Sirois log cabin near the airstrip at Dean River was built by Gerry Silver of Bella Coola. The cedar trees were logged from near the road washout at the top of the hill leading to the canyon at 2.5 Mile. Started in April and completed in November.

References

Gildersleeve Pioneers, by W. H. Gildersleeve (Rutland, Vermont: Tuttle Publishing, Inc., 1941).

Rain People (First Edition), by Bruce Ramsey (Ocean Falls Centennial Committee, 1971).

Rain People (Second Edition), updated by Roland Neath (Kamloops, B.C.: Wells Grey Tours Ltd., 1997).

Rain Coast Chronicles: First Five, by Howard White (Madeira Park, B.C.: Harbour Publishing, 1976).

Salmon and Our Heritage, by Cicely Lyons (Vancouver, B.C.: Mitchell Press Limited, 1969).

The West Beyond the West, by Jean Barman (Toronto, Canada: University of Toronto Press, 1991).

West Coast Words, by Tom Parkin (Victoria, B.C.: Orca Book Publishers).

Woodsmen of the West, by M. Allerdale Grainger (Seattle, Washington: Fjord Press, 1988).

Books on Gildersleeves:

Willard Harvey Gildersleeve, M.A. wrote three books:

Gildersleeves of Gildersleeve, Conn., 1914.

Gildersleeve Pioneers, 1941 (no. 1 above).

Sylvester Gildersleeve Descendants, 1952: This book is about Willard Gildersleeve's grandfather's descendants and gives a history of six generations of Gildersleeves and shipbuilders. The manuscript by Willard Harvey Gildersleeve of Gildersleeve families revised is deposited at the following institutions: Library of Congress, Washington, D.C.; Long Island Historical Society of Brooklyn, N.Y.; California State Library, Sacramento, CA.; SOTRO Library, San Francisco, CA.; California Branch of State Library.

Gildersleeve-Owens, Pioneer Loggers in Coastal British Columbia by W. James Sirois, 1997, can be found at the following institutions: National Library of Canada; Mormon Archives, Utah; Vancouver, B.C. Public Library; University of B.C. Library.

More great HANCOCK HOUSE biographies

Real Life • Great Stories

Alaska Calls
Virginia Neely
ISBN 0-88839-970-7

Beyond Northern Lights
W. H. Bell
ISBN 0-88839-432-2

Bootleggers Lady
Ed Sager & Mike Frye
ISBN 0-88839-976-6

Bush & Arctic Pilot
A. R. (Al) Williams
ISBN 0-88839-433-0

Bush Flying
Robert S. Grant
ISBN 0-88839-350-4

Chilcotin Diary
Will D. Jenkins
ISBN 0-88839-409-8

**Crazy Cooks
& Gold Miners**
Joyce Yardley
ISBN 0-88839-294-X

Crooked River Rats
Bernard McKay
ISBN 0-88839-451-9

Curse of Gold
Elizabeth Hawkins
ISBN 0-88839-281-8

Descent into Madness
Vernon Frolick
ISBN 0-88839-321-0

Fogswamp
Trudy Turner & Ruth McVeigh
ISBN 0-88839-104-8

**The Incredible
Gang Ranch**
Dale Alsager
ISBN 0-88839-211-7

Gang Ranch: Real Story
Judy Alsager
ISBN 0-88839-275-3

**Good Lawyer /
Bad Lawyer**
David Nuttall
ISBN 0-88839-315-6

**Journal of a
Country Lawyer**
Ted Burton
ISBN 0-88839-364-4

Klondike Paradise
C. R. Porter
ISBN 0-88839-402-2

Lady Rancher
G. Minor Roger
ISBN 0-88839-099-8

Nahanni
Dick Turner
ISBN 0-88839-028-9

**Ralph Edwards of
Lonesome Lake**
Ed Gould
ISBN 0-88839-100-5

Real Alaskans
Lew Freedman
ISBN 0-88839-254-0

Ruffles on my Longjohns
Isabel Edwards
ISBN 0-88839-102-1

Wheels, Skis and Floats
E. C. (Ted) Burton &
Robert S. Grant
ISBN 0-88839-428-4

**Where Mountains
Touch Heaven**
Ena Powell
ISBN 0-88839-365-2

Wild Trails, Wild Tales
Bernard McKay
ISBN 0-88839-395-4

Wings of the North
Dick Turner
ISBN 0-88839-060-2

Yukoners: True Tales
Harry Gordon-Cooper
ISBN 0-88839-232-X

Yukon Lady
Hugh Maclean
ISBN 0-88839-186-2

Yukon Riverboat Days
Joyce Yardley
ISBN 0-88839-386-5